The Microdynamics of Technological Change

The emergence in recent years of a knowledge-based economy, and the structural changes it has wrought in the advanced economies, have been the subject of intense debate in economics. This volume presents a comprehensive assessment of the economic effects of the emerging information and communication technologies associated with a knowledge-based economy, and looks at how knowledge is increasingly treated as a product in its own right.

An original framework is developed to comprehend these fundamental shifts, based on three bodies of knowledge:

- the economics of path dependence and of historical time as they are elaborated in the economics of new technologies;
- economic topology based on the methodology of network analysis;
- the new economics of knowledge and the concepts of localised technological change and technological communication.

The Microdynamics of Technological Change provides a unified analytical framework for the study of the transition of advanced economic systems towards a knowledge-based economy. As such it will be welcomed by both students and researchers of the new information age.

Cristiano Antonelli is Professor and Chair of Economics in the School of Communication of the University of Turin, where he organises the Economics of Innovation Laboratory. He is also managing editor of the journal *Economics of Innovation and New Technology* and has published widely in the field of the economics of innovation.

Routledge Frontiers of Political Economy

The Microdynamics of Technological Change

Cristiano Antonelli

London and New York

First published 1999
by Routledge
11 New Fetter Lane, London EC4P 4EE

Simultaneously published in the USA and Canada
by Routledge
29 West 35th Street, New York, NY 10001

Reprinted 2001

Routledge is an imprint of the Taylor & Francis Group

© 1999 Cristiano Antonelli

Typeset in Garamond by
J&L Composition Ltd, Filey, North Yorkshire
Printed and bound in Great Britain by
Selwood Printing Ltd, Burgess Hill, West Sussex

British Library Cataloguing in Publication Data
A catalogue record for this book is available from the British Library

Library of Congress Cataloging in Publication Data
Antonelli, Cristiano.
    The microdynamics of technological change/Cristiano Antonelli
    p. cm. – (Routledge frontiers of political economy; 23)
    Includes bibliographical references and index.
    1. Information technology. 2. Technological innovations–
    Economic aspects. I. Title. II. Series.
    HC79.I55A58   1999
    338'.064–dc21   98–35407
                         CIP

ISBN 0–415–19052–5

This book is dedicated to the memory of my father.

Contents

Figures

Tables

General editor's foreword

It is often said that we live in the West in a knowledge-based world, that we participate in new forms of capitalism in which the accumulation of intangible, intelligence related assets is the key to the distribution of economic activity and the standard of living. Such economies are truly renaissance economies. Yet the treatment of the epistemological foundations of this world by economists and by other social scientists remains largely fragmented and partial. With time, Cristiano Antonelli's thoughtful and imaginative work will be seen as one of the necessarily few contributions which set us on new paths towards a more comprehensive understanding of modern capitalism and its intangible foundations. His starting point is Adam Smith's starting point, the division of labour in the generation of knowledge by a variety of mechanisms in a bewildering variety of micro contexts. Not just science and technology as conventionally defined, but knowledge of how to organise, of what consumers may demand and of where to find the necessary information. Division of labour demands co-ordination, yet such co-ordination is rarely provided by conventional market institutions alone. From this follows Antonelli's primary theme, the role of network institutions in drawing the threads together, institutions which depend upon notions of receptiveness and connectivity for their operation. These are systems with percolation properties in which patterns of interaction mutate continually, frequently settle into coherent clusters of activity but, like a kaleidoscope, may be shaken by seemingly innocuous events to constitute radically new worlds.

Now knowledge co-ordination processes of this kind are inherently restless. There is no equilibrium attractor, a coherent, relatively invariant and stable state of rest towards which our systems tend. Economic activity is open-ended, in its very prosecution it changes the conditions of its own replication and all we can say is that the future will differ from the past through the medium of the present. Such worlds are deeply historical, essentially unpredictable, and forever changing in form and structure. This is the essential, radical and perhaps uncomfortable conclusion that Antonelli guides us towards as he considers the economy as a discovery process on a grand scale.

None of this implies that the rules of economic conduct must be rewritten in their entirety. Capitalism imposes its own continuity. Thus, and centrally, the accumulation and application of new knowledge remains constrained behaviour and requires substantial and irreversible investments to bring it to fruition. Development constraints on the ability to change behaviour (switching costs), and to formulate new behaviours (innovation costs), are at the heart of Antonelli's analysis. In this light is a side issue, whether or not firms can be said to maximise anything in a side issue. What matters are the development constraints, how they vary across firms and sectors and how ineluctably they are shaped by evolving and localised network relations. Knowledge-based economics are also deeply social, they are not worlds of anonymous transactions. They are in Polanyian terms instituted worlds in which networks are major elements of social capital underpinning economic change. In turn, the significance of irreversible investments is that they lead us back to increasing returns, the absence of equilibrium and history.

To say that this is a complicated, rich agenda for empirical work is a profound understatement. Antonelli has not shied away from this issue, devoting the second part of his essay to a series of original investigations into the telecommunications and business services sectors as exmplars of the new information economy. His primary findings are that activity in these two sectors is highly, postively correlated within the OECD countries and that these activities are significant contributors to national and sectoral differences in productivity growth.

This book will surely stimulate many others to treat knowledge seriously, and to recognise its dependence on micro experience. While we may measure macroeconomically, our understanding of the economic and social process of development and transformation is to be found in the co-ordination of microeconomic change. Consequently, markets and their foundations in deeper institutional forms are at the heart of the knowledge economy.

J. S. Metcalfe
15 July 1998

Foreword

This book is the result of a long-lasting research activity.[1] Preliminary versions of many chapters have been discussed in several meetings among which: the workshops of the European Union TSER projects 'Innovation in services and services in innovation' and 'Industrial districts and localised technological knowledge'; the Fondazione Rosselli Conference on the 'Economics of path dependence' in Torino, 1992; the ICER workshop on the 'Economics of Localised Technological Change' in Torino, 1995; the European Management & Organisation in Transition workshop at the University of Durham (1996); the XXII and XXIII European Association for Research in Industrial Economics Annual Conferences in Juan les Pins (1995) and Vienna (1996) respectively; the OECD Workshops on the 'Economics of the Information Society', in Toronto, June 1995; and London (March 1997); the Second Annual Conference of the Consortium for Research on Telecommunications Policy 'Public Policy and Corporate Strategy for the Information Economy', in Evanston, May 1996; the WIFO (Österreichisches Institut fur Wirtschaftsforschung) Conference 'Competition Policy in the New High-Tech Global Market Place' in June 1996 in Vienna; the III Rencontre 'Economies des Institutions' of the INRA in December 1996 in Dourdan; the Accademia dei Lincei Conference 'Sviluppo tecnologico disoccupazione e trasformazione della struttura economica e sociale' in Rome, January 1997; the meetings of the group 'Technologies de l'information et de la communication: performances économiques' of the Commissariat General du Plan in the fall and winter of 1996 and 1997 in Paris; the seminars at the PREST of the Victoria University of Manchester in January 1996; and the ENST (Ecole Nationale Supérieure de Télécomunications) of Paris, in March 1996; the Fondazione Rosselli workshop 'New Information and Communication Technologies: Growth and Employment' in February 1997, in Torino; the Ecole d'Eté d'Economie Industrielle at Cargese in August 1997; the CRIC (ESRC Centre for Research on Innovation & Competition of the University of Manchester) 'Systems and Services: Innovation Workshop' in March 1998.

The comments of the many attendants at the workshops, conferences and seminars are gratefully acknowledged. The author is especially grateful for the stimulating discussions with many friends and colleagues among whom: Robert Boyer, Jean Michel Dalle, Dominique Foray, Ned Lorenz, Pascal Petit, Michel Quéré, David Allen, John Cantwell, Robin Cowan, John Enos, Bill Lazonick, Steven Martin, Dennis Mueller, Dick Nelson, Ian Steedman, Peter Swann, Nick von Tunzelmann, Daniele Archibugi, Mario Calderini, Elena Cefis, Aldo Enrietti, Aldo Geuna, Alessandra Lanza, Martin Marchesi, Roberto Marchionatti. The author is particularly grateful for the detailed suggestions and repeated discussions with Paul David and Stan Metcalfe. The recursive comments of two anonymous referees have been especially useful. The help of David Hill in polishing my 'English' deserves a worthy mention. The usual disclaimer applies to all remaining errors.

The support of the European Union TSER projects 'Services in innovation and innovation in services' and 'Industrial districts and localised technological knowledge' and of the Consiglio Nazionale delle Ricerche (Research grants N° 96.03949.PS10 and 97.05173.CT10) is acknowledged.

Introduction

After years of neglect, the theory of economic growth is again at the centre of much interest in economics. The endogenous growth theories have contributed much to focus attention on the endogenous creation of knowledge and on its key role in assessing the rates of growth of total factor productivity and output of economic systems (Aghion and Howitt, 1998; Romer, 1986 and 1990).

Two complementary hypotheses have been developed in this theoretical context: the production of knowledge, based upon learning processes, is 'automatically' linked to output, via investment and/or human capital, and growth takes place in equilibrium. These hypotheses deserve a deeper analysis (Amendola and Gaffard, 1988; Metcalfe, 1997).

First, the microeconomics of the creation of new knowledge and the introduction of new technologies is a far more complex process. It is exposed to a variety of influences and takes place in a context of dynamic discontinuities. Although learning does play a major role, an intricate web of complementary factors needs to be taken into account in order to be able to assess the actual rate and direction of new knowledge, the actual pace of introduction of new technologies, their characteristics and hence their effects on the economic system. A variety of results of such microeconomic complexity of the dynamics of technological knowledge, at the aggregate level, should be taken into account: catching up, forging ahead and falling behind are all possible outcomes (Abramovitz, 1986).

Second and most important, growth takes place in a context characterised by structural change, that is the endogenous change of utility and production functions, and out-of-equilibrium conditions where firms, exposed to changes in their economic environment, at each point in time, consider not only the opportunity to adjust quantities to prices and vice versa, but also evaluate the scope for the creation of new knowledge and the introduction of new technologies.[1] The creation of new knowledge and the introduction of new technologies is induced by out-of-equilibrium conditions, takes place in an out-of-equilibrium context and generates new out-of-equilibrium conditions. In this process, path-dependence, articulated in externalities and irreversibilities, plays a major role.

This book elaborates upon these two hypotheses and tries to contribute a more comprehensive theory of endogenous growth which focuses on the role of firms, industrial structures, technological changes and regions, and appreciates the role of historic time in order to elaborate on an interpretative framework where the dynamics of technological knowledge, technological change and general structural change is better accounted for.

To achieve these results the Marshallian and the Schumpeterian traditions are brought together. Specifically, the Marshallian legacies about increasing returns and partial equilibrium analysis are intertwined with the Schumpeterian tradition about structural change, that is the endogenous creation of new knowledge and the introduction of new technologies. Because of irreversibilities and indivisibilities, exchanges out-of-equilibrium do take place in Marshallian markets but again, because of irreversibilities, indivisibilities and structural change, i.e. the endogenous creation of knowledge and introduction of technological and organisational innovations by agents acting out-of-equilibrium, the convergence towards equilibrium is continuously altered by the changing structural elements of the system. In such a dynamics a sequence of virtual equilibria can be traced, but no equilibrium point found.

In this context, following the track opened by *Technical Choice and Economic Growth* by Paul David, the process and the path along which the system evolves become the single, relevant units of analysis.

The evidence provided by advanced economies at the end of the century confirms the relevance of our hypotheses. Advanced economies are facing fast structural changes characterised by two parallel and interacting dynamic processes: the diffusion of new information and communication technologies, and the growing economic role of the production of knowledge as a good, specifically an economic good.

The emergence of the new knowledge-based economy, specialising in the production and distribution of knowledge, draws attention to three characteristics:

1   The role of historical time in the processes of accumulation of the competence and capability necessary to generate new knowledge and introduce technological and organisational innovations. This increases the need for analytical tools which better integrate the role of historical time in economic analysis;
2   The role of technological communication, that is the effects of the circulation of information and elements of knowledge in the economic system among innovators and between innovators and adopters. This increases the need to understand the dynamic laws of the spillover of technological information;
3   The role of new information and communication technologies, which are increasingly emerging as the basic infrastructure on which the knowledge-based economy builds.

To analyse these issues the book builds upon three strands of literature: first, the industrial economics literature[2] and the recent advances made possible by the economics of path-dependence and the analysis of the implications of historical time; second, the contributions of economic topology based upon the methodology of network analysis and spatial stochastic interactions; third, the new economics of knowledge and the notion of localised technological change.

The notion of localised technological change plays a key role. Technological change is inherently localised in that it consists of changes in the technical capability of the production process and the structure of organisation that are limited to a well defined set of characteristics: size, age, location, industrial specialisation, levels of integration and diversification, distribution and access conditions to property rights, mix of complementary and interrelated inputs, cumulated competence, skills, and factor and output market strategies of firms. Localised technological change builds upon two different forms of knowledge: tacit and codified. The latter is based upon structured information that, as a public good, is available to everybody with low, though not negligible costs of imitation and acquisition (since these require competence and dedicated capability). Tacit knowledge is the result of lengthy learning processes; it is idiosyncratic and specific to the organisation and business environment of the firm.

Technological change is more or less localised according to the mix of internal and external, codified and tacit knowledge on which it depends, but neither form may be dispensed with. Technological knowledge may be considered a highly impure public good with relevant elements of excludability and rivalry that relies upon a continuum of specifications of different forms of knowledge: at one extreme one finds the notion of codified scientific knowledge, at the other the notion of tacit knowledge. In the generation of localised technological change firms rely on the complementarity between tacit and codified knowledge, which are both internal and external to each firm (Antonelli, 1995a).

Localised knowledge is idiosyncratic as it emerges from daily routines and from the experience acquired in using capital goods, producing and manufacturing, and interacting with customers and suppliers as well as other manufacturers and service firms. Localised knowledge consists of specific pieces of technological know-how obtained by means of learning by using and doing. It incorporates the experience and skills of labour as well as the opportunities of improving products and production processes generated by highly circumstantial factors and events: as such it is characterised by high levels of cumulativeness. Consequently localised knowledge is specific with respect to the set of topological factors that shape the learning process.

As soon as it is not possible to reduce all the interactions in the economic system to market transactions, perfectly cleared by prices, a variety of externalities become relevant. In these conditions, the location, proximity and interdependence in multidimensional spaces of firms becomes relevant

(Perroux, 1935 and 1964). The process of accumulation of knowledge is heavily influenced by the topological location of firms and because of this it is highly path-dependent in that it reflects the specific learning opportunities each firm has come across over time (David, 1975; Nelson, 1987; Antonelli, 1995a).

Since localised knowledge is mainly tacit: because it is implicit and embedded in the memory of organisations and in the economic, regional and industrial environment of each firm, it is difficult to learn, imitate, transfer, adopt and use. It is more proprietary and its use is more excludable than is generally assumed in the 'Arrovian' tradition. Its circulation and communication, however, play a key role in the general innovative capacity of a system. The capability of a system to respond to changes in demand levels and factor costs through innovation depends on the amount of knowledge, tacit and codified, each agent in a system has access to.

The generation of localised technological change is characterised by increasing returns, which are both internal and external to each firm. The former consists of the dynamics of learning to learn and in the cumulativeness of the competences necessary to acquire and manipulate the available information and blend it with the specific conditions of each firm. The latter consists of the dynamics of technological externalities which spill over from firms co-localised in regional and industrial spaces. Technological externalities, shaped by the economic topology and the network structure of relations among firms, within regions and industries, account for increasing returns external to firms. Firms relying on localised knowledge can implement their technological capability not only by means of R&D expenditures and internal learning, but also by the systematic absorption of technological and scientific externalities available in their environment. The transfer of tacit knowledge is impeded by strong institutional problems of disclosure: such knowledge is embedded within organisations and is unknown to the majority of participants actually in them (Arrow, 1996).

An economic topology articulated on the methodology of network analysis and spatial stochastic interactions can provide important insights into the dynamics of localised technological knowledge and change. The methodology of spatial stochastic interactions, originally introduced in physics, is increasingly used in economics to analyse dynamic processes, where the outcome of communication processes in economic systems, characterised by networks of communication links, is understood to depend upon the quality of connectivity among agents, their receptivity to external information, their density in multidimensional spaces, and the extent of external pressure.

The elaboration of an economic topology warrants much efforts to appreciate the role of multidimensional spaces into which each firm is embedded. The topology of the economic spaces into which firms' behaviour can be understood in turn is the outcome of a path-dependent process of accumulation. The application of spatial stochastic interaction models seems particularly useful here: it makes it possible to appreciate the role of communication within innovative systems and, specifically, connectivity and receptivity. The former measures the number of connections in place among the agents in a structured system, and the latter the capability of each agent to absorb the information received. This book uses the methodology of network analysis and spatial stochastic interactions to identify the implications of the structural characteristics of innovation systems as communication networks, on both the economics of innovation and technology policy. Analysis of the dynamics of localised technological changes and spatial stochastic interactions explains the role of innovation systems in fostering the rate of technological change and the clustering of innovations in well defined technical and regional spaces.

Building on these premises, the book provides a general assessment of the economic effects of new communication and information technologies, considered as the enabling technological system on which the new knowledge-based economy is founded. New information and communication technologies change the domain of the spatial interactions structure of innovation systems by their effect on the appropriability, divisibility, and marketability of information. They increase the opportunity for greater technological co-operation and social division of labour so that the production of knowledge is less and less embodied in manufactured products and may be produced and delivered by specialised firms.

In this context, the emerging knowledge-intensive business service industry appears to exert a key role as an interactive agent between tacit and codified knowledge components, intensifying the connectivity and receptivity of firms perceived as learning agents.

The structure of the book

This book follows an interpretative framework based upon the notions of localised technological knowledge and change, path-dependence and the methodology of spatial stochastic interactions, in order to provide appropriate analytical tools for the study of the transition of advanced economic systems towards a knowledge-based economy. The aim is to identify the general characteristics of the dynamics of localised technological knowledge and change, and apply them to the analysis of the emerging knowledge-based economy. With this in mind, the book is structured in two parts. Part 1 elaborates the theoretical framework and lays down the basic tools for the study of the dynamics of localised technological change. It consists of five chapters.

In Chapter 1 the general conditions of path-dependence are defined and their relations with the industrial economics literature are made explicit. Path-dependence represents the set of dynamic processes whereby small events have long-lasting consequences, which economic action may modify at any moment, but only to a limited extent. Path-dependence is analytically generated by the overlapping of irreversibility, indivisibility and the structural actions of agents. It allows for both the effects of past behaviour of agents on the structure of the environment and the Lamarckian survival of agents by learning and adaptation to the character of the environment; thus it provides a framework by which to understand and to model the effects of historical time on the behaviour of agents who are able to modify their evolution at each point in time.

Chapter 2 explores recent developments in the new economics of knowledge and summarises the relevant issues in the ongoing debate between the 'Arrovian' and the Schumpeterian and Marshallian traditions. According to the Schumpeterian and Marshallian traditions, the development of knowledge within firms is characterised by the mixing of four specific forms of knowledge – tacit and codified, internal and external – and by different processes of acquisition. Localised knowledge is based upon tacit knowledge as it emerges from tacit learning procedures; it is augmented by the absorption of external tacit knowledge and requires broad efforts – consisting of R&D activities and of the absorption of external codified knowledge – to be fully articulated and applied to the specific operational context of each economic agent.

The core of Part 1 is devoted to the analysis of the dynamics of localised technological change. It includes three chapters. Chapter 3 explores the introduction of localised technological change as the endogenous outcome of the interplay between substitution costs, producer switching costs and learning processes. All changes in relative prices and desired output levels can be accommodated by firms via either technical changes in a given map of isoquants or localised technological change. In this context, the dynamics of localised technological change is analysed as the result of the interaction between Schumpeterian rivalry, factor substitution costs and demand-pull pressures. Out-of-equilibrium exchanges and localised technological changes drive a recursive, path-dependent process. The introduction of localised technological change is now viewed as part of a more general dynamic process, where the accumulation of competence and knowledge, and the changes identified at both the firm and system levels, are strictly intertwined.

Chapter 4 analyses the important effect of the increasing returns from the generation of new knowledge on discontinuous growth. The dynamics of endogenous technological change, induced by changes in the economic environment and characterised by cumulative learning processes and technological externalities can be used to explain the clustering of innovations in time and new technological gales and thus actual business cycles.

Chapter 5 provides the first elements of an economic topology to explore the sources of technological communication using the methodology of network analysis and spatial stochastic interactions. A proper understanding of the communication structure of each innovation system and the resulting spatial stochastic interactions, i.e. the combination of connectivity and receptivity, which define the levels of effective communication within that system, constitutes a major factor in assessing both the rate and direction of technological change. The conditions of access to relevant technological externalities within network systems influence the rate and direction of the introduction of localised technological change. The actual rate and direction of the introduction of localised technological change in turn affects the communication structure among agents in each system so as to shape a recursive path-dependent process of structural change.

Part 2 analyses the emergence of a knowledge-based economy in the context of a number of applied and empirical issues, where the dynamics of localised technological change and the analytical tools so far identified, i.e. path-dependence and technological communication, seem to offer relevant insights. The factors likely to affect the rate of introduction of technological change, as well as its direction, are investigated in the specific context of the growing role of knowledge as a good in itself. Both the causes and effects of the structural change in the European economy are analysed in an attempt to understand the evolution towards a knowledge-based economy.

Chapter 6 explores the emergence of advanced telecommunication technology, a key component of the new information technology system, as the result of the introduction of complementary radical innovations that have drastically altered the role of telecommunications in the economy. Today, the use of telecommunications-based advanced services is associated with the opportunity to extract significant quasi-rents, and this has in turn pushed users to innovate in order to become major players in the arena of technological change within telecommunications and information technologies. In such a context, the notion of a network of networks, implemented in the European Union, seems appropriate to encourage the dynamic efficiency of the system, accommodating both centrifugal and centripetal innovations, yet still retaining network inter-operability and interconnectivity.

Chapter 7 develops a Schumpeterian approach to analyse the interaction between unemployment and localised technological change within the global competitive process. With reference to the effects on the globalising economy of new information and communication technologies, the model articulates the relation between technological change, the duration of competitive advantage and global pressure, based around the process of generation, adoption and imitation of innovations. Using OECD statistics, results indicate that a country's competitiveness, and thus its world market share and level of employment, is determined by its innovative capacity. In terms of implications for industrial policy, investment in innovation and R&D clearly becomes important, as do efficiency wages (although wages alone cannot establish full employment conditions). Both the cause of and 'cure' for unemployment is considered to be the fall-out surrounding technological change on a global scale: the generation of technological innovations requiring renewed innovative capability via research and learning can uphold competitive advantage and reduce unemployment.

Chapter 8 depicts the emergence of the new knowledge industry as the outcome of the introduction and diffusion of new information and communication technology. The influence of this new technology on the organisation of the production of knowledge has resulted in the growth of specialisation. We are witnessing the institutional formation of a knowledge economy by the separation of research activities from corporations, the identification of a derived demand for technological knowledge, and the subsequent specialisation of firms in the production of knowledge. This process fuels and is fuelled by new innovative technology. The chapter also considers the different and conflicting claims on the knowledge industry, from incentives to innovate on the one hand and the social welfare of knowledge on the other.

Chapter 9 is devoted to the analysis of a major innovation in the organisation of research and development activities, such as technological co-operation. Here, the analysis focuses the time stratification of the historic sequence of interactions of innovative agents and the path-dependent evolution of the different forms of technological co-operation along the classic product-cycle.

Chapter 10 analyses the emergence of standards as part of the more general process of the generation of new knowledge and the introduction of institutional and technological changes. The introduction of standards plays a key role in the conversion of tacit into codified knowledge and it is an essential component in the generation of new localised knowledge. The various aspects of the standardisation process, are seen as the range of actions which a firm has available, over and above price adjustment, in response to its changing environment. The outcome of standard-setting is heavily influenced by specific characters on both the demand and supply sides. Identifying the factors leading to standardisation, this chapter considers the implications of standards on both the industrial system and market structure. The long-term effects of standards, on such things as transaction costs, specialisation and the rates of introduction and diffusion of technological innovations, are recognised as a feature of innovation systems.

Chapter 11 offers empirical evidence in support of a basic thesis about the knowledge economy and the influence of new information technology. As factors of connectivity and receptivity, communication and business services themselves are 'products' of the new technology and enable the generation of innovation by means of the interaction between competence and the tacit and codified knowledge components that make up localised technological innovation. The rate of diffusion of such services is considered to be an indication of an industrial system's innovative capacity and ultimately, therefore, productivity. An increase in the spread of communication and business services should lead to an increase in the growth of total factor productivity, and the mechanics of this process were visible in the European economy at the end of the 1980s.

The conclusion, Chapter 12, delineates the analytical procedure followed, summarises the results and assesses the numerous implications.

Part I
The theory

1 Path-dependence in industrial economics and the economics of innovation

Path-dependence defines the set of dynamic processes whereby small events have long-lasting consequences, which economic action can modify but only to a limited extent. The trajectory of a path-dependent process cannot be fully anticipated on the basis of the original events. Path-dependence is different from past-dependence because the former is able to accommodate the consequences of actions at each point in time. Path-dependence analysis is systemic and dynamic, because it focuses attention on the process of change that is generated by the interaction of a variety of agents whose behaviour is constrained by their localisation in time and space. Path-dependence is analytically generated by the overlapping of irreversibility, indivisibility and structural change, that is the endogenous change of utility and production functions, as opposed to parametric behaviour (David, 1975, 1985, 1988, 1992c, 1997).

Analysis of the various classes of interactions and combinations of irreversibility and indivisibility provides elements for building a new approach to understanding industrial change and economic change generally: an approach in which irreversibility and indivisibility are the basic components of an evolutionary process of change, where what matters is historic time rather than merely the factors of some well circumscribed classes of market failure.

In this chapter, the first section outlines the generation of path-dependence and its effects, drawing from the existing industrial economics literature. The five most significant attempts to understand the role of path-dependence in industrial dynamics: diffusion and selection of the new technologies; economies of growth; structure-conduct-performance; industrial retardation; menu and consumer switching costs, are analysed in the second section. This section highlights the complexity of interactions that take place and their reciprocal effects when excess inertia and excess momentum are taken into account. The third section considers the effects of path-dependence on the distribution of agents in a multidimensional space and the role of an economic topology in market dynamics. In the fourth section a generalisation of industrial evolution over time is formulated with path-dependence as the protagonist. In the conclusion the

various dynamic processes encompassed by such a generalisation are itemised and its role in understanding the dynamics of technological knowledge
is highlighted.

The process of path-dependence

Within the context of path-dependence, irreversibility and indivisibility
assume a radical new shape. Although irreversibility and indivisibility *per se*
are noted tools for economists, their combination with structural change
uncovers a new area of economic analysis. Irreversibility and indivisibility
are at the origin of well-known classes of market failures. The overlapping of
the different classes of indivisibility and irreversibility with structural
change, however, generates dynamic processes whose effects are displayed
over time with important consequences in terms of multiple equilibria and
discontinuity. The transition from out-of-equilibrium conditions towards
equilibrium can be impeded or delayed indefinitely.

Irreversibility is familiar to industrial economics. It may be defined as the
difficulty of changing a given behaviour or choice. Hence it can be measured
by the opportunity costs that arise at time $t+1$ from any attempt to change a
commitment to a given behaviour or choice made at time t. A variety of
phenomena can be classified under the heading of irreversibility, including
switching costs for both consumers and producers when changing the mix
of products or production factors that enter their current bundle, and sunk
costs associated with the difference in the market value for assets *ex-ante* and
ex-post their purchase (Boyer, Chavance and Godard, 1991).

Indivisibility among production factors leads to a variety of well-known
phenomena, such as, technical and pecuniary economies of scale; externalities and economies of scope. Indivisibility and irreversibility become
significant when economic analysis focuses on the role of information as
an economic good. Reputation is the outcome of irreversibility and information impactedness. Transaction costs are clearly the outcome of a special
class of indivisibility. Low levels of appropriability and learning can both be
portrayed as aspects of the more general problem of indivisibility. In turn,
inappropriability has important dynamic implications in terms of interdependence among innovators and user-producer interactions, which lead to
the clustering of innovative activities in innovation systems, such as technological districts and industrial 'filières' and spillovers, providing opportunity for imitation and technological recombination, and hence free rider
behaviour.

Standard economics is built on strict assumptions about the scope of
economic action. Economic agents are induced to act only by optimisation
procedures and their action is strictly parametric in that it consists only in
adjustments of prices to quantities or quantities to prices. Structural action,
that is the intentional change of either technology in the production
function or tastes in the utility function, remains outside the scope of

standard economics. Tastes and technology can change, but strictly in response to exogeneous forces and endowments.

When structural change is instead brought in, tastes and technology become endogenous variables that are determined by the interaction of agents who can deliberately change their own production and utility functions. Learning processes play a major role among the determinants of structural change. Learning consists of a peculiar class of indivisibility in that agents, while manufacturing or selling, also learn about technologies and market conditions. A large literature has explored the different categories of learning: learning by doing; learning by using; learning by consuming; learning to learn and learning by forgetting (Arrow, 1962a; Stiglitz, 1987; Malerba, 1992). Beside the effects of learning, the utility and production functions of each agent can be influenced by the actions, both intentional and unintentional, of other agents. Structural change may thus be viewed as the outcome of the autonomous effort of learning agents as well as the result of a change in conduct induced by the action of other parties. In this approach firms do more than adjust prices to quantities and *vice versa*: they are also able to manipulate interactively the basic structure of the system. Technologies and tastes at time t are the outcome of the strategic interaction in the market place of agents at time $t-1$. Hence strategic market interaction determines not only quantities and prices but also new technologies and tastes.

When economic growth is path-dependent, stationary-state theory is an inadequate analytical framework (Rosenstein Rodan, 1934; Abramovitz, 1938). Agents are exposed to changes in a way which affects their behaviour and expectations. Path-dependence should be considered a process of which each agent does not necessarily have a full understanding nor a clear command of the sequence and timing of each stage. Time matters as a source of uncertainty about the consequences of each action. When path-dependence is at work, time also matters because of irreversibility: the sequence of growth stages cannot be reversed and the time profile of each action has important effects. Consequently, time matters because it affects selection processes: the 'tendency' towards equilibrium is dramatically altered by changing market conditions. Finally, time matters because the outcome of any adjustment process of market dynamics is dependent upon the characteristics of the initial conditions of market forces and the behaviour of agents at any point in time. When path-dependent growth takes place, stationary economics has little to say about the real dynamics of market forces and the behaviour of firms for given initial conditions of disequilibrium.

In the industrial economics tradition, economic agents are assumed to be able to change the basic structure of their system, that is the production and utility functions. A variety of models and empirical studies have explored the effects of R&D expenditures on the growth of total factor productivity of firms, the relation between demand pressures and the direction of technological change, and of changes in the relative prices of production factors as inducement mechanisms to foster the rate of introduction of innovations as well as their direction in terms of factor intensity.[1] A large literature has also assessed the effects of advertising expenditures on the elasticity of demand curves for the products of firms.[2]

Industrial structures are characterised by high levels of heterogeneity among sectors, regions and firms. Sectors differ in terms of levels of concentration, number of firms, exit and entry rates, forms of competition and rivalry, conditions of access to technological knowledge, rates of growth of output and productivity. Firms differ in terms of size, age, organisation, innovation and learning capabilities, input costs, market conduct, distribution of property rights and, most importantly, in terms of performances such as profitability, productivity and output growth. Regions differ in terms of the mix of sectors and firms and, most importantly, in terms of the specific conditions of input and output markets, including the local innovation systems. Such diversity is persistent and self-reinforcing. Industrial economics has analysed in detail various partial dynamic processes in an attempt to understand the causal factors behind the evidence of the variety of cumulative growth processes that characterise advanced economies. Yet, it has failed to provide a general framework capable of accommodating these partial analyses. Path-dependence can help build such a framework in order to better study the evolution of industries and firms.

The dynamics in industrial economics

Industrial economics has long analysed the implications of the interactions of different classes of structural change, indivisibility and irreversibility, and has generated a variety of important models that are usually found dispersed in different chapters of textbooks.

The dynamics explored by industrial economics consists of two different process: the endogenous process of change and the endogenous persistence of out-of-equilibrium behaviour. Both reveal that the system is characterised by a plurality of attractors and forces that go well beyond the limits of standard equilibrium analysis (Greenwald and Stiglitz, 1989).

Important models have been built on the interaction between different classes of structural change, irreversibility and indivisibility, all within the theory of the firm, the theory of demand, the theory of markets, the economics of structural change and industrial dynamics, the economics of regions, and, more recently, the economics of knowledge and the economics of innovation and new technology. More generally, industrial economics has tried many times to appreciate the significance of the overlapping of irreversibility and indivisibility in an attempt to produce a theory of industrial dynamics that would integrate their effects rather than simply listing them as special classes of market failure. Notable attempts so far have been developed along five axes:

1   the diffusion of innovations and the selection of new technologies;
2   the notion of economies of growth in the theory of the firm;
3   the structure-conduct-performance approach and its dynamic applications;
4   the structural change and industrial dynamics approach;
5   the notion of consumer switching costs.

From the diffusion of innovations to the selection of new technologies

The diffusion of innovations has long provided the basic field of analysis to understand and appreciate the long lasting effects of increasing returns and irreversibility (Mansfield, 1961).

The diffusion of innovations, that is the distribution of delays in the adoption of new technologies, has long been understood in terms of the increasing returns due to externalities in the assessment of the information necessary to evaluate the new products being introduced into the market place. The larger the number of users of a new product, the lower the information costs necessary to appreciate the characteristics of that product. The adoption of new goods among consumers is first delayed by transaction costs originating in the lack of reputation of the new products and the difficulty of assessing their actual utility. Eventually, however, when a critical mass of new consumers has been built up, a fast diffusion process among users can take off. This 'epidemic' contagion is the outcome of the flow of information made available in the market place by each new user. Moreover, increasing returns on the demand side, due to complementarity with other products or skills, favour the reduction of the hedonic prices for products that happened to be selected first, and hence their diffusion. Irreversibility plays a major role in the selection of a new product: both producer and consumer switching costs delay the adoption of new technologies that are superior only when sunk costs are not accounted for, while increasing returns on the supply side favour the reduction in costs and prices of new products which happened to be selected first, and hence their diffusion.

For a long time the diffusion of innovations had been analysed as if only one new superior technology had been introduced at each moment. A major shift took place in the literature when it became clear that the diffusion of an innovation is the outcome of a complex process whereby a wave of new rival products is introduced into the market place, intense competition takes place, a subset progressively wins out in the selection process against similar rival new goods and is eventually diffused, i.e. adopted by a large number of potential users.

Increasing returns from adoption and positive feedbacks are important in such a process. Increasing returns from adoption stem from the combination of four distinct classes of dynamic forces: learning to use and learning by doing; network externalities; economies of scale in production;

and technological complementarities and interrelatedness. The dynamics of the interdependent diffusion of new complementary products on the demand side, and imitation processes on the supply side, leads to irreversibility. Technologies that happened to be selected first have greater chances of being diffused faster and eventually becoming the standard (Katz and Shapiro, 1986; Farell and Saloner, 1985; Foray, 1989). Economic systems may be locked into technological choices that are actually inferior to other possible alternatives (David, 1985; Arthur, 1989; Cowan 1991).

The new economics of technological choice under the conditions of increasing returns, indivisibility and irreversibility, enables appreciation of the pervasive role of two classes of dynamic processes (Foray, 1997):

1 excess momentum, i.e. hysterical processes of change and growth. The persistence of dynamic behaviour, even when agents are not stimulated to adjust to any exogeneous change, is the outcome of some endogenous dynamic force that cannot be reduced to adjustment processes;
2 excess inertia and inelastic adjustments, i.e. the lack of proper reactions to given incentives. Behaviours that have been chosen in certain circumstances are retained even when the parameters of the system change, due to some attrition forces that need to be properly analysed.

The extension of the analysis of replicator dynamics can play an important role in this context. Replicator dynamics is an interesting extension of the biological metaphor proposed by Fisher-Prye (Fisher, 1930), much elaborated by Stan Metcalfe (1992, 1997), who suggests that the more efficient firms, like performing species, grow rapidly at faster rates than the average. Specifically, the rates of growth are a function of the spread, with respect to average levels, of efficiency levels. While performing species grow in terms of higher rates of reproduction and survival, more efficient firms grow in size because of higher levels of liquidity, via retained earnings on extra profits and higher rates of investment. Higher rates of investment lead to faster growth in output and size and consequently market shares. When the replicator dynamics is augmented by the analysis of adoption, diffusion and innovation, excess inertia and, consequently, path-dependence, exert a powerful influence in industrial dynamics.

The basic distinction between adoption and diffusion in the interaction between growth, investments and performance is relevant in this context. Adoption measures the capability to choose the new technologies as given by the ratio of innovative machines to traditional ones for given flows of purchase. Diffusion measures the actual penetration of innovative machines, shown by the ratio of innovative machines to the stock of machines in place. Investment makes the difference. Young firms with fast rates of growth and small stocks of machines can fund the high levels of net investment necessary to adjust their production capacity to the larger, desired levels of output. Growing firms, expanding their capital stock, can purchase new vintages of capital stock which embody better technologies, have a larger flow of new machines and experience high levels of actual penetration of innovative machines. In old, stagnating firms, on the other hand, the flow of actual purchase of new machines is slowed by sunk costs of existing, large capital stocks and consequently, the ratio of innovative machines to the stock of machines in place is low. Hence, firms with faster rates of growth can embody faster, better technologies, experience a reduction in costs and, for some sticky market prices, can increase output, in turn leading to new investment, faster adoption and diffusion of new technologies and further cost reductions. Firms with lower rates of growth, although able to make correct choices (i.e. adoption) about the new technologies embodied in new vintages of capital goods, are less able to fund investments to expand their production capacity and replacement of existing capital stock with older vintages is slowed by sunk costs. Average costs are higher and market shares decline together, with net investment capacity (Salter, 1966; Antonelli, Petit and Tahar, 1992).

On a similar topic, the interaction between market performance and innovative capability leads to path-dependence. It is sufficient to assume that growing firms have higher chances to invest larger resources in R&D activities and hence to introduce faster, new technologies. Hence they can increase their size and market share and further invest in activities that eventually lead to the further reduction of costs and a general increase in performance. Firms which, at one point in time, happen to benefit from some specific and highly idiosyncratic competitive advantages may enjoy for a long time, the positive feedback of excess momentum, while firms, accidentally trapped in competitive disadvantage, may be caught in the downward spiralling effects of excess inertia (Iwai, 1984a and b).

The analysis of replicator dynamics, combined with the distinction between adoption and diffusion in the interaction of growth and investment, and the relationship between innovation capability and performance, reproduce the basic ingredients of excess momentum, excess inertia and path-dependence (Metcalfe, 1997 and Chapter 3).

Economies of growth in the theory of the firm

In the theory of the firm, the notion of growth economies has been dealt with at different times and with different specifications. The basic argument is that unit costs tend to decrease along with the rates of output growth. Formally this can be expressed by the following equation:

$$AC = F(dY) \text{ with } F' < O \tag{1}$$

where AC are the average costs and Y is output

This notion is at odds with the received theory where firms produce in equilibrium. In the received theory, firms can experience economies of growth only when they are small and the optimum size is large. In such a case, the faster the growth rates the closer firms get to the equilibrium output. Because of growth, firms are then expected to be able to shift along a given L-shaped average-cost curve that reaches a minimum after which no further economies of scale are attainable. The relationship between average costs and rates of growth is clearly spurious here, hiding the more substantial difference between actual (small) sizes and optimum (larger) ones.

The evidence available on the dynamics of firm size confirms the importance of the so-called Gibrat's law, according to which growth is proportionate to size independently of the relative size of each firm. Gibrat's law states that both small and large firms grow at a rate which is simply proportional to their size, with no actual convergence in the distribution of sizes towards a given optimum size. In this context there is no trend towards convergence in the firm size. On the contrary, the given initial spread of sizes tends to persist over time. Hence economies of growth lead to a classic case of excess inertia and hysteresis in the composition of the population of firms in a system (Hart, 1962; Hymer and Pashigian, 1962; Mansfield, 1962).

The evidence of continuing advantages from growth is applicable equally to the full spectrum of small and large firms and calls for an alternative explanation, one where dynamic forces are at play. The emergence of the notion of economies of growth at the firm level, elaborated by Edith Penrose (1959), parallels the analysis of endogenous processes of growth elaborated at the system level by Kaldor (Kaldor, 1957; see also Momigliano, 1975). Their analytical foundation consists of rejecting the basic assumptions about the exogeneous and static character of technology in production functions and tastes in utility functions. Instead, endogenous technological change, the endogenous formation of consumer tastes and competencies, learning processes, indivisibility and irreversibility constitute the analytical blocks on which economies of growth are currently built.

The irreversibility of production factors generates the basic incentives for a firm to grow. Density economies account for economies of growth when substantial expenses are anticipated and sunk, not only in fixed capital (Sutton, 1991) but also in reputation, R&D activities, and marketing outlays that can be used by large quantities of incremental output, with no additional expense. Moreover, according to Arrow (1974), information channels necessary to manage a firm are the result of long-lasting investments and constitute a substantial piece of dedicated capital stock, highly specific and idiosyncratic, which is difficult to replace or reutilise in other circumstances. The capacity of communication channels is also very large, and additional information flows can be sustained with limited levels of additional investment. Once firms have made such an irreversible commitment and poured funds into building communication channels, the advantages of making intensive use of them are endless. Thus firms have a clear incentive to grow, because the larger their size the better use is made of dedicated resources sunk into communication channels, which constitute the actual fabric of organisations. Lazonick (1990) stresses that the irreversibility of large amounts of capital stocks sunk in fixed production factors and anticipated in organisation and intangible capital, accounts for the steep negative slope of average and marginal cost curves. The larger the output, the lower the costs and the larger is the amount of internally-generated funds available to finance new generations of fixed capital and, in particular, to introduce better and more sophisticated technologies and organisational structures (Simon, 1982; Langlois, 1986).

All learning processes favour the emergence of economies of growth. The basic assumption here is that the larger the levels of cumulated output and the larger the experience acquired by agents, the larger is the reduction in costs. Learning economies have many implications for industrial economics. First of all, the age of firms becomes an important issue in understanding the distribution of sizes in the population of firms and the related dynamics. The interaction between technical economies of scale and learning leads to variety among firms. Old firms can be small and yet as efficient as young, larger ones which benefit from technical economies of scale. Second, for some levels of market prices, which may be sticky in the short term, a self-propelling process of growth takes place. The larger the cumulated output, the larger the experience, hence the lower the costs and market prices of each learning firm, and the larger the potential growth in size. Larger size, via learning processes, induces new reductions in costs and prices and thus increases of output. Third and most important, a variety of learning processes has been detected and each stresses different aspects of the behaviour of firms. Learning-to-do relates the learning process to production activities, learning-to-use to investment activities, learning-to-learn to research activities, and learning-to-interact to user-producer interactions. Analysis of the relationships between these different classes of learning opens the way to understanding economies of growth as an interdependent process, organically developing the competencies and capabilities acquired from managing current business (Rosenberg, 1982; Stiglitz, 1987; Cohen and Levinthal, 1989; Malerba, 1992).

Interaction between economies of scale and economies of scope results in economies of growth by diversification. According to Chandler (1990), the very engine of economies of growth is the interaction between economies of scale and scope. Production processes are characterised by indivisibilities and bundles of specific and strictly interrelated techniques, which exhibit clear potential for economies of scope. Firms have an incentive to increase their size in order to reap the advantages of technical economies of scale. The new size, however, uncovers a potential for hidden economies of scope. The larger the size in one given line of business, the larger the incentive to increase the division of labour within the firm and to convert combined production units into specific production processes. Specialisation enables the reduction of production costs. Each production process so far specified is in turn characterised by economies of scale, inducing firms to grow in each newly-specified production process.

The interaction between inappropriability, learning and economies of scale produces multinational growth. A specification of the process elaborated by Chandler has been provided by Dunning (1981) and Caves (1982) to explain the multinational growth of firms. Here, the building of competence and technological capability plays a central role, together with the notion of transaction costs for technological know-how. Firms are learning organisations able to build up a technological capacity. Tradeability of technological know-how, especially in international markets, is hindered by inappropriability problems and the related high risks of opportunistic behaviour. Firms are thus induced to establish affiliates abroad in order to take advantage of the technological know-how generated, while managing current business in domestic markets.

Structure-conduct-performance and structure (t + 1)

In the traditional structure-conduct-performance analysis, the conduct of firms was determined by the industrial structure, particularly in terms of barriers to entry and concentration. In turn, the performance of firms was determined by conduct.

This original representation was essentially static and to a large extent reproduced the basic elements of the neoclassical paradigm which assumed that the behaviour of firms could have no bearing on the structural characters of the system. This representation underwent major changes when the term 'structure $(t + 1)$' was added by Almarin Phillips (1970 and 1971) to the traditional sequence. Now the structure of the industry could no longer be regarded as a given exogenous state but, rather, part of a dynamic process which was exposed to the effects of the behaviour of agents. A recursive process emerges in which firms at the same time decide their conduct on the basis of the present features of the structure and select a behaviour that generates improved performance as well as some changes, both intended and unintended, in the structure of the system.

The introduction of endogenous technological innovations that reshape the cost curve, and increase the advantages of incumbents with respect to potential entrants, as well as the long-lasting consequences of advertising strategies on the reputation of firms, are simple examples of a recursive process of change, where the features of the system at time $t + 1$ are influenced by the conduct of firms at time t.

When the structure of a market is the endogenous product of the behaviour, both explicit and unintended, of firms, the actual notion of barriers to entry needs to be explored further. Increasing returns and sunk costs associated with reputation reduce the risks of failure for incumbents, thus offering barriers to exit. Irreversibility and sunk costs reduce mobility of firms across sectors, creating mobility barriers.

In general, the notion of dynamic barriers is re-emerging. Dynamic barriers are barriers to growth for marginal competitors. Within dynamic barriers, marginal competitors have slower and more irregular rates of growth, while incumbents are able to take full advantage of economies of growth. In the 1960s, a large empirical literature documented the advantages in terms of steady rates of growth for large firms with market power, as opposed to irregular growth cycles for smaller, marginal firms (Caves and Porter, 1977; Kamien and Schwartz, 1982; Jacquemin, 1985).

Within this theory of markets, entry barriers, arising from absolute cost advantages, economies of scale and reputation, delay the entry of newcomers and hence protect the quasi-rents of incumbents, which in turn feed new investments in R&D and reputation-building activities, increasing the unit costs for small potential entrants. Here barriers to entry are the outcome of both the conduct and performance of incumbents. When strategies associated with high levels of sunk costs, learning opportunities and large optimum sizes are selected, the conduct of incumbents is oriented towards the erection of barriers to entry. In fact, all these strategies imply significant, asymmetric differential effects for smaller newcomers who can spread the fixed costs over smaller volumes of output. Moreover, the selection and endogenous generation of new technologies with large optimum sizes and steep negative portions of cost curves for small firms becomes an essential factor in the height of new barriers to entry. Past performance has a structural effect on the increase of the height of barriers to entry, particularly in terms of the interaction between high levels of economic profits and lower constraints, due to the funding of risky and uncertain activities such as R&D, where external financial markets incur high information costs in the assessment of the profitability of borrowing for such undertakings (Mueller, 1986; Stiglitz, 1988; Geroski, 1991).

Increasing returns and sunk costs, combined with the introduction of innovations, favour the persistence of profits above the norm even with low levels of barriers to entry, if there are significant barriers to imitation. The interaction between barriers to entry, profits above the norm and learning leads to the persistence of innovative activity. This is the famous Schumpeterian Mark II model, where firms that happen to be able to introduce an innovation at time t are able to earn profits above the norm for a long period of time. Quasi-rents generated by an early innovation can be partly used to fund high levels of R&D expenditures. High levels of R&D expenditures increase the chances of generating a new wave of innovations: hence the possibility of maintaining high levels of profit and high rates of introduction of innovations simultaneously. Larger R&D activities, for a given distribution probability are likely to generate faster rates of introduction of technological innovations. When economies of scale in conducting research activities are admitted, larger R&D budgets can generate more than proportionate rates of introduction of technological innovations. Moreover, each successful innovation enables the costs of

R&D expenses to be spread over large quantities of cumulated output, reducing unit cost and so increasing further profitability. Barriers to imitation can be built by innovating firms selecting and generating new technologies, with high levels of information impactedness and complexity, which reduces the risks of unintended leakage (Sylos Labini, 1962 and 1984; Malerba, 1992).

Endogenous changes of utility functions, where tastes are influenced by reputation effects, caused by the bounded rationality of consumers and 'gregarious' imitation, advertising and other intentional strategies of firms, now become relevant. The interaction of economies of scale in advertising and increasing returns from demand externalities makes for the emergence of a new class of self-sustaining barriers to entry. Firms that enjoy the advantages of barriers to entry at time t can invest internally-generated funds in reputation-building, perpetuating or even increasing their profitability and cost advantage over potential competitors. Economies of scale in advertising play a major role. Reputation engendered by demand externalities can actually provide long-lasting advantages to incumbents even without advertising expenses. It is sufficient that learning processes occur on the demand side when tastes are assumed to be endogenous.

In this case, the demand externalities can take a variety of forms. The utility each consumer extracts from a product is greater according to the number of consumers of the product; the quantity of products sold in the market place; the utility each consumer extracts from that product; the length of time the product has been sold; and the stock of products sold, that is the cumulated quantity of goods still used by other consumers.

Under these conditions, the demand curve for such products is larger and steeper than that for rival goods. Proper advertising strategies can supplement the processes of endogenous taste formation, so that small amounts of advertising expenses have a long-lasting influence when associated with solid reputation effects engendered by demand externalities. Subsequently, self-propelling barriers to entry are generated. The larger the output at time t, the larger the reputation at time $t + 1$, hence the higher the barriers to entry and the greater the quasi-rents, which may be partly used to fund advertising expenses, that help to further increase the height of new barriers to entry (Schmalensee, 1986; Spence, 1980; Jacquemin, 1985).

The interaction between externalities, economies of scale, and birth and entry rates of new firms favours the clustering of economic activities within industrial districts in limited regions, with the emergence of asymmetric dynamic barriers to entry. The dynamics of the specialisation and division of labour of interrelated production processes encourage the emergence of regional and industrial clusters. Dynamic externalities become relevant when the natality of firms is considered. New firms are born in clusters and along technological 'filières', where new opportunities spill into the regional and technological innovation system. Indivisibility and inappropriability are causal factors of increasing returns, both internal and external to firms. The demand effects exerted by incumbents and the externalities spilling from their current activities interact so as to attract new firms in well-defined regional or technological niches. The classical conditions for self-propelling processes are again well in position. Economies of scale push firms to grow internally and to increase the derived demand for intermediate inputs, which provides additional demand for new specialised firms. Interdependence among innovators and user-producer inter-actions leads to the clustering of innovative activities in regional innovation systems, such as technological districts and in technological systems. Technological, technical and pecuniary externalities favour the birth and entry of new firms, which in turn is likely to create new waves of externalities attracting new waves of entrants. Firms outside these clusters face increasing barriers to entry, while firms within them experience the lowering of such barriers (Becattini, 1987; Krugman, 1992).

Structural change and industrial dynamics: industrial growth retardation

Traditional industrial economics has long considered the idea of retardation in industrial growth, particularly in the 1930s. The empirical evidence about retardation indicates that industrial growth follows a definite 'secular' movement according to three well defined phases: a first phase of slow growth; a short dramatic surge in output; and a prolonged phase of slow growth that tends to an asymptotic level of cumulated output. One of the clearest analyses was provided by Simon Kuznets (1930), who noted that retardation characterises the growth of single industries:

> As we observe the various industries within a given national system, we see that the lead in development shifts from one branch to another. The main reason for this shift seems to be that a rapidly developing industry does not continue its vigorous growth indefinitely, but slackens its pace after a time, and it is overtaken by industries whose period of rapid development comes later.
>
> (Kuznets, 1930: 5)

The problem of retardation, so clearly identified both by Kuznets (1930) and Burns (1934), has been substantially overlooked in the postwar literature, except for applications to the theory of international trade and foreign direct investment, termed the product life cycle by Vernon (1966). It has recently been rediscovered in order to explain the evolution of industrial structures. Many growth industries which had characterised the postwar period, such as the motor-car, aeroplane and chemical industries, have, in most industrialised countries experienced a significant decline in the rates of growth of output, productivity and employment since the mid-1970s, after reaching asymptotic levels of cumulated output (Freeman, Clark and Soete, 1982).

A broader approach to structural change and economic dynamics has been built upon the retardation hypothesis. This literature relies on three basic ideas: a theory of endogenous technological change; a theory of demand based on endogenous changes of utility functions, where the evolution of consumer tastes is influenced by income levels and gregarious behaviour; and a theory of indivisibility and complementarity in production processes and consumption patterns.

The analysis of Kuznets has received growing attention in recent years and a large body of literature has explored the causes and effects of the distribution of innovative activity within industries. Technological change is inherently characterised by the features of competition and learning processes (Pavitt, 1984; Sahal 1981; Metcalfe, 1989).

Innovative activity within firms selected by the competition process is based on localised knowledge acquired by means of learning by doing and by using, and is geared towards the introduction of process innovations that help beat off competitors, mainly in terms of cost reductions (Antonelli, 1995a; Utterback, 1994). The introduction of process innovation on the supply side and saturation on the demand side, following the fast growth of the first periods of the diffusion process, pave the way to retardation.

In the market place, two quite distinct dynamics exist within the diffusion process of new goods; from monopoly to competition and from competition to monopoly (Klepper and Graddy, 1990). When the appropriability of process innovations is high, the new market has a strong monopolistic character, which eventually degrades into competition via the entry of new firms able to invent, i.e. to imitate and introduce process innovations that make it possible to reduce the cost difference – built upon reputation and size – with respect to incumbents (Flaherty, 1980). When the selection process among many independent innovators is very strong and many parallel product innovations confront one another in the market place, the opposite shift may take place: process innovations introduced by firms that had a chance to make transient economic profits pave the way for the selection of products and firms, so that the market evolves from competition to monopoly.

The outcome of the interdependence between demand diffusion and supply diffusion, and between processes of innovation and processes of selection, is such that process innovations become increasingly important: as an industry matures, the number of firms shrinks and the opportunities for growth decline.

A theory of demand based on the endogenous evolution of utility functions lies at the heart of the approach to structural change and industrial dynamics. As Kuznets noted, demand plays a major role: retardation is driven by the rate of introduction of incremental innovations, but is actually determined by the inelastic portion of demand curves that is 'necessarily' met by a sequence of lower and lower supply curves. The basic assumption here is that income elasticities are influenced by both income levels and the novelty of products. In a general equilibrium approach, stable income elasticities should compensate for the decline of production costs and keep the overall levels of output constant. However, when Engel curves are considered, the relationship between consumption and income changes according to income levels and, hence, endogenous changes in the articulation of consumer tastes. An industry characterised by a decline of income elasticity, gregarious consumer behaviour and the introduction of incremental process innovations, is exposed to a secular decline in output. An industrial system characterised by a block of old declining industries and only a few new emerging ones is also exposed to secular decline, especially when it is integrated in international markets that provide the new goods at low cost (Pasinetti, 1981 and 1988).

Utility functions may also change endogeneously because of the gregarious behaviour of agents, whose belief is influenced by the aggregate levels of consumption of new goods. Positive and negative externalities are significant in shaping the evolution of consumer beliefs, particularly with regard to the expected utility of new goods: positive externalities induce consumers to attach a greater value to a new good when the number of lead-users is still small, and it is perceived as a status symbol, or when actual complementarities in usage highlight the good (this is naturally the case of telephones and communication services generally). Eventually however, when the number of users and goods already used increases, congestion may reverse the positive effect and actually reduce expected utility (Marris, 1964).

The analysis of industrial and structural change concentrates on the strong complementarities and interdependencies among industries and products. Industrial structures are characterised by a system of interdependent and specific complementary production activities which rely on each other for the provision and purchase of intermediate production factors. Increasing returns to scale and specific thresholds characterise each industry (Milgrom and Roberts, 1990). Significant externalities, both pecuniary and technical, spill from one industry to another in the matrix of inter-industrial exchanges. For some combinations of output values in vertically-integrated sectors, an industrial system may achieve very high levels of efficiency. Complementarities in consumption play a similar role, so that the demand for different products is strongly interrelated, in that each demand exhibits positive cross-demand elasticities. Complementarities in production and consumption account for big push effects, i.e. discontinuities in growth rates due to the emergence of the correct combination of inter-industrial linkages. The dynamics of structural change are guided by the endogenous evolution of the technical coefficients in the input-output matrix, the cross-elasticities among products and the income elasticities of bundles of complementary products (Rosenstein Rodan, 1943; Hirschman, 1958; Simon, 1951; Durlauf, 1993).

Kuznets was the first economist to explicitly import the logistic curve into economics from demography and population studies, in an attempt to provide a synthetic and simple statistical tool to model the dynamics of the long-term output growth of industries. The logistic specification he proposed, to fit the empirical evidence about retardation in industrial growth, is comparable to the Schumpeterian tradition regarding the sequence in technological change between the punctuated introduction of radical technological innovations and the subsequent declining rates of introduction of incremental innovations (Mokyr, 1990).

The logistic specification of retardation can be formalised as follows:

$$P(t) = a - b \cdot Q(t) \qquad (2)$$

The revenue equation is:

$$R(t) = P(t) \cdot Q(t) = [a - b \cdot Q(t)] \cdot Q(t) \qquad (3)$$

Let us now assume that in a competitive market, a share Z of the total revenue of the industry at each point in time is devoted by all firms to fund R&D activities, making it possible to reduce the costs of the output in the ith industry and consequently – because of the effects of perfect competition – the market price in that industry:

$$P(t) - P(t - 1) = -\lambda \cdot Z \cdot R(t) \qquad (4)$$

where $Z < 1$ measures the share of revenue devoted to R&D activities and λ the effects of those activities on production costs and, consequently, market prices.

Substituting equation (3) into (4) we see that:

$$P(t) - P(t - 1) = -\lambda \cdot Z \cdot [a - b \cdot Q(t)] \cdot Q(t) \qquad (5)$$

Since the increase in demand depends on the reduction of prices:

$$Q(t) - Q(t - 1) = -B \cdot [P(t) - P(t - 1)] \qquad (6)$$

Substituting equation (5) into (6) we have:

$$Q(t) - Q(t - 1) = \lambda \cdot B \cdot Z \cdot [a - b \cdot Q(t)] \cdot Q(t) \qquad (7)$$

which can be expressed as:

$$\frac{Q(t) - Q(t - 1)}{Q(t)} = B \cdot \lambda \cdot Z \cdot [a - b \cdot Q(t)] \qquad (8)$$

Equation (8) indicates that the percentage rate of growth of output is a negative function of the levels of output already reached, that is to say it reproduces the basic dynamics of retardation. When expressed as cumulated output, the growth equation with endogenous technological change, funded with a fraction of the revenue each time to reduce production costs and market prices for the product of the industry, exhibits an S-shaped process of growth[3] which shares the essential characteristics of the logistic curve, and is directly obtained via simple hypotheses from the standard demand equation.

Equation (8) has as its solution the well-known logistic function:[4]

$$Q(t) = \frac{\alpha}{1 + C_2 rme^{\alpha \cdot \lambda \cdot Z \cdot t}} \quad \text{where } \alpha = \frac{a}{b} \tag{9}$$

It is clear from equation (9) that the dynamics of the absolute rates of growth contain three distinct regions: for low levels of cumulated output they are very low, they are particularly high in a central region; and finally they are very low again for high levels of cumulated output. Specifically, with respect to equation (8) we see that industrial growth is retarded, that is it follows a distinct product life cycle along a sigmoid time path shaped by the values of:

Z, the share of revenue used to fund R&D activities and generate process innovations;

λ, the effects of R&D activities on production costs and consequently market prices;

B, the demand slope.

Similar results are obtained when the endogenous formation of the utility function is considered to be the outcome of the gregarious behaviour of consumers. Let us take a simple Cobb-Douglas utility function with constant returns, where the utility elasticity of a good (x) for each consumer (i) is influenced by the levels of the aggregate stock (X) of the same good already sold. The relationship between the stock and the flow accounts, for positive externalities up to a certain threshold and negative externalities beyond that level, can be modelled as a quadratic function (Marris, 1964). Thus:

$$U_{it} = f(x_t^a, y_t^b) \quad \text{with } a = (X_t - X_t^2) \tag{10}$$

Standard maximisation of the utility under a budget constraint (I_{it}) leads to the following demand equation for each gregarious consumer:

$$x_{it} = I_{it}(X_t - X_t^2) / P_{xt}(b + (X_t - X_t^2)) \tag{11}$$

The equilibrium levels of aggregate demand at each point in time can be considered as a flow added on to the stock:

$$dX/dt = I_t(X_t - X_t^2) / P_{xt}(b + (X_t - X_t^2)) \tag{12}$$

where once more we see that the rate of growth of the dependent variable is shaped by a quadratic function of the levels of the same variable.

With respect to equation (10), for given levels of income and prices, we see that industrial growth is retarded by the alternation between the positive and negative effects of gregarious consumer behaviour on the evolution of both consumer beliefs about the expected utility of new goods and, hence, demand.

The effects of the income elasticity of demand, especially when the Engel Law applies, can be appreciated if a in (2) is $a(t)$ with, in the inverse demand function, $d(1/a)/dt = A$. A measures the effects of the income elasticity in terms of shifts of the demand function over time. The general function (9) in such a case generates an envelope of logistic paths, where each S-shaped process shifts rightward.

When the endogenous aspects of consumer taste formation are taken into account we see that a variety of path-dependent growth alternatives are likely to emerge. According to the endogenous evolution of tastes, the distribution of income elasticities for different products will vary across economic systems, and with it the growth opportunity for the system itself. The time distribution of all efforts to manipulate the formation of tastes and their effects plays a central role in such dynamics, along with the matching between endogenous taste formation and endogenous technological change. Furthermore the interactions of structural change and the dynamics of industrial markets can lead to a variety of outcomes. Industrial structures are also exposed to structural changes that parallel retardation: in the stages of fast growth rates, barriers to entry, based on the ratio of minimum efficient size to total demand, R&D and reputation-building sunk costs, should shrink so that entry is easier and concentration levels subsequently lower. Within such phases, non-price competition is systematically used by firms in order to acquire larger shares of the market. Conversely, selection is more severe when retardation emerges; consequently concentration levels rise together with the decline in the number of firms and market place rivalry. Along the product life cycle, markets change because of endogenous changes in technology (Mueller and Tilton, 1969; Vernon, 1966; Winter, 1984).

Menu costs and consumer switching costs

The debate about wage stickiness and related macroeconomic fluctuations has led to the notion of menu costs. Menu costs include the administrative costs in adjusting payrolls and the transaction costs associated with all changes in wages. Because of menu costs firms are reluctant to fully adjust wages to prices and output levels. The debate on menu costs has re-introduced in recent economics the appreciation of rigidities and excess inertia in agents' behaviour on the demand side in labour markets (Akerloff and Yellen, 1985; Mankiw, 1985). Recent advances in the theory of consumer behaviour have made possible the appreciation of the role of irreversibility in consumer choice. Irreversibilities in consumer choices led to a new theory of demand where the purchase of a product at time t is allowed to have some effects on the choice set of the same consumer at time $t + 1$. This application of irreversibility on the demand side leads to the important notion of consumer switching costs, introduced and elaborated by Paul Klemperer (Klemperer, 1987a, 1987b, 1995). Consumers who have already purchased a product at time t from one firm may experience switching costs when considering new goods from another firm at time $t + 1$. Consumer switching costs arise from a variety of factors: need for compatibility with existing equipment, transaction costs of changing suppliers, costs of learning how to use new brands; uncertainty about the quality of the new brands. In this literature consumers' switching costs may be objective, actual costs or only subjective, perceived costs. While in the former case they still belong to the notion of costs, in the latter instead there is an implicit assumption about the endogenous change of the utility function which is rarely spelled out. The consumer preference for a product would be allowed to change because of the previous purchase of that product. In this case irreversibility would lead to structural change, that is the endogenous change of utility functions.

This literature concentrates its analysis of irreversibilities in demand only on the markets for final products and their effects on market competition, focusing much attention on the oligopolistic behaviour of suppliers, who are assumed to be aware of the switching costs of their consumers and hence, able to act strategically. Firms fix the price for their product at time t taking into account the negative effects on the choice set of consumers at time $t + 1$. Consumers are expected to experience a reduced scope of choice among products because of the costs of switching from one product and brand to another. With high levels of switching costs consumers can be locked into their original choice. Hence firms can extract quasi-rents from their consumers, as far as switching costs last over time. The time profile of the prices of new products and the marketing strategy of firms are clearly affected: firms have an incentive to attract consumers at the beginning with discounts and special offers and then to increase their prices. Intertemporal oligopolistic reaction functions can be elaborated upon these premises and the equilibrium values calculated accordingly.

According to this approach, consumer switching costs have important negative effects in terms of welfare losses: they discourage entry, reduce the incentive to differentiate and introduce product innovations, and induce firms to diversify and to offer excessive product variety. Potential positive effects, such as those generated by learning curves are not even mentioned.

The literature on consumer switching costs, however, provides important insights into the effects of irreversibilities on the demand side and raises important issues, which had been poorly dealt with. As a matter of fact, this literature leads to the complementary notion of producer switching costs, that is expands this approach to the analysis of the determinants and consequences of the costs of changing the current mix of inputs on the derived demand for production factors and the related issues of technical choice, technological change and market strategy of firms (See Chapters 3, 4 and 10) (Beggs, 1989; Antonelli, 1994b; Antonelli, 1994c).

Path-dependence and economic topology

The combined effects of irreversibility, indivisibilities and structural actions shape the multidimensional economic space into which the economic action of agents is embedded. The behaviour of agents in economic time has lasting consequences on their characteristics, and on their conduct, as well as on the features of the economic environment into which they are embedded via the powerful effects of local externalities. As a consequence, it is clear that an economic topology, that is the analysis of the characteristics of the distribution of firms in multidimensional economic spaces, is crucial to understanding the market dynamics as well as the dynamics of technological change.

Standard microeconomics assumes that markets are able to push firms towards the use of homogeneous techniques and organisations. Variety can emerge out of temporary dis-equilibrium conditions brought about by changes in technology or tastes. Some firms can earn extra profits, which will alert new competitors. The entry and exit dynamics, however, will select the best performing agents, out of the population of firms. Eventually, all surviving firms will imitate the best-practice and less adaptive firms will be sorted out by competition. Hence variety is reduced to uniformity by the selection process. Market dynamics select the best technologies and the best firms.

This selection process in the market place can work only under specific conditions that have rarely been taken properly into account. The transition to equilibrium from temporary disequilibrium implies strong assumptions about variety across firms, rather than homogeneity. The argument can be summarised as follows. Let us assume that (some) incumbents earn extra profits. According to standard assumptions, extra profits attract the entry of new firms, the entry of new competitors shifts the industry supply curve to the right so that the equilibrium position with no extra profits is reached. New firms are assumed to be able to imitate the product, the technology and the organisation to replicate the cost conditions of incumbents.

This process becomes complex when we consider that the standard assumptions are that large numbers of firms are attracted even by low levels of extra profits. When entry elasticity is high, and hence a large number of firms react to the stimulus exerted by extra profits, the effects on the supply curve can exceed the equilibrium point. Now, most (if not all) firms incur losses. If, once more, supply elasticity of firms to losses is high, a mass exit can take place. Only a few firms (or actually none), those more efficient than average, will be able to resist. The few survivors will eventually earn extra profits and hence new signals will attract many new entrants. An endless process of entry and exit would take place in a system which is never able to actually stabilise on equilibrium conditions, but only to pass through equilibrium values just for short time periods while attracted by the two extremes of the market possibilities, consisting of either high levels of extra profits or low levels of losses, both for the most efficient firms.

This analysis of the complexities of the competition process, which are actually necessary to reach equilibrium conditions, when out-of-equilibrium exchanges are assumed as a starting point in the process, is extremely important. The standard process can work only when additional qualifications are added (Arrow, 1959). The herd behaviour built into mass reactions, assumed by standard theory, is the main problem.[5] Variety matters in analysing market selection processes, not only *ex-post*, but also and, most important, *ex-ante*. Firms would not react as members of a herd to extra profits or losses only when their variety, in terms of localisation in multidimensional economic space and hence performances and productivity is assumed as a qualifying character.

Firms with differentiated access to information and differentiated competences and capabilities use different techniques and methods of organisation. Different firms have differentiated chances to survive at the time when most firms exit because of excess entry and, conversely, weigh cautiously their entry according to their specific cost conditions. Entry and exit then take place in an ordered sequence which makes it possible to reach and remain around equilibrium conditions. The closer such equilibrium, the slower would be the flow of entries (and exits), so that mobility would slow down in the proximity of equilibrium.

The notion of a rugged economic space with hills and valleys through which it is costly to walk, and hence the notion of economic topology articulated in such specifications as distance, density, network relations and communication channels among firms, makes it possible to replace herd entry and exit with sequential entry and exit. The notion of variety and localisation in a multidimensional economic space, defined in terms of cost conditions, technological maps, product specificities, marketing features, skills, competences and idiosyncrasies, in turn becomes essential to understanding the process of sequential entry and exit. The signals of extra profits and losses are now emanated by a well defined location in the economic space: only firms close to that source of information will be able to collect the signal and to take advantage of it. For a signal of a given intensity, only a limited number of co-localised firms will be able to react. Signals of increasing intensity will attract larger numbers of firms, for a given distribution of firms in the economic space at any point in time.

Limited mobility of firms in this rugged economic space is measured by the information costs necessary to collect and evaluate the signals and the producer switching costs necessary to make the existing and localised characteristics of each firm compatible with the opportunities of the specific location from which the signals are emanated. Entry implies some mobility from a previous state, exit requires some mobility from the existing location.

The number of firms which happen to be co-localised becomes an important structural feature of the system. More generally, the entire distribution of firms, both real and virtual – that is potential firms that are to be created – their density and the distance among them in a multidimensional economic space, is an important structural feature of the system.

In sum, variety in the population of firms, expressed by the distribution of firms in multidimensional spaces, is a necessary condition for markets to work. In turn the distribution of agents within a multidimensional economic space is not an exogeneous characteristic of the economic system but is in itself endogenous. The distribution of economic agents in a multidimensional space is the outcome of economic action in previous times, featured by irreversibility, indivisibilities, local externalities and the capability for structural change (that is to introduce changes in technology and tastes) of each agent.

The distribution of agents in multidimensional economic spaces is the path-dependent product of economic action in historic time. Distance, structural holes, density, connectivity and receptivity of links and information channels among agents and, more generally, all the features of the direct and indirect communication flows and hence of the information channels conceived of as nodes of a network, can be thought of as the long lasting and partially irreversible, often unintended, consequences of the specific conducts of economic agents in historic time such as: entry (and exit), internal and external growth, specialisation, diversification, vertical integration, adoption of specific technologies, accumulation of knowledge, capital structure, competence, strategic action in product and input markets, and institutional set-up.

According to Arrow (1974) the distribution and access to information within economic systems seem to be especially sensitive to the notions of irreversibility, path-dependence and economic topology:

> One might attempt to formalize the capital aspect of information in this way. A signal hitherto unheard is useless by itself; it does not modify any probability distribution. However, a preliminary sampling experiment in which the relationship between the new signal and the more

familiar ones can be determined or at least estimated will serve to make valuable further signals of the new type. This experiment, which may be vicarious (education, scientific literature), is an act of investment. *Such investment, being locked up in an individual's mind, is necessarily irreversible.* It can of course be transmitted to others, but it remains in the possession of the individual and cannot be alienated by him, though, like most irreversible investments, is subject to depreciation. In the last twenty years, there has developed some theoretical literature on irreversible investment. Obviously irreversibility is of no consequence when the future is one of steadily growing demand for the capital good; but it becomes of importance when there are fluctuations, particularly stochastic fluctuations. Now by its very nature the value of an information channel is uncertain, and so we have an economic problem which resembles the demand for inventories under conditions of uncertainty. We may venture on some possible generalizations. One is that the demand for investment in information is less than it would be if the value of the information were more certain. *The second, most important I would guess, is that the random accidents of history will play a bigger role in the final equilibrium.* Once the investment has been made and an information channel acquired, it will be cheaper to keep on using it than to invest in new channels, especially since the scarcity of the individual as an input, already alluded to, implies that the use of new channels will diminish the product of old ones . . . A third basic characteristic of information costs is that they are by no means uniform in different direction. At any given moment an individual is a bundle of abilities and accumulated information. He may find it cheaper to open certain information channels rather than others in ways connected with these abilities and this knowledge. Thus, an explorer in hitherto unknown territory will find it easier to explore new areas near to those he already covered. *Geographical propinquity is but a special case.*

Arrow (1974: 40 and 41 *italics added*)

The topology of economic spaces into which firms are embedded becomes a central issue in understanding their conduct and their aggregate dynamics. Standard tools, elaborated in the neoclassical tradition, assume microeconomic rationality applies, but to agents is embedded or localised in well defined multidimensional economic spaces. Because of irreversibility economic action is shaped by such important dimensions as producer and consumer switching costs, in order to move in the economic space, and information costs, in order to acquire relevant information about 'sites' which are distanced from the localisation of each agent: Local externalities affect the profit function of each agent according to his/her own specific localisation and context of action. Finally, structural change, consisting of the generation of new knowledge and the introduction of technological and organisational innovation, often leads to unintended consequences which become clear in historic time. Substitution at the margin and optimisation can be useful tools in such a context, provided that the causes and consequences of the localisation of agents in the relevant economic spaces are understood. More specifically the notion of localised rationality, as opposed to Olympian rationality, seems appropriate to analyse the conduct of agents who are rooted in economic space and time. Optimisation is local and amounts to no more than making the best of existing circumstances.[6]

The causes and consequences of the distribution of agents in economic spaces become relevant issues because of the intertwined effects of irreversibility, externalities and endogenous structural change, that is the endogenous change of utility and production functions of agents and of their distribution. Hence, an effort to elaborate a methodology to study the topology of economic spaces seems necessary. Network analysis and the methodology of spatial stochastic interactions appear promising tools in such an undertaking. Network analysis is well practised in social science and provides an array of tools to study the relationship among agents localised in structured spaces. Spatial stochastic interactions models, originally studied in physics, can be used to understand the outcome of the aggregate dynamics of the structured context into which heterogeneous agents are embedded (See Chapters 2 and 5).

Towards a generalization: path-dependence as a general model of evolution and change in industrial economics[7]

The complex dynamics recalled so far have long been known to industrial economists, yet disregarded due to the difficulty of handling their effects analytically. As Brian Arthur notes, even Schumpeter pointed out that:

> Multiple equilibria are not necessarily useless but from the standpoint of any exact science the existence of a uniquely determined equilibrium is, of course, of the utmost importance, even if proof has to be purchased at the price of very restrictive assumptions; without any possibility of proving the existence of a uniquely determined equilibrium – or at all events, of a small number of possible equilibria – at however high levels of abstraction, a field of phenomena is really a chaos that is not under analytical control.
>
> (Schumpeter, 1954 quoted from Arthur, 1994: 4)

Many processes explored in the industrial economics literature can be accommodated by the methodology of Markov chains:

> The condition of the industry in each time bears the seeds of its condition in the following period. It is precisely in the characterization of the transition from one period to the next that the main theoretical commitments of evolutionary theory have direct application. However

those commitments include the idea that the process is not deterministic; search outcomes, in particular, are partly stochastic. Thus, what the industry condition of a particular period really determines is the probability distribution of its conditions in the following period. If we add the important proviso that the condition of the industry in periods prior to period t has no influence on the transition probabilities between t and $t + 1$, we have assumed precisely that the variation over time of the industry's condition – 'state' – is a Markov process.

(Nelson and Winter, 1982: 19)

Within the broad category of Markov processes, a distinction can be made between homogeneous Markov chains and inhomogeneous Markov processes. This distinction plays a major role in our analysis.[8] Dynamic processes, where the transition from one state to another depends only on the state at time $t - 1$, can be termed 'state dependent' and are suitably accounted for by the methodology of homogeneous Markov chains. Here the events at time $t + 1$ can be fully predicted on the basis of the knowledge of the state at time t. The probability of transition from the state at time t to the state at time $t + 1$ is unaffected by the characters and features of the previous states. These processes are past-dependent, but not necessarily path-dependent. In fact the condition of non-ergodicity does not apply in a full sense. A process with such features is partly deterministic: the intentional actions of agents and the conduct of firms in the past are not able to change the probability of transition from one state to another. The methodology of homogeneous Markov chains offers interesting insights into the dynamics of industrial systems, but seems inadequate to represent the complexity of outcomes of the interactions of agents, who are fully embedded and localised in the structural characteristics of the system, yet still able to influence the evolution by means of a variety of structural actions, which also affect the transition probability from one state to the following ones (Krugman, 1996).

Dynamic processes where the probability of transition from one state to another is influenced by the memory of the process, that is by the specific conditions of the states at time $t - 1$, $t - 2$, $t - n$, are non-ergodic and fully path-dependent. Transition clearly depends on the state at time $t - 1$, but also on the changes that the path to state $t - 1$ has exerted on the probability of transition. The methodology of inhomogeneous Markov processes may be applied to this second class of dynamic processes. A path-dependent dynamic process can be described as a process where there is a multiplicity of rest states and the transition from one to another of many of these cannot be fully predicted solely on the basis of the conditions of the state at time $t - 1$: at each point in time the state also exerts an effect on the transition probability to the following state. Such a definition of a path-dependent process seems to accommodate the specific self-propelling processes which characterise the growth of firms and the evolutions of markets and industries that have been identified in the industrial economics literature. In all these processes agents are assumed to be 'state dependent' yet able to generate structural changes, either intentionally and directly or unintentionally via interactions which reflect the conditions of the system at time $t - 1$ and at the same time can still modify its evolution in an unpredictable way. The behaviour of agents, via both aggregate and local changes, can alter the probability of transition at each point in time and push the system towards a variety of alternative states.

Within Markov processes, the interaction between Markov chains or routines and global changes, as determined by the collective behaviour of all the agents, has already found many applications. Newman and Wolf (1961) elaborated one of the first applications of Markov processes in order to represent the dynamics of industrial selection and adjustment within the Marshallian tradition (Marchionatti, 1992). They assumed that for each firm the probability of increasing or decreasing output depends upon the levels of temporary equilibrium prices. The transition matrix, that is the probability for each firm of transition from one size to another for a given distribution of firm sizes, is affected by the interaction between a global variable, such as the level of prices, which reflect the levels of aggregate supply, and the economies of growth internal to each firm. Nelson and Winter (1982) used Markov processes to study the evolution of routines within firms and the introduction of innovations within the Schumpeterian tradition. Within the dynamics of Markov chains, the introduction of technological and organisational changes is influenced by the features of a global factor such as the selection environment of the market. Firms are induced to innovate, and hence alter the reproduction of routines along natural trajectories of growth, by the failure of their performances as determined in the market place where heterogeneous agents confront one another.

In fact several dynamic models relying upon Markov processes have recently been applied to economics, such as the models of diffusion and the selection of new technologies based upon Polya Urns, also generalised to consider *n* colours (Arthur, 1989; Cowan, 1991). Among Markov processes, special attention has been given to Random Markov Fields with multiple absorbing states such as Spin systems, stochastic Ising dynamics, and percolation analysis. Random Markov Fields seem particularly useful in the analysis of the dynamics of firms and technologies where variety is continuously reproduced together with selection and standardisation. Methodological interest in Random Markov Fields consists of the existence of a plurality of absorbing states where the dynamics of the process ends. The process declines when all the agents converge on the assignments of one of the many elements of the finite set.

In this context, three methodological approaches seem especially promising: spatial stochastic interaction analysis, the adaptive-recursive approach and the survival methodology. The latter two appear to be directly useful in empirical work. The former provides an interesting framework for conceptual analysis and simulation applications.

Spatial stochastic interaction analysis has been pioneered by David (1988, 1992) who relies systematically on local Random Markov Fields. This class of dynamic processes is characterised by the outcomes of local interactions as opposed to global ones. A system is now viewed as a network of asymmetric relations among agents (Dalle, 1995, 1997), and economic action shapes the system only via the structure of local interactions. A local path-dependent process has three basic ingredients:

> (a) a source of local positive feedback that will systematically reinforce the action of agents . . . (b) some source of fluctuations or perturbations that remain independent of and weak in comparison with the systematic effects of the system . . . and (c) something causing the progressive diminution in the comparative strength of whatever forces are perturbating the system.
>
> (David, 1988: 29)

Within this application of Random Markov Fields, spatial stochastic interactions models seem particularly relevant (Chapter 5). The dynamics of market selection, the formation of expectations especially in financial markets, technological rivalry, complementarity among industries with respect to input-output inter-industrial flows of intermediary inputs, decisions on location of new plants and entry into new industries all constitute examples of processes where the outcome of the interaction of agents at the global level can be thought to be determined by the specific topological context in which each round of interactions takes place. Moreover, all these processes involve some co-ordination equilibria to an extent that decision-making is influenced by co-ordination with neighbouring agents located in the same economic niche.

In physics the outcome of spatial stochastic interactions, in terms of the conversion to a given state of a heterogeneous population described by disordered local states, is influenced by such factors as: external pressure; connectivity probability and receptivity probability. For given levels of external pressure, the interaction probability is measured by the combined result of the probabilities of receptivity and connectivity. The methodology of spatial stochastic interactions may be used to study the probability that flows of exchange of goods, information and effective communication take place within local networks. A variety of applications has been elaborated ranging from the study of the adoption of communication standards (David and Foray, 1994), to the spillover of innovations; the effects of technology transfer on the productivity of a firm's research and learning efforts, to the evolution of technological co-operation among firms (Chapters 5 and 9).

The application of an economic topology articulated in network analysis and the methodology of spatial stochastic interactions to the study of dynamic processes in economics is based upon the assumption that at each point in time the behaviour of each agent is significantly influenced by its topological context of action: the behaviour of each agent depends upon the decisions of its neighbours in multidimensional economic spaces (Perroux, 1935 and 1964).

The analysis becomes dynamic and path-dependent when the reverse causation and its time stratification are taken into account. The conditions prevailing at each time bear a significant effect on the conditions at time $t + 1$ both directly and indirectly, that is affecting also the transition probabilities. The outcome of each spatial interaction is dependent upon the distribution of agents' behaviours in a given topological context. At each point in time, however, this structural distribution can be changed by the intentional action of agents, whose performances and behaviours are themselves influenced by the results of previous spatial interactions. For small changes in the structural features of local interactions, the outcome may be either full homogenisation or 'hysteresic' differentiation in behaviours. In this context, the historic sequence of spatial stochastic interactions based upon the basic properties of the Markov Random Fields becomes relevant.

Among the many different models of spatial stochastic interactions, the methodology of percolation deserves much attention. In fact percolation can be defined as 'interdependent Markov chains with locally positive feedback or additively interacting Markov processes' (David, 1992). Percolation captures nicely the outcome of localised interactions, where each agent is exposed to the influence of its neighbours rather than to the global influence of the entire system. The time stratification of different percolation structures is easily obtained when it is assumed that the basic structural conditions can be changed, because of the effects – such as the increased rates of introduction of technological innovations – of the results of the previous interactions – the mixed percolation probability – at each point in time. The time stratification of different percolation structures generates 'percolation processes' which capture the essence of a path-dependent process where the conditions prevailing at each point in time are likely to affect both the probability of transition to the following state(s) and the following state(s). The implications of these approaches in the development of new applied research strategies are important. As Krugman (1996: 1, 70) notes, percolation models have already been applied in more than fifteen scientific fields though (practically), not yet in economics. Krugman (1996) shows how percolation theory may be applied to business cycles (Scheinkman and Woodford, 1994) and regional economics.

In the adaptive-recursive approach elaborated by Day and Nelson (1973), Day (1986) and Foster (1991, 1993), an evolving system characterised by path-dependence can be described as follows:

$$X_t = X_{t-1} - Z_t + W_t \tag{13}$$

where: X_t is the structure of events analysed at time t; X_{t-1} is the structure of events as they took place at time $t - 1$; Z_t represents the part of the X structure exposed to decay over time t; and W_t is the part of the X structure that is new, due to new actions undertaken over period t.

With an adaptive recursive approach it appears possible to analyse the structural dynamics underlying the time distribution of events, controlled by the behavioural factors that both reinforce and contrast it. Nonlinearity in the dynamics of the process is easily captured by the manipulation and qualification of the relationship between the events at time $t - 1$ and the outcome at time t:

$$X_t = (X_{t-1}) - (X_{t-1})^2 - Z_t + W_t \qquad (14)$$

According to equation (14), past conditions exert their influence on current events within a quadratic relationship, privileging the role of some thresholds before which the relationship takes a positive sign and beyond which a negative one.

In the survival or duration approach, following Kiefer (1988), an evolving system is directly characterised as an entropy process where the duration of an event, or the rate of survival of the same event, is assumed to be conditional upon its state at time 0 and a vector of characteristics that evolve through time. A standard duration model takes the following form:

$$L(t; Z) = L_0(0) \exp(Z; b) \qquad (15)$$

where L is the instantaneous rate of failure conditional upon survival over time t; L_0 is an arbitrary and unspecified base-line hazard rate at time 0; Z is a vector of characteristics of the agents; and b is a vector of coefficients.

Survival methodology enables the calculation of how long it takes before a given behaviour or event occurs, and which features of the state at time 0 affect its evolution, together with those characteristics of the agents and structural determinants of the behaviour analysed that are associated with the time distribution of the events.

These new empirical approaches appear able to accommodate the effects of both hysteresis and evolution in the study of a large range of dynamic processes, including natality, entry, growth and retardation, profitability, investment and capacity expansion, productivity, integration and speciali-sation, concentration and fragmentation, advertising and marketing strategies, and innovation and technological change; all of which are in-fluenced by the characteristics of the economic topology of the environment and yet are also likely to affect that environment's evolution. Within the industrial economics tradition and the economics of innovation and tech-nological change, path-dependence enables further elaboration of the assumption that the behaviour of agents at any point in time is the outcome of the structure of events as they were at time $t - 1$ and the part of the structure of events that changes through time.

Conclusions

Path-dependence offers a general framework capable of accommodating a variety of dynamic processes which have occupied industrial economics such as the growth and diversification of firms, the role of sunk costs, the inertia and excess momentum of industrial structures and the long-term persistence of profits above the norm.

Specifically, path-dependence provides a useful methodology in the analysis of the individual dynamics underlying both the generation of localised technological knowledge and localised technological change. The key role of cumulativeness in the generation of new knowledge and competence is highlighted, as is the pervasive activity of irreversibilities, complementarities and learning processes in their accumulation (Chapter 2). Irreversibility of both tangible and intangible capital stock and competences is a major factor, accounting for the emergence of the key notion of economic distance and related producer switching costs engendered by all changes in the current size and input combination of firms. The trade-off between producer switching costs and localised technological knowledge pushes firms to introduce localised technological change when either factor costs or demand levels change within competitive markets, characterised by rivalry among the variety of firms and hence the excess momentum of the augmented replicator dynamics. This results in the persistence of innovative activities along technological trajectories, as defined by agents' input intensity, and their specialization across countries (Chapter 3). Industrial growth is also affected by the dynamics of positive feedbacks in the generation of localised technological knowledge and hence, the introduction of localised technological change within regional and technological innovation systems, because of high levels of indivisibility and irreversibility within localised and dynamic complementarities among firms, with respect to existing production processes and new technologies (Chapter 4). In the assessment of the innovative output of economic systems exposed to environmental changes, such as price fluctuations in production factors, a major influence is identified in the local technological externalities and other topological characteristics of innovation systems, defined in terms of network structures and spatial stochastic interactions. In this context the analysis of historic and endogenous sequences of different but related Random Markov Fields seems relevant to an understanding of the path-dependent dynamics of the communication flows and the related rate and direction of the introduction of new localised technologies (Chapter 5). Finally, somewhat in tandem, the emergence of new information and communication technologies and the attendant knowledge-intensive business services furthers the specialisation of countries and the production of knowledge as an economic good, implementing and enhancing the relations between learning agents in innovation systems (Part 2).

2 The new economics of knowledge

This chapter elaborates on the distinction between information, knowledge and competence and provides the basic elements of the dynamics of localised knowledge. It considers information as an input in the process of the creation and use of new localised knowledge together with the competence of each firm and the amount of technological communication which flows into the environment. Localised knowledge consists of the capability to combine the competence, built upon tacit learning processes, with codified knowledge and to use existing information in the specific topological contexts of the actions of each agent. This chapter also provides the basic elements of the role of both internal and external positive feedbacks in the production of localised knowledge as shaped by the dynamics of learning to learn, lays down the first elements of an economic topology to study the multidimensional spaces into which firms' action is embedded, identifies the role of technological externalities available in the innovation systems into which each firm is embedded and considers the notion of intellectual property rights regimes.

The first section considers competing definitions of knowledge and the growing distinction between technological knowledge and technological information, resulting in the emergence of the notion of localised technological knowledge. The second section concentrates on this recent development, identifying the four specific components of such knowledge. A new industrial taxonomy is proposed according to the relative weight of each component of the knowledge creation process and their dynamic implications are elaborated. Within this conception, the third and fourth sections assess the respective effects of efficiency wages, positive feedbacks and increasing returns in the generation of technological knowledge, on the rates of generation of technological knowledge. The role of the distribution of economic agents in multidimensional spaces relevant to analyse the causes and consequences of technological externalities and more generally the need for an economic topology is considered in the fifth section. The sixth section develops this approach to understanding the relevant domains of innovation systems. The last two sections outline the respective reciprocal relations between localised technological knowledge, new information, communication technology (and the related knowledge business services) and intellectual property rights. The conclusion summarises the whole analysis, linking the constituent parts, and illustrates the likely outcome of this co-evolutionary model.

The economic definitions of knowledge

Standard 'Arrovian'[1] microeconomics assumes that technological knowledge and information coincide. Hence technological knowledge, like information, should be considered a public good, in that its use is non-excludable and non-rival and its production and use are characterised by high levels of indivisibility; it can also be easily transferred and learnt at little cost. Hence it cannot be fully appropriated by innovators, but it can be applied to a wide variety of uses. Finally, it cannot be traded without some disclosure; hence its value is difficult to assess.

In this approach, the generation of technical knowledge is the result of a deductive chain that utilises scientific discoveries and general methodological procedures developed mainly in pure research; such knowledge is then applied to the specific activities of each firm. Learning is automatically associated with the new vintages of capital goods and human capital. The actual flow of technological information is considered to be a spontaneous aspect of economic systems. Intellectual property rights can increase appropriability but reduce the scope for the socialisation of innovation benefits (Arrow, 1962b and 1969; Jaffe, 1986; David, 1993a and 1994; Geroski, 1995). The new endogenous growth theories rely systematically on these assumptions. (Aghion and Howitt, 1998).

This 'Arrovian' view of technological knowledge, as information, is being increasingly challenged by recent developments of the Schumpeterian and Marshallian approaches, which stress the distinction between information and knowledge; for information is an input in the production of knowledge. Specifically, the notion of localised technological knowledge contrasts with the 'Arrovian' notion of generic knowledge and elaborates an approach where technological knowledge is considered a non-pure private good with higher levels of appropriability and excludability, generated by a process characterised by cumulativeness and path-dependence (Antonelli, 1995a; David, 1975; Atkinson and Stiglitz, 1969).

According to this growing literature, there is a distinction between technological knowledge and technological information, in that the former implies the competence and capability necessary to use information, within the specific context of each agent, as well as to participate in communication and, eventually, to generate additional information. Knowledge is 'localised' in tacit learning processes that are embedded into the background and experience of each innovator and hence highly idiosyncratic. It is thus largely excludable and its use is partly rivalrous. In particular, technological knowledge tends to be localised in well-defined technical, institutional, regional and industrial situations: it is specific to each industry, region, firm and individual or team of individuals and consequently costly to use elsewhere. The localised character of technical knowledge increases its appropriability, but reduces its spontaneous circulation in the economic system (Lamberton, 1971; David, 1993a and b; Mansfield, 1985; Jorde and Teece, 1990; Rosenberg, 1990).

Since technological knowledge tends to be highly specific and is costly, if not impossible, to use elsewhere, communication conditions become very important: relevant communication efforts are necessary both to transmit and acquire it. The transfer and adaptation of technological knowledge from one firm to another involves specific costs, that according to many empirical analyses almost amount to the cost of first introduction (Nelson, 1990; Rosenberg, 1990). In turn however, the generation of localised knowledge is increasingly viewed as the outcome of a collective undertaking strongly influenced by the effective availability of information and the quality of communication channels among learning agents (Von Hippel, 1988; Allen, 1983).

The division between the standard and the Schumpeterian-Marshallian approach also applies to the production of technological knowledge. In the standard approach, the generation of technological knowledge is the outcome of institutionalised efforts geared towards the introduction of innovation, which occurs in a deductive chain originating from scientific discoveries and general methodological procedures, easily understood by all potential users and elaborated mainly in universities. A growing number of authors have recently challenged the traditional view of technology as a pure public good, arguing that technology has a strong proprietary character. In fact, each unit of technological knowledge can be created, used and exchanged only by means of specific competences acquired by firms, now viewed as learning organisations, within a larger framework, which includes a whole array of complementary and interrelated units of knowledge generated by other firms, universities and research institutions.

The Marshallian tradition provides basic guidance in this direction (Richardson, 1972; Loasby, 1991 and 1994; Zaratiegui, 1997; Casson, 1997). Alfred Marshall (1890, VIII) had already grasped much of the complex interactions between capital, knowledge and organisation and the implications of the distinction between the public and private nature of knowledge:

> Capital consists in a great part of knowledge and organization: and of this some part is private property and other part is not; it enables us to subdue Nature and force her to satisfy our wants. Organization aids knowledge; it has many forms, e.g. that of a single business, that of various businesses in the same trade, that of various trades relatively to one another and that of the State providing security for all and help for many. The distinction between public and private property in

knowledge and organization is of great and growing importance: in some respects of more importance than that between public and private property in material things; and for that reason it seems best sometimes to reckon Organization apart as a distinct agent of production.

(Book IV, I, 1)

In the Schumpeterian view, the generation of new knowledge is mainly the outcome of the efforts of innovators drawing on learning processes, which are localised and specific to their individual history and experience. Localised technological knowledge contains elements of highly specific and tacit knowledge, possessing a high degree of idiosyncrasy. Drawing on daily routines and from the tacit experience of using capital goods, producing and manufacturing, and interacting with both customers and other manufacturers, localised technological knowledge is implemented via formal activities of R&D.

The capability to innovate appears to be strongly conditioned by both access to available technological information and learning opportunities, and by the accumulation of tacit knowledge both internal and external to each firm. The new analyses of the innovation process highlight the important distinctions between information, knowledge and competence and identify the significance of the innovation system into which each firm is embedded.

Knowledge, information and competence

The dynamics of localised knowledge

Technological information in the form of codified knowledge, tacit knowledge acquired by means of repeated action and the technological externalities from the technological and regional innovation system which is acquired with systematic communication efforts, represent the basic ingredients in the process of the creation of new knowledge. Knowledge is the result of a complex process of creation of new information, guided by the competence of each agent, building upon the mix of tacit knowledge acquired by means of learning processes, the socialisation of experience, the recombination of available information and the conduct of formal R&D activities.

Specifically, technological knowledge, as it is used and generated by firms, draws upon four different forms of knowledge and four distinct processes. It is useful to distinguish between the relevant forms of knowledge along two axes: tacit or codified and internal or external (to each firm). Hence we have internal and external tacit knowledge and internal and external codified knowledge. Internal tacit knowledge consists of skills and rules which 'cannot be articulated' (Nelson and Winter, 1982: 76), it is generated by means of processes of learning by doing and learning by using. External tacit knowledge is acquired through informal exchanges and socialisation, which require dedicated efforts and enable the internalisation of the technological externalities spilling into the technological and regional innovation systems in which each firm operates: membership into technological and standardisation clubs plays a key role here, as well as the location within technological districts. Internal codified knowledge is the result of formal activities of R&D. Finally, external codified knowledge, consisting of structured information available in generic forms, is acquired as such, but eventually re-organised by means of the recombination of bits of technological information and applied to different contexts than those originally conceived, and often implemented with a variety of formal co-operation schemes between firms with their own R&D laboratories or between firms and universities, including standardisation processes, co-localisation within technological districts and membership into technological clubs (Chapters 8, 9 and 10) (see Table 2.1).

Competence consists of the capability of firms to implement such a complex mix of inputs, where each element is complementary and indispensable.[2] Some substitution among the different components and related processes is possible but only to a limited extent. Tacit knowledge is necessary to generate new localised knowledge, both directly and indirectly, as it is essential to acquire and learn new codified knowledge, because of the high levels of natural excludability of codified knowledge. Rarely can codified knowledge, even when it consists of the results of scientific undertakings, be reduced to a simple set of instructions. Codified knowledge can be acquired directly on the shelf and yet the direct and intimate relationships between researchers plays a central role in its assimilation (Quéré, 1994; Zucker, Darby and Amstrong, 1994). As a result codified knowledge is necessary for the accumulation and elaboration of both localised knowledge and new tacit knowledge. External codified knowledge is necessary as a source of new ideas to feed the recombination process (Pavitt, 1991). External tacit knowledge is required to implement internal knowledge, both tacit and codified.

In the generation of new localised knowledge, competence consists of the specific activity shaping the relationship among these four forms of information processing. Such an activity can be specified as follows:

$$\text{LTK} = (\text{LEARNING}^a, \text{SOCIALISATION}^b, \text{R\&D}^c, \text{RECOMBINATION}^d) \quad (1)$$

Table 2.1 The four components of localised technological knowledge

	Tacit	*Codified*
Internal	Learning	R&D
External	Socialisation	Recombination

In equation (1) LTK stands for localised technological knowledge; a, b, c, d, measure the marginal productivity of each respective component. Each component is indispensable. This clearly implies that no form of knowledge, out of the four considered, should fall below a minimum level without putting the full process at risk. Substitution can take place, but only to a limited extent.

This analysis has important implications for assessing (from both a social and private viewpoint) the organisation of knowledge production. The strong complementarity between internal and external sources of knowledge stresses the trade off between the positive effects of property rights on innovation incentive and negative ones on information dissemination and the key role of communication among firms and other research institutions.

Enhanced appropriability regimes for inventors, secured by intellectual property rights, like, long-lasting patents with a large breadth or lead times, barriers to entry and generally pre-existing monopoly power of incumbents, delay the disclosure of the information and the decay of quasi-rents associated with the innovation. As such, they are a fundamental incentive for agents to innovate, undertake inventive activity and last, but not least, secure financial resources both in internal and external financial markets to fund risky research and search activities.

At the same time, however, protection to inventors, consisting of either *ex-ante* patents or *ex-post* market-power, has a significant negative effect, with regard to both the private efficiency and the social welfare, on the production of new knowledge. The proprietary character of the new knowledge leads to monopoly rents, which delay the diffusion of product and process innovations, and, to duplication of efforts, and therefore a waste of resources, in re-inventing knowledge which is already available but proprietary. Finally, the possibilities for the dissemination, recombination and cumulative usage of the new knowledge are also reduced with clear damages to both the social and private efficiency in the generation of new knowledge.

Since localised knowledge builds upon the combination of both tacit and codified knowledge, internal and external to firms, and it is generated by the competence embedded in the memory of organisations and in the economic, regional and industrial environment of each firm, it is difficult to learn, imitate, transfer, adopt and use elsewhere. It is more proprietary and appropriable than is generally assumed in the 'Arrovian' tradition. As such, localised knowledge has the characteristics of a non-pure private good which can be partially appropriated by those who have generated it (Romer, 1990). Its use is partly excludable, in fact its identification, imitation and re-utilisation require dedicated learning and communication efforts by prospective users. Because of this, the conditions of the circulation and communication of localised knowledge are far less easy than currently assumed and do play a key role in the general innovative capacity of an economic system (Chapter 5).

Different modes of organisation of knowledge production, such as entre-preneurship, institutional variety, vertical integration, technological co-operation, and specialisation have been experimented with historically and are still in place today. Their social and private efficiency varies according to the levels of transaction and governance costs, the character-istics of the technology being introduced and especially the dissemination and communication conditions for technological knowledge, once generated (Chapter 8).

According to the different modes of organisation of knowledge produc-tion, in the attempt to achieve complementarity, a variety of paths, characterised by the different sequences with which each component enters the process and their different relative marginal productivity, can be detected in the knowledge production process. A major distinction can be drawn between the articulation of the competence shaping the knowledge produc-tion process which prevails in skill-intensive and science-based industries respectively.

The articulation of the competence consists of the specific combination processes of the different forms of knowledge necessary to generate tech-nological innovations. The specific forms of competence, that is the speci-fications of the knowledge production process differs across industries. In all cases, the management of the interfaces among the firm and its environment is crucial to the assessment of the efficiency of the innovation process: the weight and role of each process, however, exhibit significant variations. Moreover, these processes also evolve along technology life cycles, and, with respect to skill- and science-based industries different sequences can be articulated.

The dynamics of localised knowledge in skill-intensive industries

In skill-intensive industries, tacit knowledge and internal learning processes, built upon previous vintages of already-assimilated technological knowledge, have high relative weights in absolute terms and especially so in the early phases of the technology life cycle. At this stage, excludability and appropriability are very high and knowledge has strong characteristics of a private good. Prominence eventually shifts towards external tacit learning, and sequentially to internal codified knowledge. In the maturity phases, codified knowledge bears the highest relative weight. Imitation here becomes easier and, conversely, excludability and appropriability levels decline. Technological knowledge eventually becomes 'quasi generic' in that it increasingly acquires the characteristics of codified knowledge with a high content of accessible information.

In the early phases of this technology life cycle, tacit knowledge plays a key role. It is eventually implemented by means of the pervasive effects of socialisation, that is, the sharing of competences acquired, via learning processes, by each learning agent in the innovation system. User-producer relations play a major role in this context, as a mechanism accelerating technology transfer. Labour markets for skilled labour, embodying relevant tacit knowledge, are also an important device for achieving faster and higher levels of complementarity among the different forms of knowledge. In the stages that follow, efforts are geared towards codifying the tacit knowledge and converting it into more general forms of understanding via R&D activities. Eventually, the recombination with complementary codified knowledge already elaborated in other contexts becomes the main source of additional knowledge.

In this process of the generation of localised knowledge, which consists here of a conversion from tacit to codified knowledge, a number of distinct steps can be identified. At first, tacit knowledge is firm-specific, that is, it is fully embedded in the idiosyncratic characteristics of the firm, where it was accumulated by means of learning by doing and learning by using. By means of collective processes of socialisation, engendered by regional proximity, some tacit knowledge eventually becomes region-specific, shared by firms co-localised within well-defined regions. Finally, tacit knowledge becomes industry-specific, shared and embedded into the idiosyncratic characteristics of well-defined industrial groups of firms with high levels of homogeneity in terms of knowledge base and hence products and production processes. Standardisation processes are relevant in this context. The emergence of *de-facto* standards acts as a process of conversion of tacit knowledge into codified knowledge and enables faster processes of socialisation and eventual recombination (Chapter 10).

Codified knowledge evolves along parallel ground. In the initial phases, R&D activities are mainly oriented towards the integration of insights, offered by scientific breakthroughs, with tacit knowledge acquired by means of internal learning processes. In the later phases R&D activities are focused on the recombination of scientific information offered by contiguous fields, which, when properly combined with the competences and technological capabilities accumulated by each firm, may translate into new opportunities to introduce innovations directly relevant to the products currently manufactured.

The dynamics of localised knowledge in science-based industries

A different path in knowledge blending is at work in science-based industries such as chemistry, pharmaceuticals and electronics, where scientific breakthroughs act as sorting devices, pushing the search and research processes in new directions and opening up new opportunities.

In science-based industries, localised technological knowledge is generated from a different combination and sequence of knowledge forms. The sequence is reversed in that codified knowledge spilling from new scientific breakthroughs and the existing knowledge pool acts as a vector of technological opportunities. In order to achieve the necessary complementarity, embedded in the relationship between the four different forms of knowledge, recombination is the second key process: firms must first acquire the new elements of codified knowledge made available by the scientific community.

Standardisation again plays a major role, although in a different context. The definition of *de-jure* standards helps the process of conversion from codified into tacit knowledge and allows faster processes of generation of new localised knowledge (Chapter 10).

Tacit knowledge is especially important in conducting R&D activities and in assimilating external codified knowledge: the intimate relations between the academic and the business community are influential. Technological co-operation among firms and between firms and academic institutions, with the implementation of a variety of technological clubs, plays a major role as an external source of knowledge, both tacit and codified (Chapter 9).

At the beginning of this technology life cycle, technological knowledge drawing from scientific knowledge, mainly in a codified form, is difficult to learn because it retains strong characteristics of natural excludability. In these industries recombination has a major role in the first phases of the technology life cycles. Intramuros R&D activities play a large role at the beginning of the technology life cycle, but mainly as a tool to access the science base available in universities and scientific laboratories. Eventually, the blending of external codified knowledge with internal R&D activities and the skill accumulated in each firm assumes a larger role. This sequence gives localised knowledge the features of a highly idiosyncratic good, embedded in the organisation of each firm, difficult to transfer and imitate; so possessing the properties of a semi-private good with higher levels of appropriability and excludability. In science-based industries, technological knowledge is first industry specific and eventually firm specific. Imitation is easier in the early phases of incubation of new technologies, as well as entry, but becomes more and more difficult as the selection in the market takes place and technological knowledge is increasingly localised in the idiosyncratic characteristics of the organisation, production process and competence of successful innovators.

Within the context of the technology life cycle, the intrinsic cumulativeness of the generation of knowledge, both internal to firms and innovation systems, has evidently a crucial role. At each step, the generation of new knowledge is strongly influenced, in terms of the rate and direction of the new technologies being generated and adopted, by the direction of technological changes already introduced, and by the sequential path of the specific forms of knowledge that have been generated and used in the past by each agent and the innovation system as a whole (Swann, Prevezer and Stout, 1998).

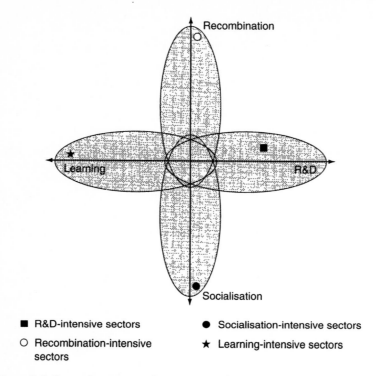

Figure 2.1 Sectoral patterns of generation of localised technological knowledge

Sectoral patterns of accumulation of localised knowledge: a taxonomy

This analysis makes it possible to implement the well known sectoral taxonomy of the patterns of accumulation of technological knowledge and introduction of technological change elaborated by Pavitt (1984) which distinguishes four types of industries: supplier dominated, science-based, scale-intensive and specialised equipment suppliers.

In our taxonomy, industries are classified according to the marginal productivity of each of the four sources of technological knowledge. Industries will be respectively R&D-intensive, recombination-intensive, socialisation-intensive and learning-intensive when R&D, recombination, socialisation and learning will exhibit the larger output elasticity respectively. More generally, we distinguish between science-based and skill-intensive industries.

In science-based industries both internal R&D and recombination play a key role: combined they exhibit a larger marginal efficiency. Clearly the chemical, pharmaceutical, biotechnological and electronic industries belong to the class of R&D-intensive activities. Software and informatics, however, can be better considered as recombination-intensive activities: the role of external knowledge is crucial.

Next, we have the skill-intensive industries, such as textile and garment, furniture, leather and shoes, business and financial services, where both internal learning and socialisation play a key role in the generation of new knowledge. Internal learning, however, appears to be the single large source of new knowledge in many engineering sectors, where important economies of growth are at work at the plant level.

Socialisation and recombination, specifically user-producer interactions, are crucial in most sectors where technological change is embodied in new vintages of capital goods, which are supplied by upstream industries. This, however, is also the case of knowledge-intensive business services which rely systematically on learning and recombination in generating new knowledge, but make little use of formal R&D activities.

Efficiency wages and the rates of generation of localised knowledge

The rates of generation of localised knowledge depend heavily on learning processes and their cumulativeness. This focuses attention on the role of the workforce, both in science-based and skill-intensive industries, in terms of levels of involvement, active participation in the production process and embodied human capital. The active participation of a qualified workforce, in implementing learning processes, makes it possible to accumulate and better valorise tacit knowledge and experience, enabling the proper evaluation of the specific context of action, and enhancing the matching between the availability of new codified knowledge and the experience of each firm. The rates of implementation of know-how, know-where and know-when rests on the levels of participation of the skilled workforce into both production and decision-making.

In this context, efficiency wages become especially relevant. Firms set efficiency wages to a level that is in excess of the short-term labour productivity levels and the opportunity cost of the effort of workers, in order to discourage shrinking and to exert a direct, positive effect on the active participation of the workforce in the learning processes (Shapiro and Stiglitz, 1984). Efficiency wages enhance loyalty and commitment, and stimulate practitioners into developing informal relations and better collective work, sharing information and accelerating the emergence of tacit knowledge (Ciborra, 1993).

Moreover, efficiency wages exert a strong influence on the levels of mobility of labour in labour markets, both with respect to new generations and intrafirm mobility. Efficiency wages make it possible to attract labour with high levels of human capital and tacit knowledge, with a cream-skimming effect on labour markets, enhancing the socialisation of tacit knowledge and, more generally the transfer of localised knowledge among firms and between training institutions and firms.

Effective internal labour markets, which favour the upgrading of competent employees within the firm, are an important complementary tool to accelerate the rates of accumulation of experience and tacit knowledge. In fact, such markets keep competent labour within the firm and act as a powerful incentive to stimulate the participation of the workforce in learning processes.

In summary, efficiency wages stimulate the opportunity for internal mobility, and activate the inductive processes of learning by doing and learning by using among the workforce. In turn, this feeds the accumulation of localised knowledge, through encouraging both, with the bottom-up process of accumulation of competence and innovative capability, and the top-down process of adaptation of new codified knowledge to the idiosyncratic context of each firm. Efficiency wages facilitate the processes of 'translation' of tacit knowledge, acquired by means of learning processes within the workforce, into codified knowledge, and *vice versa*. In doing so, efficiency wages and internal labour markets have a powerful effect, accelerating the blending of internal and external knowledge and its integration with the organisational knowledge on which the introduction of localised innovation rests (Chapter 3 and Chapter 7).

Increasing returns in the generation of localised technological knowledge

The generation of localised technological knowledge is characterised by significant feedbacks and increasing returns.[3] These are both internal and external to firms.

According to a growing amount of empirical evidence on the intrinsic cumulativeness of the generation of new knowledge, internal increasing returns are pervasive in the generation and use of new knowledge (Stephan, 1996). Internal increasing returns consist of the dynamics of learning to learn, which is in turn based upon the effects of substantial indivisibilities and irreversibilities in the production of new knowledge. In particular, two factors of internal increasing returns have been detected. Strong elements of cumulativeness characterise the production of new knowledge, which is mainly based upon the process of recombining existing bits of information with new ones, so that much new knowledge is made 'standing on the shoulders of giants' (Scotchmer, 1991). Hence the larger the skills and experience accumulated by each firm and the amount of resources invested in search and research processes, the greater the innovative output. Second, many of the costs associated with the production of new knowledge are fixed because of the difficulty in changing the destination and use of the skills and competences acquired in the production of each specific form of knowledge (Stiglitz, 1987: 125). Hence, at each point in time, the greater the additional innovative efforts that make use of that basic infrastructure, both tangible and intangible, the lower are the costs because of the classical effects of economies of density. Higher innovative output makes better use of the existing and long-lived stock of fixed infrastructure and intangible capital, consisting of the localised knowledge already commanded by the firm. Cumulativeness and economies of density lead to the dynamics of learning to learn.

Increasing attention has recently been paid to technological externalities spilling from the learning and research activities of other firms. Techno-logical externalities are defined as the direct, i.e. not mediated by market prices, effects on the technological capacity of each firm produced by the complementarity and interrelatedness of both R&D activities and tech-nological learning among interdependent firms. Technological externalities thus spill from complementarity and interrelatedness among firms and other research institutions in the generation of new technologies, rather than from complementarity and interrelatedness of the actual production processes in use.[4]

This definition of technological externalities makes it possible to appreci-ate the knowledge dimension of innovation systems, which includes all firms involved in research and learning activities that are complementary, with respect to the technologies being introduced, irrespective of geo-graphical location.

The significance of the innovation system, with regard to technological externalities and the transfer of both tacit and codified knowledge between firms and other research institutions in the production of new knowledge, leads to external positive feedbacks. For given levels of investment in research and learning activities, the amount of technology generated is likely to be larger in countries and in sub-elements of industrial systems, where complementarities and interdependence in the generation of new knowledge, based upon strong communication systems and effective infor-mation flows, are already in place. Therefore, not only the technological capability, in terms of rates of introduction of technological innovations, but also the technological specialisation, in terms of industrial and tech-nological direction across sectors and products, is likely to be shaped by strong elements of irreversibility and inertia, i.e. path-dependence. External feedbacks provide an important rationale for understanding the strong stability over time of the technological advance and specialisation of countries (Callon, 1991; Archibugi and Pianta, 1992).

Economic topology: networks and spatial stochastic interactions

The distribution of agents in multidimensional spaces becomes a relevant issue in understanding the capability of firms and economic systems to generate technological knowledge. Topological attributes of the economic environment, into which firms are embedded, such as the distance among agents; their density in each relevant space; structural holes; types and complexity of actual links among agents; their connectivity and receptivity, are all crucial in shaping the causes and consequences of technological externalities (Perroux, 1935, 1964). Recombination and socialisation are heavily affected by the distribution of agents in a variety of economic spaces (Swann, Prevezer and Stout, 1998).

Relevant topological dimensions of economic spaces include: the scientific space in terms of the complementarity of the research agenda of each firm and research laboratory; the technological dimension in terms of the proximity of the technical characteristics of production processes; the product space in terms of the relations of complementarity, compatibility, inter-operability and substitutability of products; the consumer space in terms of the distribution of consumers groups which affects the actual values of the cross-elasticities of demand for differentiated products; the industrial dimension with respect to the user-producer relations among industries within the input-output matrix; the outsourcing dimensions, especially with respect to knowledge-intensive business services that are provided in the market place; the labour markets dimension in terms of labour markets generating and distributing skilled labour incorporating relevant competencies, both codified and tacit; the geographic dimension in terms of the role of regional proximity, transportation and location costs, and last but not least the institutional context as shaped by historic time and regional policy.[5]

In turn, the distribution of actual production processes and products, and of the characteristics of product and process innovations is not an exogeneous event dictated only by some technological and scientific laws. Interrelatedness, complementarity, inter-operability, cumulability and, more generally, technical distance among technological articrafts are not exogenous specifications of the technology, but conversely should be regarded as the outcome of path-dependent processes of the introduction and adoption of technological changes while under the constraints of both the economic environment and the topological characteristics of the multi-dimensional space into which the economic and technological action of firms is embedded.

In order to understand the innovative capability of firms as well as the rate and direction of technological change, an economic topology appears to be increasingly necessary. An economic topology enables an appreciation of the economic implications of the distribution of agents, in multidimensional spaces, in the generation and distribution of technological knowledge within economic systems. Network analysis and its dynamic developments with the methodology of repeated spatial stochastic interactions seem especially promising.

The notion of networks is gaining momentum in the social sciences: it provides an appealing metaphor in the analysis of social events where the holistic and the individualistic approaches merge (Burt, 1992; Wasserman and Faust, 1994). Networks consist of interdependent nodes whose individual behaviour is influenced by the system of relations with other nodes. Analysis of networks makes it possible to appreciate the characteristics of direct and indirect interdependences among agents which are not fully cleared by market prices.[6] The methodology of the time stratification of the historic sequence of different, but endogenous, spatial stochastic interaction structures seems to provide the basic tools for an understanding of the laws of the aggregate dynamics of localised technological change. The combined use of network analysis and the methodology of spatial stochastic interactions derived from Random Markov Fields can build a first step toward an economic topology (Chapter 5).

Innovation systems and their domains

In this context, a wave of empirical and theoretical works has made a step beyond the criticism of the traditional chain of factors that link innovation capability exclusively to intra-mural R&D expenditures and has articulated the notion of the innovation system in order to highlight the systemic character of the generation of technological knowledge (Freeman, 1991; Lundvall, 1992; Nelson, 1993; Freeman, 1997).

A large body of empirical research indicates that the process of the generation and use of new knowledge in firms interacts in a reciprocal way. The introduction of a single technological innovation is conditioned by decisions regarding the adoption of complementary or related innovations by other firms. Important additional knowledge about the capability of the new products which reflective sellers are able to appropriate and subsequently elaborate upon[7] is generated by the close interaction between sellers and customers, and assistance to buyers in learning how to use the new products. Explicit co-operation among firms plays a major role in assessing innovative capability: it enhances the circulation of information, the opportunities for external learning, that is learning from the specific knowledge generated by other firms, and the scope for capitalising on potential complementarities, between both the variety of firms and the different R&D activities performed by them.[8]

Much of this evidence has been encapsulated in the notion of national systems of innovations and confirms that the performances of innovating firms, in terms of the rate of introduction of technological innovations, cannot be analysed in isolation. Innovation capability depends also on the amount of information each firm is able to receive from the innovation system, both regional and technological, in which it operates and the effective use it makes of it.

Consequently, the study of the determinants of the innovation capability of each firm, embedded within an innovation system, must take into account six classes of factors:

1   the levels of skills and experience acquired by each agent;
2   the amount of resources devoted to generating innovation by each agent in the system;
3   each agent's receptivity to technological knowledge generated by third parties in the system, and its search capacity;
4   the complementarity in the knowledge base among innovating firms in the system;
5   the properties of the system in terms of connectivity and distribution of receptive agents;
6   the properties of the system in terms of the width and substance of the scientific and technological pool, consisting of basic research and academic training activities converted into technological opportunities offered to each firm.

The systemic character of the innovation process, however, applies to a variety of domains which deserve to be specified according to the characteristics of the localised knowledge involved. Much attention has been dedicated to the national domain, so that national innovation systems have been studied in detail. Our approach to the generation of localised technological knowledge and the distinction between the bottom-up processes of generation of localised technological change in skill-based industries and top-down processes in science-based industries enables the identification and appreciation of three more specific domains of innovation systems. Namely, local innovation systems, global innovation systems, and technological systems.

National innovation systems are relevant when the general conditions of the scientific infrastructure, education and training are considered together with the communication infrastructure, the inter-industrial flows of information and the general supply of knowledge-intensive business services. The institutional setting of intellectual property rights and standardisation processes are also important in that they affect in depth incentives to codification on the one hand and the conditions for the circulation of

Table 2.2 The domains of innovation systems

	Local (socialisation)	Global (recombination)	Technolgical
Skill intensive	• Labour markets • User producer • KIBS • Technological districts	• Global KIBS	Complementarity Compatibility Inter-operability Standardisation
Science based	• University – industry • Science parks • Scientific entrepreneurship	• Scientific networks	Cross-licensing Collective R&D Technological clubs

scientific and technological information on the other. Beside the national domain, however, local, global and technological domain systems seem to be very important (Edquist, 1997).

Local innovation systems appear especially relevant within skilled-based industries. In these industries, regional proximity is a major factor in the generation of localised technological knowledge because it enables the socialisation of tacit knowledge more effectively and systematically. User-producer relations, informal exchanges and cross-imitation among competitors, creation of new firms and especially spin-offs from incumbents, and the mobility of skilled labour among firms are all influential in the generation of localised technological change, that are augmented and actually made possible by regional and territorial proximity (Feldman, 1994; Swann, Prevezer and Stout, 1998). Global innovation systems play an important role also in skill-intensive industries, a role that is made increasingly relevant by new information technologies when access to international knowledge-intensive business service companies is considered. Recent empirical findings confirm the important role of the international spillover of technological externalities (Coe and Helpman, 1995).

Global innovation systems, however, are relevant, especially within science-based industries for the opportunity they offer to co-operate within scientific networks via university researchers, research laboratories and firms active in remote geographical contexts. Local innovation systems also play an important role in science-based industries, within science parks and other institutional settings characterised by proximity, such as scientific venture capital, implementing information exchanges and relations between universities and firms, thus favouring scientific entrepreneurship.

Beside the regional domains, the systemic character of the generation of new localised knowledge is relevant also at the technology level, when technological complementarities between innovations, which are part of the same technological systems, are considered. In order to achieve complementarity, compatibility and inter-operability of new technologies, a variety of institutional actions such as cross-licensing, standardisation procedures and technological alliances are implemented (Langlois and Robertson, 1995). New information and communication technologies provide evidence about the systemic nature of technological change: information and communication technologies are themselves the outcome of the convergence of a variety of complementary innovations generated in a wide range of industries, including telecommunications, informatics, microprocessors, optoelectronics, and space industries (Chapter 6).

The higher the complementarity of innovations being introduced in each technological system the faster are the overall rates of introduction of technological innovations. The direction of technological innovations within technological systems is affected by the emergence of compatible innovations and their levels of complementarities. Moreover, the rates and directions of generation of each of these innovations are very much influenced by their levels of compatibility and interfacing with the existing capital stock. The institutional setting of standardisation processes, the implementation of cross-licensing practices, technological clubs, research joint-ventures and collective industrial research centres, are important tools, favouring the coherence of innovative efforts within technological systems (Chapters 9 and 10).

Within technological systems, as in regional systems, inertia in the direction and path-dependence in the rates of technological change are once more the outcome of local irreversibilities and indivisibilities (Antonelli, 1992; 1993a and b; Callon, 1991; Perrin, 1991; Rosenberg, 1994; Swann, Prevezer and Stout, 1998).

New information technologies and the generation of localised technological knowledge

The introduction of new information and communication technologies radically changes the processes of generation of localised knowledge because it affects the accumulation of both tacit and codified knowledge. New information and communication technologies have powerful effects on the conditions of accessing, storing, processing and communicating information. As a result firms can better exchange and trade both tacit and codified knowledge.[9] Computer communication moreover can be used to substantially reduce transaction costs associated with the market exchange of bits of technological knowledge, because dedicated communication protocols, and especially the access conditions to dedicated software and data banks, can be used as 'hostages' and hence reduce the risks of opportunistic behaviour.

The use of business and communication services in innovation systems is becoming an important factor of connectivity and receptivity among agents, thus enhancing the innovative capability of an innovation system. The generation and diffusion of innovations rely more and more upon the daily on-line interaction, communication and trading of information of learning firms, among themselves and with other scientific institutions, taking advantage of the new advanced telecommunications infrastructure and the opportunities for computer communication it offers. Knowledge-intensive business service firms, by taking advantage of new information and communication technologies, can specialise in the management of the interfaces between external and internal knowledge, operating as 'converters' of codified knowledge into localised experience and tacit knowledge and *vice versa* (Chapter 11).

The remote-controlled application of general purpose software and algorithms to specific contexts of action increases the economic value of codified knowledge, consequently accelerating the rates of its codification. At the same time however, because of the easier conditions of interaction and communication, engendered by new information and communication technologies, firms can better manage the accumulation of internal tacit knowledge and its integration with external tacit knowledge. Tacit knowledge may also be acquired from activities conducted in remote locations, or by third parties, linked by means of computer communication systems. The possibilities for 'remote' exchanges of tacit knowledge and remote socialisation of scientific and technological knowledge are also augmented by the availability of new information and communication technologies. New information technologies help firms to implement technological co-operation at a distance. Firms located in remote markets are more keen to establish effective technological alliances. The risks of opportunistic behaviour are reduced by the sheer geographical distance and by the complexities of conducting business in remote locations (Chapter 9).

In this context, the diffusion of new information and communication technologies favours the demise of the Chandlerian mode of generation of new knowledge, based upon the tight vertical integration of research and search activities within industrial firms. This is because of the increasing outsourcing of knowledge-generating activities this mode makes possible. By means of computer communication firms can rely more and more on knowledge-intensive business service (KIBS) providers, who acting as 'competent interfaces', implement the blending of the different forms of knowledge necessary to generate new localized knowledge (Chapter 8).

In turn, the remote access to KIBS, made possible by new information and communication technologies, gives these firms a global scope of action so that multinational KIBS firms can gradually emerge, combining the advantages of proximity and variety.

Hence, the speed of circulation of both technological information and technological knowledge within economic systems is likely to increase along with the division of labour among economic agents in the production of new knowledge.

Localised knowledge and intellectual property rights regimes

The notion of localised knowledge has important implications for the current debate on the appropriate regime of intellectual property rights because it enables a new approach to the analysis of the intellectual property rights trade off.

As a growing literature has pointed out, there is a trade off between the

Table 2.3 The dynamics of localised technological knowledge with new information and communication technologies

	Tacit		Codified
Internal	Learning	K I	R&D
External	Socialisation	B S	Recombination

goal of efficient use of the stock of knowledge and the need to provide an optimal incentive to the potential producer of new knowledge. To put it very simply, in the choice of intellectual property rights regimes, protection to inventors is traded off against protection to users of invention (Hirshleifer and Riley, 1992; Besen and Raskind, 1991; David, 1992; Foray, 1995).

On the one hand it seems necessary to provide protection to the inventor because of the low appropriability of technological knowledge. In an innovation system with a weak intellectual property rights regime, inventors have only a small incentive to invest resources in the production of new knowledge and hence the general rate of productivity growth will be low.

On the other hand, there is a clear incentive to enhance the dissemination of new knowledge for many reasons: to generalise and fasten its uses and applications, and hence its diffusion and related implementation; to minimise duplication of research efforts; and to increase the rates of generation of new knowledge embodying previous knowledge. An innovation system with a (too) strong intellectual property rights regime, based upon patents granted with strict novelty requirements and with a broad breadth, can experience low rates of productivity growth and yet high rates of generation of new knowledge. New knowledge is poorly used and its rates of increase can fall in the long term because of the lower opportunities for recombination.

From a social viewpoint the choice of an appropriate regime of intellectual property rights consists of elaborating the 'best' compromise between the conflicting incentives to protection and dissemination of intellectual property. An intellectual property rights regime is appropriate when it overcomes the contradiction 'between the "static" disadvantage of a patent monopoly and the "dynamic" advantage of encouraging invention' (Hirschleifer, 1971). Intellectual property rights regimes can be classified according to their balance between these two goals. Thus, an intellectual property rights regime can be defined as 'diffusion oriented' when exclusive rights to inventors will be weak and circumscribed while users will be favoured. An intellectual property rights regime can be defined as 'invention oriented' when, on the contrary, broad exclusive rights will be granted to inventors.

In the 'Arrovian' economics of knowledge, an innovation system requires a strong invention regime of intellectual property rights in order to attract appropriate levels of resources in the production of new knowledge, because of the public good nature of generic knowledge and its low levels of appropriability and excludability (Machlup and Penrose, 1950).

The producer of localised knowledge, instead, can pay less attention to the protection offered by intellectual property rights regimes: he is protected by the fact that an important component of this knowledge is tacit and consequently cannot be easily expressed outside of the research, learning and production context in which it is generated. Free riding is less dangerous if technological knowledge is localised and therefore a non-pure private good, rather than a public good as in the 'Arrovian' tradition. The producer of localised knowledge, however, depends heavily on the provision of external codified and tacit knowledge and on the conditions of access to the stock of knowledge because of the strong cumulative and systemic characteristics of the generation of localised knowledge: both external tacit and codified knowledge enter into the production function of new knowledge. The non-pure private good characteristics of localised knowledge suggest that an evolution in the intellectual property rights regime might emerge: one where the acquisition, communication and dissemination conditions of new knowledge are appreciated as important inputs of the general production of knowledge, as well as providers of necessary levels of property rights.[10]

Intellectual property rights regimes build upon three basic tools: patents, trade secrecy and copyrights. Both from a dissemination and an invention view point, intellectual property is better enforced by patents than trade secrecy for the informational function of patents. In turn, patents are granted with varying qualifications in terms of degree of novelty, breadth and duration. Copyright law, usually applied to acts of creativity rather than scientific and technological knowledge, seems more and more appealing in this context, because, on the one hand, it provides strong protection to inventors, but on the other, it reduces excludability and protects derivative applications of the original knowledge.

In this context, the excludability and breadth of the patents assigned seem especially important. When excludability implies the absolute right of the owner to impede the use of the new knowledge by third parties, as well as the right to discriminate among potential users, the goal of maximising the dissemination of new knowledge and its recombination in order to produce new localised knowledge seems especially endangered. For the same reason, a broad breadth of patents assigned to inventors risks excluding other potential users from a large portion of the new set of prospects opened by each invention and each element of additional knowledge (Kitch, 1977; Arora, 1997).

A regime of intellectual property rights based upon mandated licensing of patents, which draws from copyright law both the characteristics of non-excludability and the reward for derivative uses, seems increasingly likely to be advocated in order to make the current intellectual property rights regime more diffusion-oriented (Besen and Raskind, 1991; Foray, 1995; Eswaran and Gallini, 1996).

Mandated licensing offers a compromise between the conflicting goals of dissemination and protection, consistent with the characteristics of localised knowledge. Localised knowledge has higher levels of appropriability and excludability than currently assumed in the generic knowledge tradition, but also has higher levels of dependability on the conditions of access to external codified knowledge. It is worth noting that mandated licensing seems more and more practised in new information and communication technologies, where inter-operability, interconnection and interfacing of software and hardware play a major role in assessing the viability of new technologies and their scope for adoption and further implementation (Farell, 1995).

Mandated licensing of patents with a narrow breadth enables users of well defined bits of proprietary knowledge to access easily the stock of codified knowledge and at the same time establishes the basic conditions for rewarding inventors. The protection for derivative uses of each bit of codified knowledge help inventors of important technological novelties to reap a larger portion of the revenue generated. Hence, mandated licensing can itself become an incentive for the producers of localised knowledge to make further efforts to fully and better codify their knowledge and market it. Mandated licensing can help the implementation of marketing especially when knowledge-intensive business service firms act as interfaces between inventors and users (Chapter 8).

Conclusions

The traditional 'Arrovian' argument represents the pillar on which a large portion of the economics of knowledge has been built. It maintains that technological knowledge is grafted into 'generic' blueprints, available on the shelf to everybody with little effort (Arrow, 1962b and 1969; Stoneman, 1983 and 1987; Hirschleifer and Riley, 1992).

The standard approach stresses the purely *informational* aspect of generic technological knowledge and views it as the outcome of a scientific process, i.e. the application of general rules to a specific problem that can subsequently and almost without cost, imitated and applied by everyone else. The alternative 'Marshallian and Schumpeterian' approach emphasises instead the *technological and communication* aspects of knowledge: it concentrates on the tacit and cumulative character of the know-how necessary both to generate and use it, and on the role of communication and exchanges of information among parties involved in the generation of both their own tacit and codified components.

This debate is now being elaborated into a broader, more comprehensive approach, where the two contrasting views are combined. In our approach, technological knowledge is seen to have a strong localised character. Localised technological knowledge is very much the outcome of a systemic process of generation involving the combination and blending of the experience and skills acquired by agents in daily routines; the access and ability to absorb external tacit knowledge generated by the other members in an innovation system; formal activities of research conducted *intra-muros* and finally, the access to external sources of codified knowledge. Localised technological knowledge is the outcome of a path-dependent dynamic process in that it reflects the original 'accidental' characters of the innovation system in which the dynamic process begins, as well as the intentional behaviour of learning agents whose innovative conduct is fully embedded in the particular system of which they are part (Antonelli, 1995a; David, 1975 and 1993).

A new taxonomy of the sectoral patterns of accumulation of localised technological knowledge can be built, on these bases, according to the relative weight of the four different and yet complementary processes that are at the core of knowledge accumulation. Industries can be termed R&D-intensive, recombination-intensive, learning-intensive and socialisation-intensive according to the relative output elasticity in terms of knowledge of each of the processes.

The specificity of technological knowledge, to the firm and to the technological and regional innovation system which generates it, and the related communication requirements represent two sides of the same coin. The distribution of firms in the multidimensional topological space and their evolution in time is crucial to understanding the dynamics of technological knowledge. The methodology of spatial stochastic interactions provides important tools to understand it.

The structural and systemic conditions of the economic topology of innovation systems, that is the distribution of agents in multidimensional economic spaces, is crucial to understanding the dynamics of technological knowledge. The characteristics of the distribution of economic agents in multidimensional economic spaces become central to our analysis of the generation and distribution of knowledge within economic systems. Such topological factors as distance, density, structural holes, connectivity and receptivity probabilities of each agent, governing the interplay between internal and external tacit and codified knowledge, are central to a variety of analytical features of the knowledge economy. The uneven distribution of innovation capability over time and across countries, regions and industrial systems; the role of technological systems and regional and technological clusters of firms within industrial and technological districts; the relevance of user-producer interactions within industrial *filières*, are where both the receptivity of firms to external information and network connectivity are likely to be more effective due to the positive effects of proximity and repeated transactions[11] respectively.

In the Schumpeterian and Marshallian approach, the accumulation of localised tacit knowledge and skills, embedded in the processes of learning by doing and by using, appears to be characterised by increasing returns and positive feedbacks which are both internal and external to firms (Perroux, 1935). Specifically, two factors of internal increasing returns have been detected: cumulativeness, due to the nature of the production of knowledge, that is the recombination of bits of existing codified knowledge and their integration with new insights acquired via the accumulation of skills and experience; and economies of density due to the sunk costs associated with the infrastructure, the skills and competences necessary for the production of each specific form of knowledge. Cumulativeness and economies of density lead to the dynamics of learning to learn.

Technological externalities, spilling from universities to firms and between firms themselves, as a result of the accelerated communication flows of both tacit and codified knowledge in innovation systems within the well-defined geographical and technological domains, provide the basic engine for the emergence of important positive feedbacks external to each firm but internal to the system. Organisation at the firm and at the system levels, as shaped by the architecture and effectiveness of communication flows between units within each firm and between firms, universities and other research institutions within technological and regional innovations systems, becomes a central factor in taking advantage of the scope for increasing returns via the accumulation of knowledge and its timely conversion into technological innovations (Teubal *et al.*, 1996).

The introduction of new information and communication technologies is altering the present economic organisation of knowledge production, which was based on high levels of vertical integration of search and research processes into business firms, and low levels of market transaction of technological information because of the well known problems of non-appropriability and non-excludability. New information and communication technologies make it easier to access, store, process and exchange technological information and to better secure the conditions of tradeability based upon the definition of the conditions of access to data banks and dedicated software, which are increasingly viewed as problem-solving mechanisms.

The co-evolution of the new technological system, attended by new information and communication technologies, and the changes in the organisation of the generation of new knowledge would appear to lead towards three important and related outcomes:

1   the emergence of a new 'industry', consisting of firms specialising in the generation of new knowledge and specifically in the implementation of interfaces between the different forms of knowledge necessary to generate technological innovations;
2   increased efficiency in the management of the resources invested in the generation of technological innovations;
3   a shift towards more diffusion-oriented intellectual property rights regimes.

3 The dynamics of localised technological changes

The interaction between factor costs inducement, demand-pull and Schumpeterian rivalry

The introduction of localised technological changes relies upon the availability of localised knowledge. An analysis of the structural and behavioural conditions into which the innovative conduct of firms is embedded is a necessary prelude to the qualification of the actual dynamics of localised technological change.

This chapter presents a partial equilibrium analysis of localised technological change as it results from the interaction of four processes: factor substitution, changes in aggregate demand determined by growth, learning within firms and innovation systems and the effects of Schumpeterian rivalry on the demand of each firm. The analysis attempts to integrate localised endogenous technological change, as an adjustment mechanism at the industry-level, into the Marshallian tradition of partial equilibrium analysis, while at the same time emphasising the out-of-equilibrium conditions of the dynamics.

The textbook description of supply and demand analysis assumes that firms are fully able to change their size, production techniques, market conduct and location at any time: nothing reduces their ability to adjust almost instantaneously to changing market conditions. This theory also assumes that firms never have to spend time or money researching known technologies, because information on existing techniques is supposedly complete. Finally, firms are not able to change their technology: technology is considered an exogenous structural factor that shapes economic systems, but is not generated by the dynamics of them.

When such restrictive hypotheses are relaxed, a much broader picture emerges, where variety and dynamics play a major role (Arrow, 1994a and b; Stoneman, 1983). Specifically, when we take into account attrition forces, such as elastic barriers (David, 1975), menu costs (Akerloff and Yellen, 1985), producer switching costs (Antonelli, 1994c), and relevant information costs – e.g. search and transaction costs and learning processes within and between firms that (with research and learning activities) enable the build up of competences and capabilities – then notions of economic dynamics, structural change and specifically localised technological change clearly become pertinent.

In this chapter, the first section analyses localised technological change as the result of the interaction between excess inertia and excess momentum, represented respectively by producer switching costs incurred because of changes in factor prices, demand levels and learning processes. The second section provides a formal model detailing the dynamic interactions that actually induce innovation. The third section emphasises the implications of market entropy and localised technological change for the evolution of industrial structures and the fourth section integrates all these assumptions in order to explore the macroeconomic consequences. The reciprocal nature of these relations and the circularity of interactions is noted in the final section, and in the conclusion the diverse characteristics of economic systems so far identified are set out.

The analysis of localised technological change

The interaction between irreversibility and learning leads to endogenous processes of localised technological change along technological trajectories, defined in terms of factors intensity. The irreversibility of the mix of production factors and organisation generates producer switching costs when either relative prices of production factors change or demand increases. Both changes in factor costs and demand increases push firms to adjust their production techniques and size to the new required levels. However, producer switching costs, including menu costs, make adjustments expensive and difficult. Limited information about new techniques adds to the costs of mobility in the techniques space. On the other hand, learning by doing and learning by using generate localised competences that can be mobilised in order to cope with new economic conditions.

Under such circumstances, the trade off, between the producer switching costs necessary to adjust within a given technology and the R&D expenses necessary to capitalise upon localised learning, induces firms to generate localised technological changes which enable the retention of factor intensity and input size, yet increase total factor productivity. The interaction between producer switching costs and localised technological change leads to economies of growth when dimensional producer switching costs are important. The greater the demand-pull, the greater the amount of localised technological change; hence the greater the increase in total factor productivity and, for some, given sticky market prices for the products of the firm, the greater the opportunity to increase the levels of output, leading in turn to further increases in total factor productivity growth. Localised technological change, fuelled by demand growth, leads to excess momentum within a self-propelling process. Localised technological change induced by changes in the relative prices of production factors leads to excess inertia in production techniques and factor intensity (Atkinson and Stiglitz, 1969; David, 1975; Akerloff and Yellen, 1985; Antonelli, 1995a).

Localised technological change is the endogenous outcome of the interplay between excess inertia, represented by substitution, menu costs and excess momentum, represented by learning processes. Changes in factor costs oblige firms to alter their production techniques, which means accepting producer switching costs and menu costs arising in particular from a variety of activities such as recruiting, firing, performance appraisal and negotiations associated with all changes in wages and salary, adding compatible capital goods and scrapping. As a result, firms may wish to capitalise on their acquired tacit knowledge, exploiting learning processes, by using appropriate R&D activities to increase the productivity of each factor and total factor productivity, though leaving factor intensity unchanged. All changes in demand, engendered either by shifts of general demand levels or by the effects of competition between firms, mean that firms are induced to take measures to adjust to in(de)creased levels of output by in(de)creasing levels of input: such an action is subject to dimensional producer switching costs. Dimensional producer switching costs consist of the resources necessary to modify current input levels by taking certain actions, such as firing staff and scrapping or indeed adding new vintages of capital and new employees to the existing input mix. When demand is in(de)creasing, such costs force firms to mobilise all their learning capabilities to capitalise on acquired experience, subsequently introducing innovations that enable output to be adjusted to the desired levels without altering their input levels.

According to this representation, it follows that localised technological change is generated by the interplay between different mechanisms of inducement. Portrayed as the outcome of a trade off between substitution costs and learning, localised technological change combines four different strains of analysis: the (neo)classical mechanism of the generation of technological change induced by changes in the relative costs of production factors; the demand-pull models of the generation of technological change by the pressure of demand growth of post-Keynesian ascent; the Schumpeterian models of the generation of technological change induced by rivalry among firms in out-of-equilibrium conditions; and the resource-based theory of the firm based on the dynamics of learning.

The literature on induced technological change actually explored, at the aggregate level, the determinants of the direction of technological change rather than the causes of the rates of introduction of technological innovations. It is based on the notion that firms are pushed to introduce factor-saving innovations by the factor intensity of their current production process (Kennedy, 1964). As Binswanger (1978) says:

> Suppose it is equally expensive to develop either a new technology that will reduce labour requirements by 10% or one that will reduce capital by 10%. If the capital share is equal to the labour share, entrepreneurs will be indifferent between the two courses of action . . . If, however the labour share is 60%, all entrepreneurs will choose the labour-reducing

version. If the elasticity of substitution is less than one, this will go on until the labour and capital shares again become equal . . .

(p. 32)

The literature on demand-pull, conversely, explores the determinants of the rates of introduction of technological changes. Here the basic assumption is that firms are pulled to introduce technological innovations by the pressure of demand (Rosenberg, 1976). In fast-growing markets the rates of return of innovation are so large that they trigger accrued innovative efforts of firms and independent inventors, which eventually leads to the generation of faster rates of innovation (Schmookler, 1966). Kaldor provides an aggregate framework for such dynamics in his hypothesis that there is a positive relationship between the growth of output and the growth of labour productivity due to the accelerated introduction of technological innovation which is triggered by the rates of output growth (Kaldor, 1957; Kaldor and Mirrlees, 1962).

The Schumpeterian literature provides another set of explanations to help us understand the determinants of the rates of introduction of innovations. It provides an analysis at the firm level in out-of-equilibrium conditions, where variety among firms is seen as the leading characteristic of the market selection process. The basic incentive to innovate is market entropy, that is firm variety, in terms of efficiency, size, factor costs, age, organisational structure, technology, and innovative entry. The larger the time variance in market shares, the greater the efforts of firms to introduce innovations. Fast-growing firms with increasing market shares have larger mark-ups, so they can rely on larger cash-flows to fund internally risky projects and hence investing larger amounts of resources in R&D activities. Eventually competitive imitation reduces the extra profits of innovators. Radical innovations, however, are often associated with the entry of new firms that are able to take advantage of latent technological opportunities which incumbents are not ready to exploit (Nelson and Winter, 1982; Scherer and Ross, 1990).

Within the same Schumpeterian context, the resource-based theory of the firm emphasises the relevance of learning and competence in assessing the competitive behaviour of firms. In this approach, the firm is more than merely a production function: it is a learning agent that produces outputs by combining inputs and knowledge, adjusts prices and quantities, selects its organisation, acquires tacit knowledge and builds up its competence at implementing specific innovation capabilities, and generates innovations. Building on their competence, firms are able to change their technology.

The introduction of technological change is viewed here as part of a more general process of institutional and economic change, in which the behaviour of firms is influenced by the market structure and the more general topological characteristics of the economic environment. Any action taken is not limited to price-output adjustments, it incorporates the notion of competence as the basic intangible asset that shapes the behaviour and the performance of the firm. Competence consists of the capability to generate technological innovations and organisational change, as well as new institutions. The introduction of technological change can be viewed as part of a process of recursive structural change, during which firms, in out-of-equilibrium conditions, react to a given set of structural features. On the one hand, these are traditional price-output changes and, on the other, a range of structural changes, specifically affecting their production functions and more generally their technological and organisational knowledge (Perroux, 1935 and 1964; Penrose, 1959; Teece, 1993).

In sum, we have two classes of models at the aggregate and micro level that offer different sets of interpretations of the rate and direction of technological change. This is viewed as an endogenous process where the rate and direction of introduction of new technologies is explicitly determined by the interplay of economic stimulae. Factor-cost-induced models provide the basic analysis tool with which to understand the determinants of the direction of technological change. Demand-pull models offer an explanation of the rates of introduction of technological change, as triggered by the rates of growth of output. Factor-cost-inducement and demand-pull models are used to explore the generation of technological change at the aggregate level but little effort is made to provide a microeconomic analytical framework of the determinants of such changes. Conversely, Schumpeterian models analyse the changes in market conditions, and resource-based theories regard the competence accumulated by means of learning processes at the firm level, as the determinants of the rates of innovation, but no hypotheses are elaborated about the direction of technological change; moreover, there is little assessment regarding the effects at the aggregate levels.

It is the dynamics of localised technological change, built upon the trade off between producer switching costs and innovation efforts based upon learning opportunities, which seems able to reconcile these different lines of analysis and to provide a consistent micro-macro analytical framework, where both the firm level and the aggregate level – as well as technological rivalry – price-inducement and demand-pull, interact in such a way as to determine a cumulative, path-dependent process of growth and technological change (David, 1993a).

A formal model

This section aims to show how the dynamics of producer switching costs, induced by changes in relative prices and demand levels, localised learning and technological externalities can lead to the introduction of endogenous localised technological changes.

The notions of sunk costs and local irreversibility are central to such a theory of the firm. All existing capital stocks, both tangible, such as fixed assets, and intangible, such as reputation, experience and competence, have high levels of durability (Salter, 1966; Sutton, 1991). Thus, it is costly to change both the amount of capital stock and the proportions in which it is used with other complementary inputs due to changing market conditions. Durability of assets becomes the main factor in local irreversibility and sunk costs. Sunk costs in turn, together with learning processes, become an important focusing device in directing the endogenous generation and adoption of new technologies. Complementarity and inter-operability between vintages of fixed capital and other intermediary inputs, also in terms of labour skills, combine as a source of local irreversibility, creating major switching costs.

In this theory, irreversibility acts as a source of costs as well as a source of opportunities: the experience and knowledge, locally acquired by firms, about existing techniques and the mix of production factors through learning by doing and learning by using, represent other sources of local irreversibility. At the same time they offer opportunities to generate new technological innovations and hence increase levels of factor productivity and, possibly, total factor productivity.

It is important to stress here the characteristic features of the theory of the firm underlying the actual dynamics of localised technological change. Firms do more than take prices as given and adjust output levels accordingly. They are also able to learn from experience, build competences and hence change the structural parameters of the system, in particular their technology, according to the specific topological conditions of their environment. In this theory, firms adjust both quantities and competences; hence they are able to change their technologies and interact with their environment.

The introduction of localised technological change is the result of the optimising behaviour of myopic agents who, constrained both by endowment factors and producer switching costs, face changes in the relative prices of production factors and the desired levels of output. The notion of endowment factors refers to the opportunities firms have to generate technological change in the technique space they use. Producer switching costs are the costs of changing techniques engendered by the qualitative and quantitative substitution of labour, skills, routines and capital stock, which necessarily consists of movements in the technical space, either shifting along the isoquant when wages change, or changing output levels when demand increases or declines (Antonelli, 1994c, 1995a, 1996b and 1997c).

Our model describes the introduction of localised technological change as the outcome of the behaviour of a firm exposed to radical changes in the relative prices of factor costs and/or demand levels. Firms which face changes in the relative prices of factor costs and/or the levels of demand, incurring some adjustment costs must find a solution in the form of a new technique or a new technology. In the case of movements on the existing map of isoquants, they will incur producer switching costs (which are

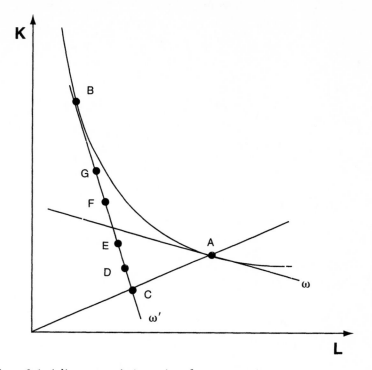

Figure 3.1 Adjustment choices when factor costs change

related to the distance in the technical space between the old and the new equilibrium points); while changing the shape of the map of isoquants, that is to say introducing technological changes, will generate innovation costs, i.e. the costs of generating and using new localised knowledge.

In particular, we consider three cases: when relative prices of production factors change; when demand levels increase; when demand levels decline.

Let us imagine that each firm, with a homogeneous production function and constant returns to scale, in a given industrial population, is – temporarily – in equilibrium in its own factor market with wages ω and capital costs R at point A (See Figure 3.1). After a compensating change in relative prices, creating a new level of wages ω' and R', the firm of the standard microeconomic textbook would choose the new technique B, where the new marginal rate of substitution equals the slope of the new isocost, i.e. the new relative prices. All switching activities necessary to move along the isoquants, representing existing techniques, command far more resources than is usually assumed. In switching from the existing equilibrium technique, defined in terms of factor intensity (and size), to the new equilibrium technique, after the change in factor costs, firms have to use important resources in order to walk the technical distance between the

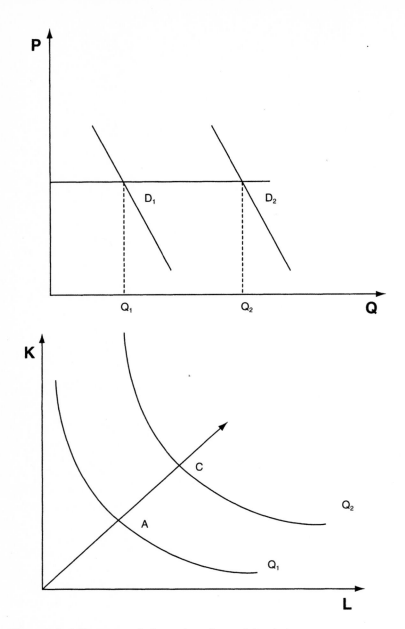

Figure 3.2 Adjustment choices when demand levels increase

two equilibrium points and hence acquire technical information about the new technique, retrain their personnel, modify their equipment, hire new skilled labour and introduce organisational changes.[1] Moreover, producer switching costs due to technical interrelatedness, in the form of technical

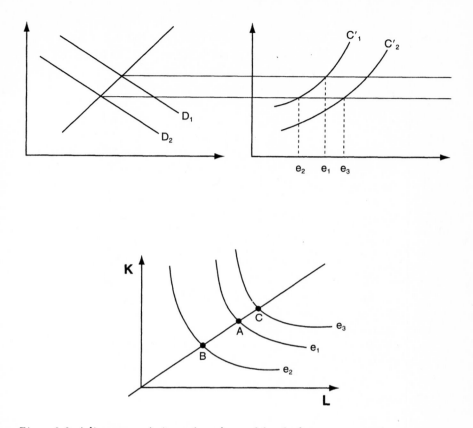

Figure 3.3 Adjustment choices when demand levels decrease

constraints, subsystem bottlenecks and complementary assets, keep a firm in a limited region of existing isoquants and make technical change, as opposed to technological innovation, more difficult and expensive.

A similar process takes place when each firm is exposed to changes in the levels of demand. When demand increases, because of the growth of aggregate demand levels or the expansion of the demand for the firm's products – due to the positive effects of Marshallian rivalry – the textbook firm should increase the levels of inputs, with a given technique, in order to expand output to the new desired levels. In this case, each firm would try and reach point C on the new isoquant further to the right on the same map (See Figure 3.2). Conversely, when demand levels shrink, again either because of a decline in aggregate demand levels or a reduction in the demand for the firm's products – this time due to the negative effects of Marshallian rivalry – the textbook firm reduces inputs in order to reduce the outputs. Now the firm tries to reach point C on the new isoquant situated further to the left (See Figure 3.3).

In both cases it can easily be argued that such changes in the levels of inputs are not free. In fact, they are expensive in many ways. The topological notion of technical distance plays a major role also in this context. The addition of new capital goods and new workforce to the pre-existing ones is not easy and implies a variety of adjustment costs. There are also higher substitution costs engendered by the efforts to reduce the levels of current inputs in order to adjust output to new lower levels. A variety of sunk costs becomes apparent, because the discrepancy between purchasing costs of capital goods and resale prices in secondary markets are especially high. The disposal of skilled labour, well-trained and experienced, with respect to the specific and idiosyncratic characteristics of the production process of each firm, all adds up and demonstrates the high levels of switching costs firms face when trying to reduce their output via a reduction in inputs. Firms are then induced to try and adjust to the factor and product market conditions by changing their technology, locally, and specifically, by changing the shape of the isoquant so as to remain in A^2 and yet continue to produce the new desired output.

It is evident that any kind of substitution movement, either along or between isoquants, implies some level of producer switching costs which may be assumed to be a function of the distance between techniques A and B. We can write, for each firm, the technical response function with respect to switching activities as follows:

$$S = f(AR) \tag{1}$$

with the usual assumptions that $f' > 0$ and $f'' < 0$. (See Figure 3.4); where S is the activity of switching and it is measured in terms of the technical distance[3] between A and B, the equilibrium points on the existing map of isoquants; AR represents the resources necessary to cover the technical distance and switch from A to B; and f measures the general efficiency of the function that enables the technical substitution of technique B for technique A.

We now turn our attention to the role of endowment factors. Endowment factors put pressure on a ray of isotechniques and create the push towards superior technology. Because of the important role of learning when acquiring the tacit knowledge necessary to innovate and when achieving the complementarity between tacit and codified knowledge acquired via R&D activities, we consider the search for new technologies especially productive along the ray OA. All technologies along the ray OA enable productive factors to be used rationally, while the technique in use before changes in relative prices and demand levels is retained. All movements along the ray OA imply an overall increase in efficiency and correspond to the introduction of technological innovations.

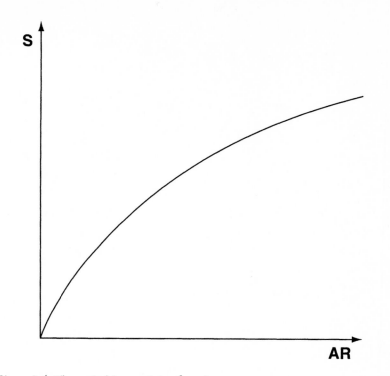

Figure 3.4 The switching activity function

The introduction of new and better technology is costly, however. In order to capitalise on the tacit knowledge acquired by means of the learning involved with the techniques in use, and to absorb the relevant external codified and tacit knowledge, firms have to invest in formal R&D activities. Job profiles have to be redesigned and part of the fixed capital has to be upgraded. Movements along OA are also costly because of the necessity to search for new knowledge and capitalise on tacit knowledge. The research process can stop when the new technology is such that the firm reaches:

1 Point C, in Figure 3.1, for firms exposed to changes in factor costs. The firm is again in equilibrium because the marginal rate of substitution equals the slope of the new relative prices.
2 Point C, in Figure 3.2, for firms exposed to an increase in demand level.
3 Point C, in Figure 3.3, for firms exposed to a decrease in demand level, where the former equilibrium level of inputs can be retained because of higher efficiency and hence lower costs.

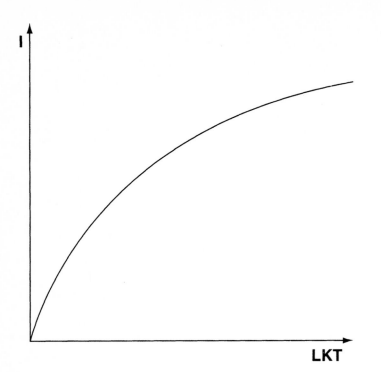

Figure 3.5 The innovation activity function

The production function for innovation activities is mainly made up of the research, learning and search expenses necessary to move the isoquant along OA up to the point C; so that we have:

$$I = g(LTK) \qquad\qquad (3)$$

with the usual assumptions that $g' > O$ and $g'' < O$ (See Figure 3.5).

In equation (3), I stands for localised technological change; LTK represents the resources, in terms of localised technological knowledge, necessary to generate technological innovation; and g measures the efficiency of the technology response function that makes it possible to generate new technologies. In equation (3) resources are used to perform the four different tasks of learning, socialisation, R&D and recombination, as already elaborated in Chapter 2. Specifically, I represents the bundle of activities leading to the introduction of technological change necessary to move OA from equilibrium technique A (before changes in the economic environment such as increases/decreases in wage or in demand) towards the new equilibrium point C (after the increase/decrease in wages or demand).

A firm choosing technique B incurs producer switching costs but avoids all innovation costs. Conversely, a firm that chooses technique C avoids all producer switching costs – the technique remains constant on the ray AC – but incurs substantial innovation costs. The firm choosing the inferior technique B clearly has an advantage over the firm that remains with technique A. This advantage is measured by the opportunity costs arising from the price inefficiency (when wages change) or losses in terms of sales, mark-ups and market shares (when demand changes).

Let us now assume that the new technology which the firm has developed, by taking advantage of learning processes and exploiting technological opportunities, enables the firm to produce at point C, with the same total costs as at point B. The gross revenue equation for the firm, considering the alternatives between A to B or A to C respectively, may be expressed as follows:

$$R = W(I) + Z(S) \tag{4}$$

where R stands for the gross revenue obtained from adjusting to the new factor prices, measured in terms of reductions in production costs, with respect to technique A. Gross revenue results from switching and innovating respectively, but before switching costs and innovating costs are actually accounted for. W expresses the unit gross revenue derived from innovating, and Z expresses the unit gross revenue derived from switching:

$$W = (TCA - TCC)/AC \tag{5}$$

$$Z = (TCA - TCB)/AB \tag{6}$$

where TCA, TCB, TCC are the total costs of production using techniques A, B and C respectively. When firms are coping with changes in relative prices of production costs, TCB = TCC; when firms are coping with either increases or declines in demand levels, TCB > TCC. The isorevenue will thus have a unitary slope only in the first case. Finally, AB and AC are the Euclidean distances.

For a given level of fixed resources dedicated to implementing learning procedures, and building communication channels and R&D laboratories, firms can either minimise the levels of adjustment costs or maximise the innovation flows. For any given level of revenue arising from adjustment to new relative prices and demand levels, the choice between full switching, i.e. B, and full innovation, i.e. C, or a combination of both, that is any point between B and C, depends on the relative costs of innovating. In turn, for given levels of factor costs, these costs are determined by the marginal productivity of innovating activities with respect to relative costs and the marginal productivity of switching.

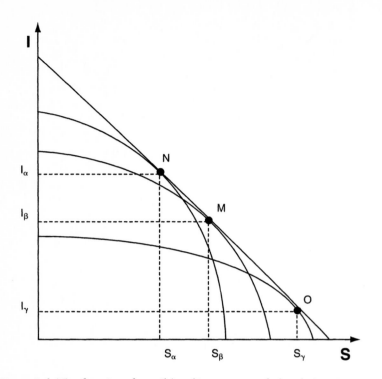

Figure 3.6 The frontier of possible adjustments and the choice set

In order to represent such a decision process analytically, we can build a Frontier of Possible Adjustments (FPA) (See Figure 3.6) with the usual properties expressed by the following equation:

$$S = h(I) \tag{7}$$

with $h' < O$ and $h'' > O$, where S is the switching distance and I the innovation distance.

If the amount of resources that can be saved by each firm by either switching or innovating is constant, we get a map of FPA and one iso-revenue line. In such a case, the firm will minimise adjustment costs. The firm is operating under the constraint of severe budget limitations: a fall in profitability and liquidity arises from new relative prices and average costs higher than market prices. On the contrary, if the amount of resources dedicated to implementing its innovation capabilities is constant, and the firm tries to maximise the outcome, we obtain a map of isorevenues and one FPA. In both cases, the firm will select the combination of switching activities and innovating activities that corresponds to the tangency between the slope of the FPAs and the slope of the isorevenue. This is defined by the ratio of the revenue of the switching activity to the revenue of the innovation activity:

$$h'(I) = -(W/Z) \tag{8}$$

In Figure 3.6, it is clear that the value of I, i.e. the level of innovation activity selected, will depend on the ratio of the marginal productivity of innovation activities to switching activities, as measured by f (in Equation 1) = g (in Equation 3) in M, $g > f$ in N, and $f > g$ in O, and consequently on the costs of introducing innovations with respect to switching costs. The firm will choose from among a range of points D, E, F, G, . . . (in Figure 3.1), each representing various combinations of innovation and switching.

When the efficiency of the innovation function is far higher than the efficiency of the producer switching function, and firms maximise the innovation flow,[4] the outcome of the adjustment process will be the generation of a completely new technology with all the characteristics of a Leontieff production function. Hence, technological change is both radical and entirely localised. The introduction of (fully) localised technological changes enables firms to cope with: an increase in demand levels, by increasing output with low levels of increase in inputs; a decline in demand levels, reducing costs so as to retain current levels of inputs and increase output at lower prices; and changes in the relative prices of production factors, by adjusting the ratio of marginal productivity while still retaining their factor intensity.

In the latter case above, the new technology will be locally neutral with respect to the old relative factor prices, but highly labour-intensive with respect to new higher wages or, instead, highly capital-intensive with respect to the higher costs of the use of capital. The new technology and technique will be in proximity to the isotechnique ray OA, so that the factor mix remains unchanged. With the high relative efficiency of the producer switching function, on the other hand, technological change is less important and weakly localised, but is not neutral. The new technology is labour-intensive for wage increases with respect to old wage levels.[5]

The minimising firm searches for the lowest FPA; the new technical solution is found on the new isocost, consequently the new solution will be as efficient as the standard one in B. The maximising firm, instead, can go beyond the new isocost and introduce a new technology that actually increases total factor productivity. An increase in total factor productivity is always obtained when a firm copes with changes in the desired level of output by means of the introduction of localised technological change.

The dynamics of localised technological change and market entropy

The dynamics of localised technological change can successfully implement the evolutionary and post-Schumpeterian theory of market competition.

Variety and out-of-equilibrium behaviour, in a context where competition is seen as a process characterised by the replicator dynamics, and the failure-inducement mechanism, are the key conditions to understanding how markets work (Metcalfe, 1989, 1992 and 1997).

At any point in time a heterogeneous population of firms is found in the market place. Competition takes place among a variety of firms of different size and age, with different factor costs, different techniques defined in terms of factor intensities, different technologies, competencies, organsations, factor costs and productivity levels. Such markets bear both Marshallian and Schumpeterian characteristics: they are defined by a selection environment in which heterogeneous players, as in the Marshallian tradition, confront each other; but players are able to change their technology, as in the Schumpeterian tradition.[6]

Supply curves are shaped by the horizontal summation of the marginal cost curves of the different firms. For a given demand curve, a market price is determined and exchanges in the market take place according to this price: subsequently, there is a variety of profit conditions. Exchanges take place in out-of-equilibrium conditions, far away from the contract curve. Some firms will have average costs well below the price, others will operate with average costs close to market prices; finally, a number of firms will be incurring significant operating losses because their average costs are well above market prices. The interest in focusing attention on the Marshallian hypothesis of market entropy and the related dynamics of market selection in out-of-equilibrium conditions, consists of the analysis of the dynamic effects across a variety of firms on the levels of performance and innovation.

Both exit from and entry into the competitive arena are slow because of relevant irreversibilities and related barriers to entry and to exit. Specifically, firms are reluctant to exit because of the high levels of sunk costs, determined not only by fixed capital, but also by the high levels of reputation and competence built up and acquired through strong learning opportunities, all closely associated with current production and techniques. Only firms with very high levels of current losses will be forced to leave the market rapidly: firms able to recover variable costs will remain in the market for a longer time span. Firms will also be reluctant to enter because of the risks associated with entry into highly unstable markets and the attendant danger of being locked into unknown markets by sudden changes resulting from shifts in industry demand curves or from the unanticipated entry and exit of other competitors. Within this approach, the interaction of the replicator dynamics and the failure-inducement mechanism enables a strong Lamarckian characteristic to complement the traditional Darwinian flavour of selection processes.

The basic replicator dynamics can be formalised by using a simple model which allows the steps up to this point to be fixed. The growth of output of firm i, for a given market size, depends on the relative levels of wages W_i and technological capacity T_i with respect to the average (A) of competitors:

$$X_{it} - X_{it-1} = f(T_i / T_A, W_i / W_A) \qquad (9)$$

where X_i represents the market share of firm i.

However, selection takes place not only on the basis of the growth of the most efficient firms, fed as they are by investments. This is the distinctive Darwinian mechanism translated into the formal modelling of replicator dynamics. Selection, and growth, are also the result of the failure-inducement mechanism, which retains the characteristics of Lamarckian adaptation. Least efficient firms will not be forced out of the market providing they are able to introduce new technologies. Within this approach, technologies are sorted out instead of firms: exit applies to inefficient technologies. The failure-inducement mechanism assumes that poorly-performing firms, drawing on the learning capabilities and the accumulation of competence, try and reduce their weakness, by means of systematic innovative efforts leading to increased rates of introduction of technological changes, which become stronger as the losses become greater. As Figure 3.7 shows, B firms are able to change their technology so that their average cost curve shifts downward, while A firms exit.

An important step forward can be made by coupling the replicator dynamics and the failure-inducement mechanism, with the dynamics of localised technological change. This enables full appreciation of both the role of localised knowledge in the generation of new technologies and the vigorous interaction between the dynamics of market entropy and the processes of technological rivalry and technological accumulation.

When the hypothesis of market entropy is retained it is clear that at each point in time the performances of firms are distributed around an average. Firms, which are both more and less efficient than the average have an incentive to introduce localised technological changes in order to cope with the adjustment costs arising from necessary changes in size. The concept of dimensional producer switching costs is important here. In the first case, the replicator dynamics is at work, and in the second, the failure-inducement mechanism.

For each firm, with performances above average, the incentive to react to demand pressure – generated by the selection process within the market – by increasing the levels of inputs, is offset by the fast-rising cost of the additional inputs, and the cost of integrating them into the existing size of the plants. Instead of extensive growth based solely on an increase in inputs, a firm will consider the opportunity of capitalising on its experience, acquired by means of learning by doing and by using, by developing it with appropriate funds invested in learning, search and research activities.

Under these conditions, the replicator dynamics is augmented by the localised character of technological change, exerting a major cumulative effect. In this process, excess momentum and path-dependence become a central issue. Firms with average cost curves below the market price have a

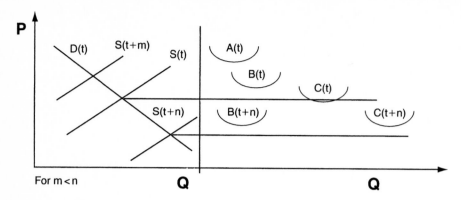

Figure 3.7 Market entropy and the selection process

clear incentive to adjust their size to the market conditions. The exit of the least efficient firms, unable to innovate, leaves new room for their growth (see both the right and leftward shift of the supply curves in Figure 3.7). Moreover, it is clear that firms with an average cost curve below market price have high mark-ups and large cash-flows. The augmented replicator dynamics explains not only the faster rates of growth of most efficient firms, with a given technology, but also their faster rates of introduction of innovations. As Figure 3.7 shows, C firms will be able to increase both their size and their efficiency so that their cost curve will shift both downward and to the right.

The replicator dynamics is augmented by the dynamics of localised technological change because, for given levels of producer switching costs, the efficiency in the generation of new technologies is enhanced and the costs for introducing innovations are lowered by three forces. First of all, important shares of extra profits can be retained by managers and used, after paying normal dividends to shareholders, to fund – internally – not only investment in fixed capital, as in the standard replicator dynamics, but also intangible capital and more risky projects, such as R&D activities, which would be difficult and more expensive to finance externally, in terms of rates of interest.

The conditions of financial markets also play a major role. The more reluctant the financial markets are to fund R&D activities and the more risk-adverse the banks are, the more important will be the internal sources of funds to finance research and learning projects; hence the more important will be the positive effects of large cash-flows on the rates of introduction of innovations and the stronger the links between quasi-rents and rates of introduction of localised technological changes. Lower financial costs and lower risks of credit rationing make it possible, with given resources, to accelerate the blending of tacit and codified knowledge, both internal and external, and increase the accumulation of localised knowledge. This clearly, with given producer switching costs, leads to faster rates of introduction of localised technological change.

Second, it may be assumed that the larger the size of the operation and, even more important, the larger the market share, the better will be the appropriability conditions for innovation returns. Moreover, larger market shares and sizes enable the average fixed costs of R&D activities to be reduced. Better appropriability conditions and lower average costs, due to economies of density and scale in conducting search and research activities, in turn lead to lower innovation costs and, for given levels of producer switching costs, to higher rates of introduction of localised technological change.

Finally, firms earning extra profits can better afford to pay efficiency wages, that is wages set in excess of the short-term levels of labour productivity and above the opportunity costs of the direct visible effort of workers. Efficiency wages stimulate the participation of employees in the production process. They also attract skilled labour, embodying high levels of tacit knowledge from other firms and facilitate the socialisation of tacit knowledge and, more generally, the transfer of localised knowledge. The reputation for a creative working environment increases the cream-skimming effect in the labour markets for skilled labour, favouring firms which can pay efficiency wages in terms of quality and levels of human capital. Clearly, efficiency wages accelerate the processes of learning by doing and by using on which the accumulation of localised knowledge rests. All this exerts a direct positive effect on the rates of accumulation of competence and tacit knowledge, which in terms of the costs of localised technological knowledge is far larger than the total difference between efficiency wages and short-term equilibrium wages. Thus, for given levels of producer switching costs, the efficiency wages which most efficient firms can afford to pay, lead to faster rates of introduction of localised technological knowledge and thus higher rates of productivity growth.

In summary, most efficient firms have higher incentives and opportunities to accumulate localised technological knowledge and consequently introduce localised technological and organisational changes. This further increases their productivity levels and feeds a recursive process, where productivity growth is the result of an endogenous and typically self-sustaining process. The replicator dynamics augmented by the dynamics of localised technological change has all the characteristics of excess momentum and path-dependence (See Chapter 1 and Chapter 7). In these conditions, equation (3) can be re-specified as follows:

$$I = \gamma \, (LTK) \tag{10}$$

where $\gamma > g$.

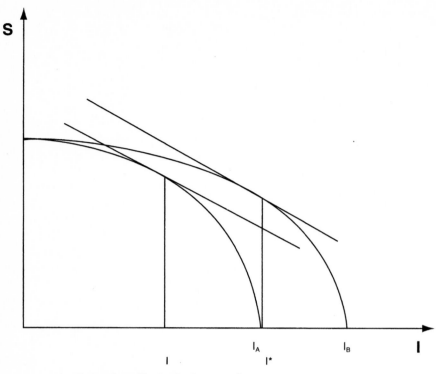

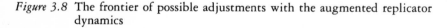

I_A = Innovation with standard assumption

I_B = Innovation with the augmented replicator dynamics

Figure 3.8 The frontier of possible adjustments with the augmented replicator dynamics

Consequently, as it can be seen in Figure 3.9, the FPA acquires a new shape when the augmented replicator dynamics is accounted for. Innovation activities are far more effective and, for given resources, the amount of localised technological change is larger, hence the equilibrium levels of localised technological change are also larger and the mix of adjustment actions selected by the firm is tilted towards the introduction of innovation.

The failure-induced introduction of localised technological change is at work with respect to the least efficient firms. Least efficient firms that have managed to survive in the short term quickly realize that they can avoid exit and subsequent heavy losses of sunk costs only by systematic efforts to innovate and hence reduce costs.

The failure-inducement mechanism is very effective when the survival of the firm is at risk: all intangible capital, as well as large portions of fixed capital, risk being lost. The levels of dimensional producer switching costs

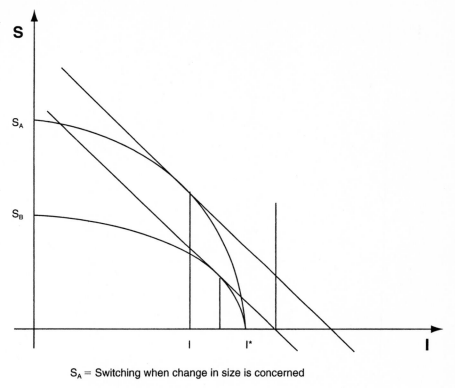

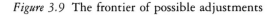

S_A = Switching when change in size is concerned

S_B = Switching with exit threat

Figure 3.9 The frontier of possible adjustments

increase exponentially when such outcomes are threatened. In these conditions, for given innovation costs, the firm will choose much higher levels of introduction of localised technological change than a firm coping with short-term reductions in size, reductions which do not imply the waste of intangible capital. With higher equilibrium levels of introduction of localised technological changes, all competences are mobilised towards the generation of innovations which enable the firm to cope with adverse market conditions, survive and avoid exit in the longer term.

In these conditions equation (1) can be specified as follows:

$$S = \phi(AR) \tag{11}$$

where $\phi < f$.

Consequently, as can be seen in Figure 3.10, the FPA acquires a new shape when the failure-inducement mechanism is taken into consideration. Switching is far more expensive and, for given resources, the equilibrium

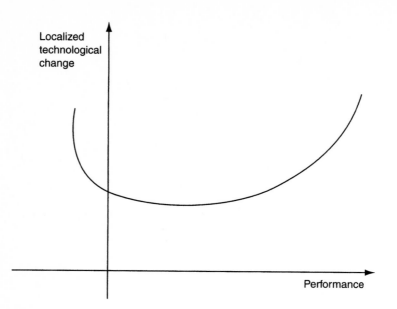

Figure 3.10 The relationship between performances and localised technological change

levels of localised technological change are once again larger, pushing the mix of adjustment actions selected by the firm towards the introduction of innovation.

The profile of the innovative efforts of least efficient firms is also dictated by constraints in capital markets, which directly affect the breadth and prospect of their search and research projects. Specifically, failure-induced technological changes are likely to consist mainly of incremental innovations based upon the adoption of process innovations designed to reduce the risks of R&D activities and obtain quick results in terms of cost reduction. Profit-induced technological changes are instead likely to be more radical, being the outcome of long-term R&D strategies and consisting of product innovations.

In summary, in this market theory, there is assumed to be a quadratic relationship between the changes in market conditions – that is to say the combinations of profits, size and shares – and the efforts to introduce new technologies and total factor productivity growth (See Figure 3.10).

Both negative and positive changes in market conditions are a strong inducement mechanism of technological change: most efficient firms, earning extra profits, can fund more innovation activities in order to take advantage of the currently favourable conditions. But also less efficient firms are forced to innovate in order to survive. In both cases the equilibrium levels on the FPA will dictate larger levels of localised technological change and hence an increase in total factor productivity. This argument can be easily formalised, elaborating on equation (9) as follows:

$$T_{it} - T_{it-1} = f((T_{it}/T_{it-1}, W_{it}/W_{it-1}) - (T_{it}/T_{it-1}, W_{it}/W_{it-1})^2) \qquad (12)$$

where T represents the level of general technological efficiency.

The selection process in these Marshallian-Schumpeterian markets now has three important consequences:

1 the scrapping of the least efficient techniques and the exit of the least efficient firms, i.e. those unable to innovate;
2 the rapid diffusion and introduction of incremental process innovations in the population of declining firms and the failure to adopt new technologies and generate incremental innovations in order to survive;
3 the accelerated generation of localised technological changes involving the introduction of more radical processes, and, especially, product innovations, by the more efficient firms. Such firms face major dimensional switching costs, but can take advantage of internally-generated resources to fund long-term R&D activities, which in turn can be used to mobilise the existing learning opportunities acquired in the course of past activities.

At the industry level, the introduction of localised technological change engenders a shift to the right of the supply curve and hence a decline in market prices; in turn causing the exit of a number of extramarginal firms, those both less efficient and slower at generating localised technological changes. However, their exit in turn engenders a new leftward shift of the supply curve and a new jump in market prices, leading to increases in market shares, output and profitability for intramarginal, technologically-dynamic firms.

The interaction of the introduction of localised technological changes and the exit of extramarginal firms is likely to generate systematic fluctuations in market prices, market shares and output levels for those firms able to remain in the market place (Dixit, 1992). The process of generation of localised technological change within the augmented replicator dynamics is conceivably endless, so there is a continual increase in productivity at the aggregate level.

The rate of introduction of innovations will vary across industries according to the specific features of the market structure, which in turn is dependent on the variety of firms with respect to cost conditions, age, size, factor costs, and their innovative performance, as determined by the levels of producer switching costs, learning capacity and hence innovative capability.

From the point of view of the inter-industrial flow of exchanges of intermediary inputs and capital goods, it is clear that the relative prices of different goods will keep changing over time as a result of two important sets of factors, namely the out-of-equilibrium conditions in which competition takes place in each industry and the uneven rates of innovation between industries and, consequently, the uneven reduction of best-practice costs.

Market entropy may be considered the main engine of aggregate growth. The rates of introduction of technological change are evidently influenced by the degree of entropy within and between markets. To this extent, disorder at the firm level would appear to be the necessary underlying condition for orderly processes of growth at the aggregate level. The replicator dynamics, together with the failure-inducement mechanism, augmented by the dynamics of localised technological change, leads the industrial distribution of firm size towards greater concentration, with a limited number of efficient firms becoming more and more innovative, thus even more efficient and more profitable and consequently growing in size.

Profits above the norm lead to higher market shares and higher rates of growth. Instead firms with average efficiency levels have lower profits and thus weaker incentives to innovate, therefore remaining small in size. The least efficient firms are induced to innovate in order to survive. Failure-induced innovators are eventually able to re-establish some profitability levels. Profit levels for firms with below normal profits eventually rise. Innovative survival can – up to a point – be substituted for exit. The findings of Mueller (1986) on the dynamics of the distribution of profits across firms, in the long run, provide strong empirical evidence in support of this interpretation. And with respect to the evolution of industrial structures, the empirical analyses confirm that, as industries mature, a skewed distribution in the size of firms emerges, where there are only a few large companies – most likely to be the early innovators – and a great number of small and medium-sized firms (Gibrat, 1931; Simon and Bonini, 1958; Nelson, Winter and Schuette, 1976; Sutton, 1997).

Within the context of industrial economics, this approach characterises industrial dynamics as the outcome of the interaction between industrial structures and firm strategies (Carlsson, 1987; Baldwin, 1995). It is clear that the traditional 'structuralist' chain of arrows which links the industrial structure – defined in terms of concentration, barriers to entry, exit and mobility, and diversity of firms; to conduct – defined in terms of firms strategies; and eventually to performance – defined in terms of rates of growth and profitability levels – now also has a strong recursive character. Conducts, namely innovative and growth strategies, affect performances, which eventually shape a new industrial structure. Industrial structure can no longer be considered an exogeneous parameter since, on the contrary, it is clearly influenced by the conduct and performance of firms in previous historic times.

Within industrial economics, this methodology paves the way to an approach that may be termed dynamic structuralism, where both inertia and excess momentum are at work. Dynamic structuralism is both past-dependent, in that a firm's conduct is affected by the original features of the industrial system, and path-dependent, because, over time the features of the industrial structure are re-shaped by the intentional strategies and interaction of the firms in the market place (Phillips, 1970 and 1971; Caves and Porter, 1977; Carlsson, 1989; Eliasson, 1989).

The coupling of the replicator dynamics and the failure-inducement mechanism with the dynamics of localised technological change is assumed to have an important role also at the macroeconomic level. Market entropy should favour economic growth: with high levels of market entropy, the dynamics of economic growth is enhanced by the effects of the innovative efforts of both the most- and the least-efficient firms (Metcalfe, 1995).

Productivity growth, factor substitution and demand-pull localised technological change

Long-term productivity growth generated at the firm level, by the inter-action of localised technological change with the replicator dynamics and the failure-inducement mechanism, has important dynamic consequences at the aggregate level. Productivity growth produces three effects that lead to the introduction of further localised technological change (Sylos Labini, 1984). Market entropy, localised technological change, and subsequent productivity growth, is likely to induce:

1 a reduction in the prices of manufactured goods, and an increase in total output of both quantities and value (See Figure 3.11a); which leads to
2 long-term growth of derived demand for labour, a consequent increase in real wages across the economy (See Figure 3.11b) and the reduction in market prices of capital goods;[7] so producing
3 a long-term increase in aggregate demand (See Figure 3.11c).

Let us analyse the dynamic consequences of each of these effects in terms of the introduction of localized technological change.

Productivity growth and output growth

The increase in real wages and the reduction in market prices of capital goods, induced by the overall growth of total factor productivity, should force firms to substitute capital for labour and switch along the production function. Switching is expensive: sunk costs, together with learning processes, act as a major focusing device in directing the endogenous generation and adoption of new technologies, encouraging technological change in a very narrow range of techniques. Firms introduce localised technological changes that enable the retention of the existing techniques and factor intensity, while at the same time increasing the efficiency of each factor so as to cope with the new relative costs (See Figure 3.12).

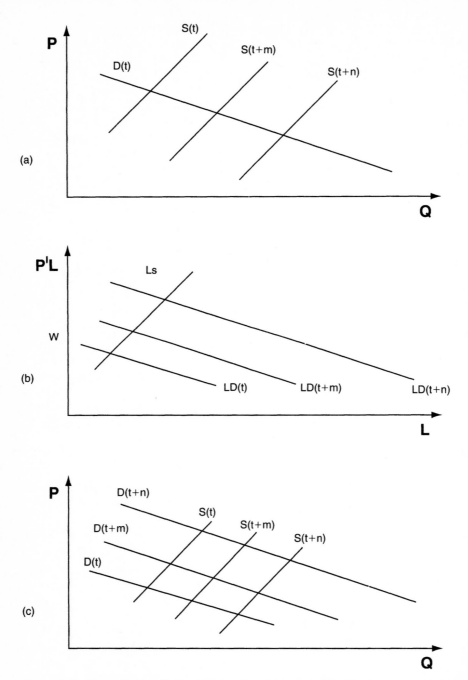

Figure 3.11 The relationship between productivity growth and output growth (a), wage increase (b), and demand growth (c)

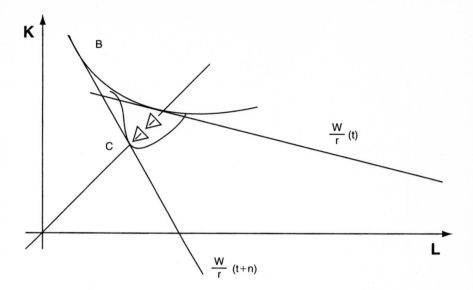

Figure 3.12 Localised technological change induced by factor price changes

Wage increase

The direction of technological change is now influenced by the new conditions of the factor markets and, more precisely, the rate of change of real wages and the reduction of rental costs of capital goods. Technological change will be more labour-saving in terms of output intensity, and with respect to the previous technology, the increase in wages will be greater. It is interesting to note, however, that the more localised the new technology is, the more neutral it will be in terms of factor intensity.

The rate at which technological changes are introduced is also influenced by the rates of change in the mix of production factors, specifically the rate of increase in wages and the rate of reduction in market prices and hence rental costs of capital goods. The rate of price-induced localised technological change is influenced by the actual amount of the increase in wages: the larger the wage increase and the greater the reduction in the rental costs of capital goods, the larger will be the switching necessary, and hence the larger the innovative effort along the isocline defining the factor intensity of the firm. This effort is required in order to retain factor intensity while coping with the new relative prices of production factors. It becomes clear that the amount of innovative effort, and its direction, is also determined by the size of the increase in wages.

For given levels of factor-market heterogeneity, the general increase in wage levels has one other important effect, namely the accelerated diffusion of previous waves of technological changes which had already been introduced but were localised in more capital-intensive techniques. These technologies reduce the profitability of adoption for those firms operating in labour-abundant segments of the economy with low wages, i.e. in equilibrium with the labour-intensive portions of the spectrum of techniques. Such diffusion reinforces the positive effects of feedbacks from increases in wages and reductions in the market prices of capital goods, resulting in the further growth of total factor productivity levels.

Demand growth

The increase in wages and the reduction in market prices of capital goods[8] also have important effects in terms of the level of aggregate demand. Together with the increase in wages, the income multiplier causes the aggregate demand curve to shift to the right. Back in our Marshallian-Schumpeterian industry, not only does the supply curve shift to the right, because of the dynamics of technological rivalry in the selection environment and the competitive entropy, but the demand curve also moves that way because of changes in the aggregate conditions (See Figure 3.11c). Irrespective of their profitability, all firms will now face an increase in market prices and demand.

The process of introduction of demand-pull localised technological change is of relevance here. Once again, firms facing pressure to adjust their size to the new levels of aggregate demand will have to consider the trade off between increasing their size by means of extensive growth, based on an increase in the levels of input, or by means of intensive growth, based upon an increase in the levels of the general efficiency of their production technology (See Figure 3.13).

The rate of introduction of demand-pull localised technological change is directly related to the size of increases in demand levels, levels of dimensional switching costs, and levels of opportunities to generate innovations dependent upon the experience and local knowledge acquired by means of learning by doing, learning by using and R&D activities.

The overall increase in demand levels, that is the rightward shift of the demand curves, has another important effect on the diffusion of previous waves of technological innovations. Higher levels of investments, required to adjust output to the new desired levels, enable firms to adopt technological innovations that had been delayed because of the sunk costs of existing fixed capital. All additional investment may now be used to purchase new capital equipment embodying the new technologies. The diffusion of such new capital goods reinforces the rates of growth of productivity of the system, stimulating further increases in real wages and raising the level of the demand curves.

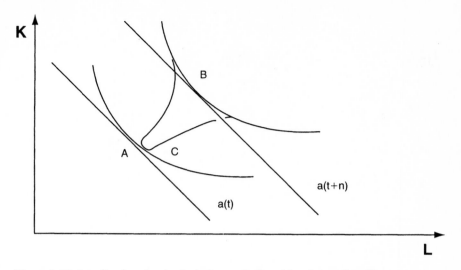

Figure 3.13 Localised technological change induced by demand-pull

The recursive interaction between different forms of localised technological change

The interaction of the three forms of localised technological change so far described, and the additional momentum produced by the acceleration of diffusion processes will probably generate a recursive process of cumulative growth; a process which is highly sensitive to both the initial conditions, i.e. a past-dependent process, and the individual behaviours of each of the agents involved at each point in time, i.e. the features of a strong path-dependent process (Young, 1928; David, 1975 and 1993a). This interaction is acutely and repeatedly affected by a large variety of structural conditions and their evolution over time and by the contingent behaviour of the large variety of firms involved in the system (See Figure 3.14).

At the firm level, the distribution of market shares and, more generally, the dynamics of market conditions are highly influential in the interaction, together with the characteristics of the financial markets, the propensity of managers to fund risky undertakings, the willingness of shareholders to exert only a loose control on the destination of profits and the intensity of failure-induced reactions. The effects of irreversibility as expressed in the levels of producer switching costs and, conversely, the relative ease with which localised technological changes are introduced, also play a central role. The importance of the introduction of localised technological change in turn depends on learning processes and the ability of firms to capitalise on them, bringing into consideration factors such as the build-up of specific

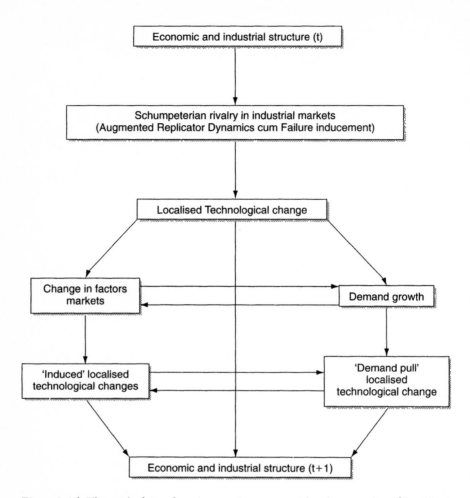

Figure 3.14 The path-dependent interactions among the three modes of localised
technological change

competences, the relative weight of technological opportunities and the
general possibility of introducing important innovations involving only
limited expenditure on R&D activities.

At the system level, the dynamics of localised technological change are
strongly affected by this three-way interaction of productivity growth, i.e.
the increase in wages and the reduction of market prices of capital goods and
the resulting increase in aggregate demand. When and where productivity
growth leads to, either, low increases in wages due to high levels of
unemployment, or flat labour-supply curves, and/or low levels of aggregate
demand due to low increases in wages, low levels of income multipliers and

low levels of new investment, the aggregate effects on localised technological change are likely to be much weaker.

Within this general context, the static and dynamic conditions governing the institutional definition of the competitive arena in which firms interact has a special role. The wider the variety of firms, and hence the greater the variance of their competences and performances, the larger will be the number of localised technological changes introduced by firms feeding the process of technological rivalry and shifting the demand curves. Consequently, all interventions that change the institutional borders of the competitive arena – such as the evolution of international economics, the process of economic integration and disintegration in global markets, and the emergence of new limitations on competition – are likely to reduce/increase the degree of technological rivalry.

The same changes are also likely to affect the extent of the feedback effects of productivity growth. There is an important trade off between the positive effects of all processes of integration and globalisation on the one hand, in terms of increased variance and thus increased rates of introduction of technological change, and on the other hand, the negative effects generated by the loosening of the macro-micro feedbacks. The effects of local technological rivalry on wages and aggregate demand, measured in terms of productivity growth, are likely to be diluted in the global macroeconomic environment.

Conclusions

The dynamics of localised technological change consists of a recursive cumulative process, where the replicator dynamics, augmented by the demand-pull introduction of localised technological changes combined with the Lamarckian failure-inducement mechanism, acts as the microeconomic engine of the system. At the aggregate level, productivity growth generated by the dynamic effects of market entropy, induces both an increase of wages and, in turn, an increase in demand levels.

Both these increases activate the introduction of localised technological changes of different sorts: the price-induced localised technological change engendered by modifications to factor markets, and the demand-pull localised technological change due to changes in the conditions of aggregate demand. Moreover, both processes also affect the rate of diffusion of innovations: all changes in factor-market conditions encourage the adoption of capital-intensive technologies, as well as changes in aggregate demand levels, favouring new waves of investment and the adoption of new capital goods embodying technological changes.

Interaction takes place at the macro level as well as the micro level. On the market side, the introduction of new localised technologies, together with the well-known limitations to their instantaneous adoption by all firms, leads once again to exchanges out-of-equilibrium, situated off the contract curve and away from tangent positions on the frontier of production possibility. Exchanges out of equilibrium-cum-localised technological changes lead to selection processes that are highly sensitive to both the situation prevailing in the system at that time, and the effects of the agents' interactions at any point in time, thus to high levels of path-dependent irreversibility (David, 1993a; David, Foray and Dalle, 1998).

When the results of our analyses are brought together it seems evident that entropy and variety are at the origin of both disorder and waste – which should not be ignored – and fast rates of productivity growth.

A system characterised by a great variety of firms, within markets that are modelled along both Marshallian and Schumpeterian lines, will probably experience high levels of variance in total factor productivity growth and high levels of 'gross' productivity growth. The former is a result of the high levels of disruption and producer switching costs that reduce the levels of general efficiency of the system, especially those of the less-effective firms and those forced to exit. The latter is instead due to the continuous efforts firms make to react to the selective environment in which they operate by introducing technological innovations. In conclusion, the high levels of gross productivity growth should be discounted by the cost of the trial and error processes which make them possible.

Given the articulation of the entire process, where variety is first combined with the inertia of producer switching costs, competence and the excess momentum of the replicator dynamics, then augmented by the introduction of demand-pull localised technological changes, the failure-inducement mechanism and the aggregate effects in terms of wages and demand (which leads to endogenous technological change), an analytical framework may be developed, which takes into account the effects of high levels of path-dependence. Indeed, when self-propelling and endogenous processes of change are considered, it is clear that both local and global irreversibility, as well as path-dependence, play a major role in analysis of the firm, the market place, the technology and the aggregate system.

A bridge between the Marshallian and the Schumpeterian approaches has been developed. Because of irreversibilities and indivisibilities, exchanges out-of-equilibrium take place in Marshallian markets. However, because of irreversibilities, indivisibilities and structural change, Schumpeterian agents, in out-of-equilibrium conditions, building upon the endogenous creation of knowledge, are able to introduce technological and organisational innovations which change the production functions and alter the very basic equilibrium points.

Under such conditions, economic systems are likely to develop along a cumulative path that is highly sensitive both to prevailing conditions and behaviour in time. It is an evolution that is equally attuned to the effects of agent interactions on the topological features of the system, in terms of the organisation of the industries and the structure of the economy. The result is an economic system containing both multiple dynamic equilibria and

multiple regimes of growth. The convergence towards equilibrium is continuously altered by the changing structural elements of the system. The
creation of new knowledge and the introduction of technological and
organisational innovations is induced by out-of-equilibrium conditions
and leads to new out-of-equilibrium conditions where exchanges keep
taking place out of the contract curve. In such a process a sequence of
virtual equilibria can be traced, but no single equilibrium points. The path
along which the system evolves becomes the single possible unit of analysis.

4   Localised technological change and Schumpeterian growth regimes

In this chapter we aim to show how the integration of positive feedbacks and increasing returns – via the accumulation of knowledge and competence, both internal and external to the firm – into the framework of localised technological change can generate a microeconomic, discontinuous growth process. Endogenous technological change, induced by changes in relative prices and demand levels, and localised by learning processes – learning to learn and technological externalities – contributes to a microeconomic rationale which is able to explain the clustering of innovations and consequently discontinuous growth (Antonelli, 1995a and 1996b).

After years of neglect, the study of growth is increasingly turning the attention of economists to models where the endogenous creation of knowledge and introduction of technological innovations is now accepted (Aghion and Howitt, 1998). Discontinuity in the rates of growth however is still rarely considered. On the other hand, much equilibrium cycle theory is concerned with exogenous technological shocks. In this context, the analysis of the accumulation of endogenous technological change as a factor itself of punctuated growth would seem to be a more promising approach (Tylecote, 1991; Mokyr, 1990). Such a technological approach to the explanation of discontinuity in growth touches upon the Schumpeterian literature on business cycles (Freeman, Clark and Soete, 1982). As Rosenberg and Frischtak (1994) note however, the traditional Schumpeterian analysis of business cycles has many limitations, first the fact that 'the conditions which set in motion the diffusion and clustering of basic and related innovations and which would stand behind the upswing of a long wave are only loosely specified' (p. 67). Second, and most important, this literature rarely takes into account the macroeconomic context and thus the scope for macroeconomic policy.

The first section sets out the analytical model of localised technological change within a realistic context, and considers the role of innovation and switching as adjustment responses. The dynamics of localised technological change are seen to increase total factor productivity, i.e. growth, and replicate the business cycle. The second section details the implications of this microeconomic analysis with regard to a number of existing hypotheses and identifies four distinct phases in the process of discontinuous growth. The macroeconomic associations, which can account for the forces driving microeconomic discontinuity, are discussed in the third section, where the different growth regimes are identified. The conclusion articulates the chain of connection between changes in demand, efficiency in innovation and switching activities, the generation of knowledge, the dynamics of positive feedbacks and increasing returns, and subsequent productivity growth.

A model of localised technological change with learning to learn

We shall analyse the dynamics of localised technological change in a realistic setting containing a variety of markets and innovation systems. The context of global markets, characterised by international competition in homogeneous product markets, but heterogeneous labour markets and innovation systems, seems especially appropriate (Swann, 1994).

Let us assume that firms in country A at time *t* enjoy high levels of international competitiveness in industry K because of low levels of wages and the introduction of radical product innovations. Their average costs will therefore be much lower than international equilibrium prices for a given product and incumbents will earn large extra profits.

Such high levels of profitability in country A will attract new firms who will imitate the new technology of that industry and enter the market K. Firms in other countries will find it very difficult to imitate the technology and their wage levels will also be much higher; profitability will be lower, certainly not high enough to attract new competitors. Consequently, the international supply curve for the products of industry K will shift towards the right, but with a small reduction in international prices and profit margins for firms located in country A.

The aggregate demand for labour (and other intermediary inputs and primary resources) in country A will however shift consistently rightwards. Let us now assume that the long-term supply of labour (and other intermediary inputs and primary resources) in country A is characterised by a kink that separates two sections: the first part is almost flat and exhibits a small slope, the second part has a strong positive slope with a growing elasticity of wages (See Figure 4.1). Such a long-term supply schedule may be represented by an exponential curve:

$$W = w(L) \tag{1}$$

where $w' > 0$ and $w'' > 0$, and L is the long-term labour supply.

The larger the number of new firms entering the market for new products K in country A, the greater the aggregate demand for labour (and other intermediary inputs); consequently, the higher the level of equilibrium

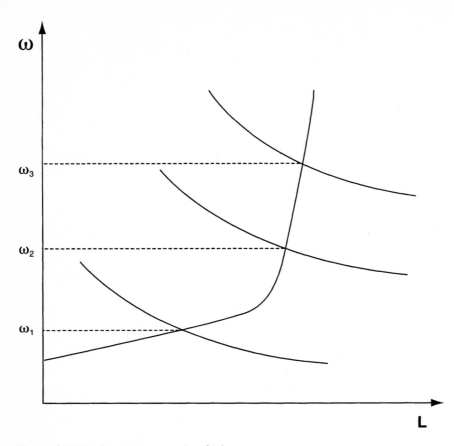

Figure 4.1 The long-term supply of labour

wages (and prices for intermediary inputs and raw materials) in industry K in country A.

Following Stiglitz (1987), we now assume that firms in industry K in country A, exposed to frequent changes in factor costs and hence to repeated adjustments in their production processes, are able to learn about the interactions between tacit and codified, internal and external knowledge so as to develop the special capability to learn to learn, experiencing the advantages of internal increasing returns in the generation of new knowledge. Within such an economic context a larger number of firms are likely to fund additional research and learning activities. Thus, increasing returns in the production of localised knowledge are likely to be reinforced by positive feedbacks, also at the system level, by the flow of technological externalities spilling among an increasing number of firms involved in the introduction of complementary innovations. Moreover, the greater the flow of internal research and learning activities of each firm, the greater should

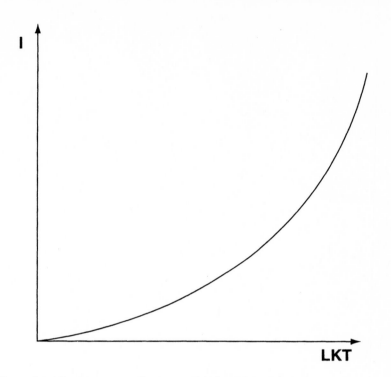

Figure 4.2 The innovation function with learning to learn

be its opportunities to access the pool of tacit and codified knowledge available in the regional and technological innovation systems. The increase in the flow of innovations should be more than proportional to the increase in the levels of internal resources devoted to research and learning activities.

Given the framework of the models of localised knowledge, described in Chapter 2, and localised technological change, described in Chapter 3, equation (2)[1] now becomes:

$$I = j(LTK) \tag{2}$$

where $j' > 0$ and $j'' > 0$ (See Figure 4.2). The FPA is now characterised by an innovation function with increasing returns and a switching function with decreasing returns. The map of FPA (Figure 4.3) takes on a very special form where, with learning to learn and increasing access to technological externalities, the slope of each frontier increases with the amount of resources available.

The selection of the equilibrium combination of switching and innovation activities is strongly influenced by the dynamics of learning to learn and technological externalities. For a low level isorevenue (See Figure 4.4),

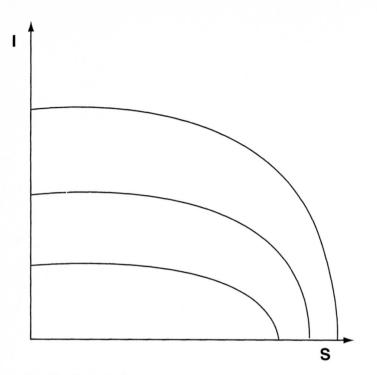

Figure 4.3 The frontier of possible adjustments with learning to learn

the slope of the FPA equals the slope of the isorevenue in region α, where switching is more efficient than innovating. Conversely, a high level iso-revenue equilibrium is found in region β, where innovating is more efficient than switching.

As entry into industry K in country A continues, because the levels of profitability and the time distribution of imitation lags that characterise the diffusion process are high, so the demand for labour continues to move towards the right, following a similar S-shaped path. In this process, wages also keep increasing by ever greater amounts, moving upward along the now, strong positive slope of the aggregate labour supply. The combination of these two stylised facts has two important results.

First, for low levels of adjustment in techniques space, which are necessary to account for (relatively) small increases in wages, firms will be induced to select technical changes rather than technological ones. At low levels of adjustment, the productivity of the switching function is by far larger than that of the innovation function. However, for larger increases in wages, and consequently, larger adjustments in techniques space, firms will find it more and more convenient to select combinations that favour the introduction of technological changes rather than technical ones.

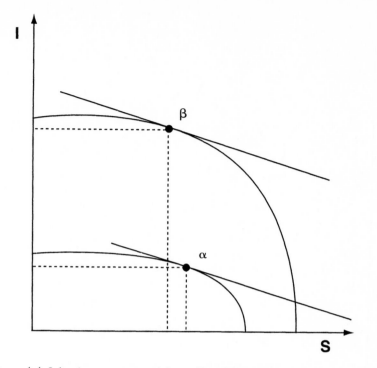

Figure 4.4 Selection processes with small and large adjustments

The changing slopes of the FPA mean that firms are likely to alternate between periods of switching, combined with the introduction of incremental localised innovations, and periods of rapid wage increases, characterised by the introduction of more radical innovations, clustered in new technological systems with high levels of complementarity.

Second, and more important, for low levels of adjustments in techniques space, firms are likely to favour the minimisation of adjustment costs: for a *given level* of the isorevenue i.e. of the opportunity costs determined by the wage changes, this consists of the selection of the appropriate combination of innovation and switching according to a standard optimisation procedure.

For high levels of adjustment, a firm's profitability declines and is eventually reduced to zero. Firms must now take into account not only the sharp increase in current total costs but also the high levels of adjustment costs. For given constant user costs of capital and increasing wages, total costs also increase; consequently, both profitability and market shares decrease. Employment subsequently shrinks and microeconomic recession sets in.

Firms that have experienced continuous rising wage levels in their recent past will have been forced to create a set of routines and fund-dedicated resources in order to cope with those continuous increases. We assume that such resources have high levels of specificity and a strong idiosyncratic nature: it is difficult to assume and incorporate a group of technical experts into a business organisation and make their activity consistent with that of the firm (Utterback, 1994). Costs of R&D laboratories can be considered long-term fixed costs. Adjustment costs belong to the class of sunk costs: hence, after a R&D laboratory has been set up it seems more rational to try to maximise its outputs rather than minimise its costs.

Confronted with a change in factor costs (e.g. a recession), a firm will fix the amount of adjustment resources devoted to either switching or innovating to levels that are necessary to switch to the new technique B, in order to move the desired distance AB. With a *given* FPA and a map of isorevenue curves, the actual point is now found on the highest attainable isorevenue. With high levels of efficiency in innovating and low levels of efficiency in switching, the equilibrium point selected can produce the conditions necessary to enable the firm to by-pass the new isocost line, generating a localised technological change that is also able to increase total factor productivity in terms of factor price. The firm in this situation is producing the same output with a smaller amount of input in monetary terms; hence its costs are lower. The map of isorevenues is bordered by levels of switching that are higher than the required distance A: beyond that level the firm has no interest in switching.

The maximisation procedure leads the firm to select the equilibrium point E (See Figure 4.5), generating an amount of innovation activity larger than that necessary to reach the new isocost ω_2. The firm is thus able to reach a lower isocost and reduce the overall costs of the production process (See Figure 4.6).

We now have a technological change that enhances total factor productivity in monetary terms. Such a technological change is itself induced by changes in factor prices (and demand levels). At the same time however, it is based upon the learning opportunities generated by the firm's competence in the techniques practiced before the changes in factor costs (and demand).

The firm not only introduces localised technological changes that penetrate and reshape the old isoquant – rather than simply moving it – it also commands a higher level of total factor productivity. The new localised technology is very close to the isocline and on the left of the new isocost ω_2. Therefore the firm is able to both retain the mix of inputs on which its learning capabilities are based and introduce a new technology that makes it possible to increase productivity.

At this point the firm is now able to regain the conditions of high profitability: market shares and growth can increase again and, with them, employment levels. In short, the basic conditions of a business cycle have been established.

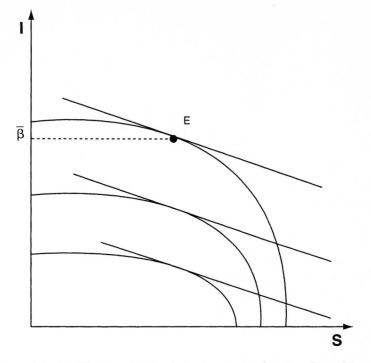

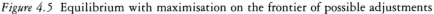

Figure 4.5 Equilibrium with maximisation on the frontier of possible adjustments

The implications of localised technological change with learning to learn

As a result of the dynamics of localised learning and localised technological change, when relative prices change smoothly firms may prefer to switch within the given technical space because of the higher costs of innovating with respect to switching. When relative prices change drastically however, firms simultaneously face a drastic drop in performance and a strong incentive to introduce localised innovations (rather than just switching). The dynamics of localised learning and technological externalities imply that firms will pass through periods of declining profitability and productivity, when relative prices change drastically. Eventually however, profitable conditions will be restored by the introduction of localised innovations. At this point, monetary policy can be particularly influential in assisting the speed of recovery, able as it is to ease the financial and liquidity constraints on firms engaged in the search for new technology.

The dynamics of localised technological change-cum-positive-feedbacks-and-increasing returns seems to offer a microeconomic foundation to the well-known Habbakuk's thesis. Habbakuk (1962) suggested that the fast

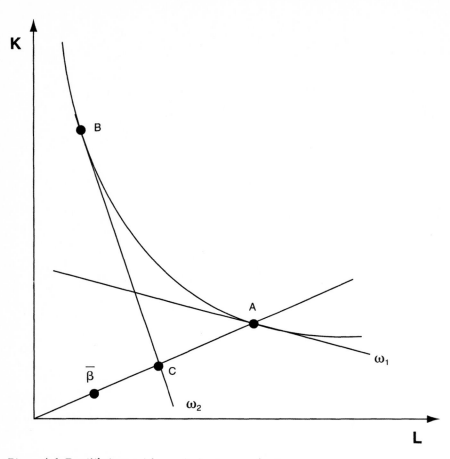

Figure 4.6 Equilibrium with maximisation on the isoquants map

rates of growth of productivity in the United States in the nineteenth century had been set off by the positive effects of the rapid increases in wages on the rates of introduction of technological changes. Von Tunzelmann (1978 and 1981) criticised this thesis based on the lack of empirical evidence on the introduction of labour-saving technological innovations in the US economy. Our model accommodates this criticism, stressing the localised character of innovations introduced in the proximities of the existing technical space, which is already occupied by the facing rapid rates of change in wages: localised technological changes thus introduced correlate with wage increases as in Habbakuk, though they are not necessarily labour saving (Fellner, 1961; Kennedy, 1964). The larger the wage increase, the more radical, localised and neutral the technological innovations.

Similarly, the dynamics of localised technological change seem consistent with the Marxist 'nutcracker' explanation of business cycles. The decline of unemployment and the subsequent rapid increases in wages together induce a reduction in profitability and growth, while at the same time stimulating technological innovations.

The clustering of innovations in time and the resilient specialisation of countries in products and, more importantly, in technological systems, is equally explained by the characteristics of inertia and excess momentum of the dynamics of localised technological change and its path-dependent rationale. At each point in time, countries specialise along well-defined technological trajectories, defined in terms of factors intensity, according to the existing mix of production techniques, products and industries. This mix depends in turn on the competences and related capability of learning to learn acquired in the particular 'loci' of the product space; here competitive advantage was gained originally through natural endowment factors (Archibugi and Pianta, 1992) and experiences over time phases of intensive and self-reinforcing innovative activity, which Schumpeter termed 'innovative gales' (Abramovitz, 1989; David, 1993).

Finally, the dynamics of localised technological change is consistent with the behavioural theory of the firm. When firms face a decline in profitability and their economic environment appears to be increasingly less sustainable, a change in behaviour becomes necessary, and economic action is directed towards modification of the structural parameters of the system, such as technology (March and Simon, 1958; Phillips, 1970; Metcalfe, 1989).

Based on the above implications, the model of the localised nature of technological change provides a powerful explanatory tool to help understand the economic dynamics of punctuated equilibria and discontinuity of economic growth, as it has been experienced in actual economic history (Mokyr, 1990). Furthermore, it offers a framework for macroeconomic analysis and intervention planning, within a microeconomic trend of discontinuous growth.

Growth regimes

In our interpretation, the alternation of growth regimes is characterised by the shift from regimes with relatively stable rates of growth and low levels of technological innovation (mainly of an incremental type with small changes in the technical coefficients of the production processes), to regimes with rapid changes in technologies, involving the introduction of radical innovations that follow sharp increases in wages and the cost of other primary inputs. The paths representing the growths in supply and demand are both S-shaped: this is due to imitation lags among producers in the former case and adoption lags among consumers in the latter. Adding these features to our model, the dynamics of localised technological change seem likely to generate four distinct growth regimes:

1   A phase of sustained growth following the introduction of new radical innovations, fuelled by the interaction of diffusion processes on both the demand and supply sides. During this phase there are increasing returns and positive feedbacks in production and consumption. New products are characterised by relevant network externalities and production benefits from economies of scale, and by technical externalities, which lead to reduced production costs and eventually lower market prices (Krugman, 1991). Employment grows very quickly and reaches full employment levels, especially with the support of appropriate macroeconomic policies.

2   A phase of recession then sets in. Profitability and investments decline. Firms are induced to switch along the production function while exhausting the last niches of labour and the other primary inputs still available.

3   Recession leads to depression, especially when the slope of the supply curve is such that wage levels increase quickly during new employment, so undermining not only the profitability of firms but also their survival. Firms are obliged to invest significant resources in adjustment costs. The adjustment reaction of firms is now tilted towards extensive technological research based upon accumulated learning and the maximisation of eventual revenues from the introduction of localised technological innovations. Here, macroeconomic policy can play a major role in two ways: by sustaining the levels of aggregate demand; and by reducing, with appropriate monetary intervention, the financial constraints which limit the search for new localised technologies.

4   The eventual introduction of radical localised technological change enables surviving firms to restore competitivity and profitability. Investment increases along with employment. The phase of recovery is in progress.

Conclusions

The general implication of the model we have explored is that technological change is both endogenous and discontinuous. This is because it is essentially a localised process characterised by increasing returns, consisting of both the dynamics of learning to learn and technological externalities, and the accumulation of dedicated competences.

The rate of introduction of new technologies is determined by the relative efficiency of switching activities and innovation activities. In order to adjust to new relative prices a firm bears a number of adjustment costs: how these are mixed depends upon the relative costs of switching with respect to those of introducing technological change. Forced to move in the techniques space because of changes in relative input prices, the firm will consider the trade off between switching, i.e. changing the production technique within a given technological area, and innovating, i.e. changing the production technology within a given technique area. The firm can change either the technology or the technique. Technology is no longer viewed as an exogenous, given structural parameter, but as a variable under the control of the firm and tightly linked to its learning capability. Along the same lines producer switching is no longer viewed as a free process that does not require any resources, but as an expensive activity which requires dedicated resources and competences.

When adjustments, induced by a rapid increase in wages, are very large, firms are encouraged to shift from cost minimisation strategies to output maximisation strategies by the dynamics of positive feedbacks and increasing returns from the generation of localised technological knowledge. The dynamics of positive feedbacks and increasing returns, and the subsequent shift from minimisation to maximisation for firms induced to select adjustment strategies, based mainly on the introduction of technological innovations rather than technical switches, are very important. The new localised technologies are now found to the left of the new isocost and thus bring about the actual increase of total factor productivity. Moreover, the generation of localised technological change clusters in time bring about the Schumpeterian 'gales' of innovation.

Macroeconomic analysis plays a major role in this context: all adjustments involve investment, and the level is clearly influenced by the level of aggregate demand and expectations; and new technologies that increase total factor productivity in monetary terms can be generated only when there are appropriate levels of liquidity, i.e. an easing of access to financial resources.

Articulation of the dynamics of localised technological change-cum-increasing returns in a context of global competition and S-shaped paths of diffusion, seems able to account for the classical Schumpeterian clustering of innovations and the sequence of recovery, sustained growth, recession and depression that shape business cycles (Schumpeter, 1939; Freeman, Clark and Soete, 1982; Tylecote, 1991), and therefore discontinuous growth. A macroeconomic policy that considers the endogenous forces leading towards discontinuous growth at the microeconomic level can be decisive in softening the negative effects of such endogenous cycles.

The strong path-dependent character of economic growth, in terms of regional concentration and technological specialisation, is also consistently explained by the dynamics of localised technological change and labour markets. This concentration and specialisation originates in small events – initial clusters of technological externalities stemming from the composition of industries, and the generation of new knowledge – which set in motion the factors of excess momentum, i.e. the dynamics of positive feedbacks and increasing returns. Subsequently, with the appropriate combination of stimuli, i.e. the large increases of wages engendered by the inelastic portions of labour supply and the capability to capitalise upon learning to learn, countries and regions can manage to reproduce their technological advantage and so remain international leaders.

Finally, the dynamics of localised technological change-cum-positive-feedbacks-and-increasing returns, its clustering in time, together with the pervasive role of complementarities in the generation and diffusion of actual technological innovations, constitute an interpretative framework capable of describing the punctuated emergence of a new technological system, such as new information and communication technology.

5   Economic topology

The role of technological
communication in the dynamics of
localised technological change

Technological communication, consisting of the socialisation of external tacit
knowledge and the access and recombination of external codified knowledge
plays a major role in the generation of new localised knowledge. Technological communication does not flow automatically within an economic
system, but requires dedicated efforts to implement the the understanding
and application of knowledge. Communication takes place when all the
agents are actually involved. Similarly, the generation of new knowledge
cannot be considered solely the outcome of the internal efforts of innovators:
relevant external knowledge is also necessary and its assimilation demands
specific actions which depend on the individual context in which firms
operate. An analytical effort to understand the economic topology affecting
the flow of technological communication in innovation systems, characterised by collective learning processes, would therefore seem appropriate.

In this chapter, we use the methodology of network analysis and spatial
stochastic interactions to explore the dynamics of technological communication. Industrial structures are conceived as a network of agents or nodes
linked by communication channels and local interaction structures where
information flows between the nodes. The generation of localised technological knowledge, based upon bottom-up inductive processes of collective learning, as well as top-down processes of blending new scientific
discoveries with available competence, is considered from the point of
view of the topological structure of economic networks shaping the communication flows of innovation systems (Antonelli, 1995a).

The first section discusses the applicability of the idea of economic
topology articulated in networks and local interaction models to the analysis
of the flow of communication within innovation systems. The degree of
effective interaction between technological externalities and their communication ultimately dictates the rate of the generation of localised technological knowledge and subsequent introduction of innovations. The
second section draws from the methodology of spatial stochastic interactions
to study the properties of communication systems: an analytical explanation
of connectivity and receptivity is presented, capable of illustrating the
variegated circulation of information within a network. A principal theory

of the work as a whole is propounded in the third section, namely that network structures and related interaction probabilities can significantly affect the outcome of the effects of changes in demand and production factors prices. The fourth section presents a stylised analysis of the cumulative, recursive non-linear, i.e. path-dependent, process which dynamically relates network structures, interaction probabilities and localised technological change. Representing the end of both the chapter and the theoretical part of the work, the conclusion draws together the main strands of the overall argument, explaining the characters of economic systems in the generation of localised technological change and the implications for technology policy and the economics of innovation.

Network analysis for communication systems

The generation of technological knowledge is heavily dependent on the relationship between: internal learning processes which lead to the accumulation of tacit knowledge; internal R&D activities which enable tacit knowledge to be codified and implemented; collective learning built upon the socialisation of experience and competence among firms; and the acquisition and recombination of external codified knowledge. In such a complex mix, each element is indispensable. Access to external tacit and codified knowledge depends on the extent to which technological externalities and effective communication among innovators percolate through the system, influencing both the research process itself and its outcome. The properties of innovation systems, perceived as network structures through which communication takes place, are therefore relevant, since they explain the capability to generate new technological knowledge.

Moreover, technological knowledge is firm-, region- and industry-specific; it is costly to use elsewhere with respect to other industries, regions and firms. The transfer and adaptation of localised technological knowledge from one industry, region or firm to another involves specific costs which are affected by the quality and effectiveness of the communication channels within the innovation system. Agents do more than exchange goods in the market place; they communicate, that is they exchange, trade and transfer information. Economic and innovation systems may also be thought of as communication networks, made up of interdependent nodes or agents whose innovative behaviour is connected to the system of relations existing between them.

In this context a first attempt to elaborate an economic topology seems necessary. An economic topology can be successfully applied at two levels: network analysis and the methodology of spatial stochastic interactions. The former seems especially useful in providing a static account of the structure of networks, as communication systems, and of the role of each firm in this context. The latter provides important elements to understand the aggregate dynamics of the flow of information and technological externalities and their effects on the production and distribution of knowledge within economic systems, when the recursive time stratification of repeated interactions is accounted for.

Interest in the network metaphor has grown rapidly in areas of economics where evidence about interdependence, in terms of externalities, complementarity, interrelatedness, and imperfect divisibility among production and utility functions, is strong. Indeed, regional economics, industrial economics and the new resource theory of the firm, as well as demand theory are increasingly using the notion of networks (Callon, 1991; Burt, 1992; Wasserman and Faust, 1994).

Network analysis can be applied to study the static characteristics of the distribution of communication links among agents in a given space. The basic assumption here is that agents are heterogeneous in terms of quality and quantity of communication links.

In a network there is a maximum number of links. For a system with n firms where all firms are connected to the others, the maximum number of links is given by a simple equation:

$$ML = (n - 1)n/2 \tag{1}$$

where ML is the maximum number of links among n firms.

In real networks, however, such a maximum number of links is rarely attained because links are expensive to build and maintain. Some firms have more connections than others and some links are more effective than others. The analysis of the actual distribution of links among agents has been developed with network analysis. A variety of tools has been elaborated to assess the characteristics of a network in terms of the typology of links in place.

The basic tools retained are: network density, mean nodal degree and degree variance across agents, specific and relational distance, degree centrality and betweenness centrality (Wasserman and Faust, 1994; Duysters, 1996). Network density (ND) is an index of systemic connection and can be easily measured by the ratio between the actual number of links or ties among agents in the network and the maximum number of potential links. Formally we have:

$$ND = 2L / (n - 1) n \tag{2}$$

where L are the link actually in place and n are the firms in the network.

Networks with high levels of density are better transmission systems: the flow of information is likely to reach all the agents.

Within networks with levels of density below 1 some agents are better placed than others. Some agents are said to have a higher degree of connectivity (d), measured by the number of communication links, than others. The mean nodal degree (D) and the variability of connectivity degree across agents (S^2) are measures of great interest. The latter makes it possible to confront networks. The former assesses the variability of connectivity levels among agents and provides a simple measure of the dispersion of ties among agents.

The mean nodal degree (D) is easily calculated as follows:

$$D = 2L/n \tag{3}$$

The variability of connectivity degrees in a network, that is the degree variance, is formally calculated as follows:

$$S^2 = \Sigma \ (d \ (n_j) - D)^2/n \tag{4}$$

Two important notions of distance emerge in this context: spatial distance and relational distance. Two agents and two points can be more or less close, in absolute terms, with respect to the relevant characteristics of the specific space which is considered. Relational distance matters when the relational space is considered.

A specific distance (Δ) – for instance in a product or scientific space defined by two important characteristics, or in the classical technical space of the production function defined by capital and labour – between points A and B, be can easily be measured with the notion of Euclidean distance (See Chapter 3):

$$\Delta \ AB = ((L_A - L_B)^2 + (K_A - K_B)^2)^{1/2} \tag{5}$$

Relational distance (d_{ij}) is defined by the geodesic distance, that is the number of links that are necessary to connect two agents i and j. The minimum geodesic distance is 1 between two agents directly linked.

Agents with a high degree enjoy some 'centrality'. Centrality in turn can be defined in a variety of ways: degree centrality and betweenness centrality are especially important. Degree centrality, is used to assess the role of each agent in the flows of information within the network. Degree centrality (C_D) assesses the importance of each agent in the network and is measured by the sum of the links in place in the adjacency matrix. Formally degree centrality for the firm i can be calculated as follows:

$$C_D \ (n_i) = d(n_i) \ / \ n - 1 \tag{6}$$

A firm with high levels of degree centrality is better able to take advantage of the flow of communication and technological externalities and can use recombination and socialisation extensively in the generation of localised knowledge.

Betweenness centrality is used as an indicator of the ability to control the flows of information within a network. A measure of betweenness centrality

(C_B) is provided by the number of times an agent is located between two other unrelated agents. If an agent has established a direct link to two other agents who are not directly linked to each other, the agent can be defined as 'between' the others. Between agents can exert a better control on the communication process and take better and more timely advantage of technological externalities spilling into the economic environment. It can be easily shown that the maximum level of betweenness centrality is achieved by the agent located at the centre of a star-shaped network. Formally, betweenness centrality can be measured as follows:

$$C_B\ (n_i) = \Sigma_{j<k}\ g_{jk}\ (n_i)\ /\ g_{jk} \qquad\qquad (7)$$

Network analysis provides important tools to appreciate the role of each agent in the economic environment. The analysis can be further enriched when the variety of communication dimensions are taken into account. As we have already considered (see Chapter 2) technological communication takes place among firms in a variety of spaces: internal and external labour markets; with informal exchanges among employees of different, even rival firms, or mobility across firms of competent employees; partnership into technological and standardisation clubs; localisation into technological districts; subcontracting relations; procurement and outsourcing; marketing and post-sales assistance and interlocking directorates.

Network analysis is less able to provide assistance to understand the aggregate dynamics of innovation systems. Moreover, within networks, interaction takes place among large numbers of players so that each agent is unable to interact strategically with others in order to anticipate un-expected consequences of the network on its own actions.[1]

Consequently, analysis of the actions of each agent in the network is only part of the story: the dynamic properties of the network itself, in which individual actions are embedded, are essential to understanding both the ultimate result of an action and the outcome of aggregate action. The properties of the system are likely to change over time, either spontaneously because of the intentional action of agents or because of exogenous inter-ventions such as network policies or scientific breakthroughs.

Spatial stochastic interactions methodology and communication systems

The methodology of spatial stochastic interactions models can be success-fully applied to the analysis of the aggregate dynamics of the behaviour of agents exposed to local technological externalities. Economics of innovation has often borrowed analytical tools from other disciplines to analyse the role of complex interactions which are not fully mediated by the price system. Epidemics provided the basis for the study of diffusion processes, and replicator dynamics, as we have seen in Chapter 3, are increasingly used to study the interactions between variety and performance in terms of market shares and rates of growth (Griliches, 1957; Metcalfe, 1989 and 1997).

Spatial stochastic interactions methodology studies the outcome of local interactions among agents characterised as disordered local states and the probability that some behaviours spread in a given context. The methodology used to study spatial stochastic interactions can be applied to economics, when local interactions, as opposed to global ones, are relevant. This methodology seems able to assess the combined effects of the amount of global codified information available (i.e. the external pressure), the topological characteristics of the environment articulated in heterogeneous firms and communication channels among them (distance and density and their effects on connectivity), and the attitude of each agent with respect to the communication (receptivity) (Kesten, 1982; Zuscovitch and Arrous, 1984).[2]

At each point in time, for a given topology of the economic space, articulated in density (i.e. the number of agents and communication channels linking the agents more or less effectively), the distribution of agents in disordered states and for given levels of external pressure, the methodology of spatial stochastic interactions can study the effects of the interaction between two classes of stochastic events: the probability that effective communication – consisting of the effective trade, exchange and transfer of information – actually takes place within innovation networks; and the probability that the results of the research and learning efforts of each firm in the system are effectively implemented by the amount of external information available in the innovation system.

The attributes of the process that leads to the generation, communication and transfer of localised technological knowledge, as investigated by the literature on innovation systems (Nelson, 1993) enable us to use the methodology of spatial stochastic interactions to understand its dynamics. This analogy between spatial stochastic interactions and innovation processes rests on the structured system in which the process takes place and the complementarity of external technological tacit and codified knowledge that is necessary to generate new localised technological knowledge and the role of communication channels among firms.

Such a methodology is able to reproduce analytically the stochastic laws of an interaction which can be successful or not, that is technological spillovers consisting of technological socialisation. Recombination can either take place or decay. Conversely, in the epidemic tradition, a diffusion process is bound to be completed once started. The methodology of spatial stochastic interactions emphasises the thresholds beyond which the system enters a 'phase transition' between absorbing states, which can help in understanding the punctuated distribution of innovation activities among technologies as well as in time and space. Traditional diffusion models based upon epidemic methodology implicitly assume only one absorbing state when adoption reaches saturation level.

An array of models of spatial stochastic interactions has been developed drawing from Gibbs Random Fields and Markov Random Fields. The general context of application are situations where the behaviour and the choices of each agent depend upon the behaviour and choices of other agents localised in economic proximity. Follmer (1974) has provided the first economic application of these models: here the evolution of the preferences of consumers is influenced by the structure of proximity and relationship. Orlean (1990, 1992) has applied the analysis of local interactions to study the dynamics of expectations based upon 'mimetic contagion' in financial markets. Kirman (1992) has explained with this methodology the coexistence of rival technologies.[3] Banerjee (1993) develops this approach to assess the uncertain value of information: each recipient in fact is not able to appreciate its economic value individually. The methodology of percolation, a specific model of spatial stochastic interaction, was first applied by David and Foray (1994) to study the diffusion of EDI standards and seems especially useful when studying the dynamics of technological externalities more generally.

The methodology of spatial stochastic interactions makes it possible to assess, for a given topology of the economic space within an innovation system – conceived as an information network – the magnitude and the impact of the local spillover of technological externalities as determined by the combined interaction between three factors: the amount of technological opportunities generated by new scientific breakthroughs (technological opportunities can be thought to exert an external pressure); the density and the distance among agents within a given technological and regional space, and the quality and effectiveness of existing communication channels among firms and other research institutions within the innovation system which all affect the connectivity probabilities of each agent; the absorptive capability of firms to actually receive and assimilate technological information in terms of both socialisation of tacit knowledge and recombination of codified knowledge which both affect their receptivity probability (Amendola, 1988; David and Foray, 1994; Antonelli, 1996a; Krugman, 1996; Dalle, 1997; Cefis and Espa, 1997).

In this context the probability that a behaviour and/or an information will spread to the whole space is determined by the specific distribution among the agents of the probability of connectivity, which in this context can be thought of as the probability that the communication channels of each agent exist and are open at the right time, and the probability of receptivity, which refers to the probability with which the technological externalities spilling into the system are actually used by each agent, i.e. the probabilities that the complementarity among firms with respect to the generation of technological knowledge is understood and properly combined by each firm with the internal research and learning process.

The characteristics of the space into which firms are embedded are very important here. In the most simple approaches the population of firms can be distributed in two states coded 0 or 1. The actual distribution of states of firms by sites in terms of: actual neighbours; distance from core regions and borders; number of links or information channels; number of firms in a given space and density, affects deeply the results of the spatial stochastic interactions. Hence, to understand the outcome of spatial stochastic interactions, it is first necessary to consider the original characteristics of the space in terms of distribution of states and other structural characteristics. The topology of the economic space in terms of actual distribution of firms, information channels and associated states, however, is not static and actually changes endogenously. It can be considered the path-dependent characteristic of the system.

Within the broad range of spatial stochastic interactions models, David and Foray (1994) have shown the powerful properties of percolation methodology. According to David and Foray (1994) the percolation probability is the probability that a firm i can effectively communicate with the other firms that form part of the same innovation system, that is the joint probability of transmitting and receiving. This approach qualifies the probability that some of the nodes can be more receptive than others and some transmission links may be more effective than others. The basic properties of the system appear therefore to consist of the actual complementarity between firms and the extent to which each firm is actually able to interact with other firms, i.e. receptivity and connectivity probabilities respectively.

According to the economic application of percolation theory, the fundamental property of percolation is the threshold generated by combinations of the critical values of the node probability (termed receptivity probability, (Pr*)) and the transmission probability (termed connectivity probability (Pc*)) beyond which there is a positive probability that percolation occurs, and below which the percolation probability is zero (See de Gennes, 1976 for the first introduction of this terminology).[4]

Specifically, the system undergoes a 'phase transition' when these underlying critical probabilities are reached. The rapid distribution of information to the whole system takes place when the local clusters, communities of agents in the same state, merge into one global cluster: the percolate cluster. There are corresponding critical values at which the receptivity (node) and connectivity (transmission) probabilities, respectively, become larger than the relevant critical values. These define the endpoints of a region above which a 'mixed percolation process' (one where it is not certain that either all nodes or all links of the network are open) will have a positive probability of achieving complete percolation (David and Foray, 1994).

The stochastic interaction properties of a system are relevant in the analysis of processes where the outcome is indeterminate, such as the 'possible' diffusion of innovations, the potential adoption of standards, the 'possible' leakage of spillovers, the 'possible' communication of external tacit and codified knowledge among firms, and the flows of inter-industrial externalities.

Specifically we see that for those levels of receptivity and connectivity probability that are below some critical values – lower than the minimum receptivity and connectivity probabilities thresholds – respectively, the general communication efficiency of the interaction system is severely damaged. Within the network, some areas, however, may experience connectivity and receptivity probability levels higher than the thresholds denoting 'maculated' networks.

In conclusion, stochastic interaction methodology seems to be a useful tool in understanding the laws that govern the circulation of information within an innovation system, particularly with regard to the following:

1   The thresholds and the 'phase transitions', absent in the traditional epidemic diffusion models, which occur when the connectivity and receptivity probabilities reach certain values.
2   The efficiency of information percolation networks as communication systems appears to be very sensitive to small changes, which may have important and long-lasting consequences (Krugman, 1996).
3   The active role of each agent in both transmitting technological information to third parties and actually absorbing it.

An important step forward can be made when the endogenous and dynamic nature of the structural characteristics of the system, such as the number of communication channels actually in place and the number of firms in a given space i.e. their density, and their effects on the interaction probability parameters themselves are considered. Connectivity and receptivity probabilities, as well as density and number of links, can be influenced by the past conduct of agents in terms of innovation capabilities and innovation activities. They can also be implemented by means of strategic and positive action designed to enforce technological clustering via either agglomeration in regional and technological innovation systems or technological co-operation.

The dynamics of localised technological change and spatial stochastic interactions

On the basis of what has been said in the previous chapters, it is now possible to put forward the principal argument that the rates of introduction of localised technological change, induced by changes in the relative prices of production factors and the desired levels of output, are actually influenced to a large extent by the communication properties of innovation systems as shaped by spatial stochastic interactions.

The properties of innovation systems, conceived as networks, in particular connectivity, receptivity and density, are especially apparent when technological knowledge is strictly localised as opposed to generic, as in the 'Arrovian' tradition. The generation of new localised knowledge is characterised by local externalities which concern only those agents which operate in close technological, industrial, regional and institutional proximity.

According to our assumptions, the production of localised technological knowledge by a firm can be formalised as the result of the interaction between internal research and learning activities and the creative access to external technological knowledge which spills over from other firms belonging to the same innovation system. These arguments enable us to better specify equation (1) in Chapter 2 as follows:

$$LTK_i = A_i \, (R\&D_i, LEARNING_i, k(IP_s, R\&D_{n-i} * LEARNING_{n-i})) \quad (8)$$

where LTK is the localised technological knowledge produced by the firm i; $R\&D_i$ and $LEARNING_i$ are the resources invested in learning and R&D activities by the same firm; $R\&D_{n-i}$ and $LEARNING_{n-i}$ are the resources invested in learning and R&D activities by the other firms in the system; IP_s is the interaction probability of the information network in which each firm is embedded; and k measures the effects on innovative output of the interaction between intramural resources dedicated to research and learning and the external knowledge flows on the innovative output.

The different levels of effective communication among innovators, as measured by the probability of the spatial interactions, are likely to affect significantly the productivity of the total amount of resources devoted by each firm to research and learning activities (Cohen and Levinthal, 1989 and 1990).

It is now clear that the shape of the frontier of possible adjustments is directly affected by the interaction probabilities of the system in which each firm operates (See Figure 5.1). Firms which operate in an innovation system with high levels of communication probabilities, *ceteris paribus*, will be more likely to face changes in the economic environment by the introduction of localised technological changes. On the contrary, firms which operate in an innovation system characterised by low levels of communication probabilities will react to given changes in their economic environment with the introduction of technical changes.

It is also evident that firms with more exposure more to high levels of communication probabilities are more likely to adopt maximisation procedures with respect to the levels of the FPA. High levels of communication probabilities are therefore more likely to be systematically associated with the introduction of actual technological innovation, which does increase total factor productivity.

To recap on the innovation generation process discussed above. The amount of technological knowledge an innovation system is able to generate will be determined by the amount of resources devoted to R&D and learning activities within firms, and the extent to which effective communication, between firms and between firms and other learning

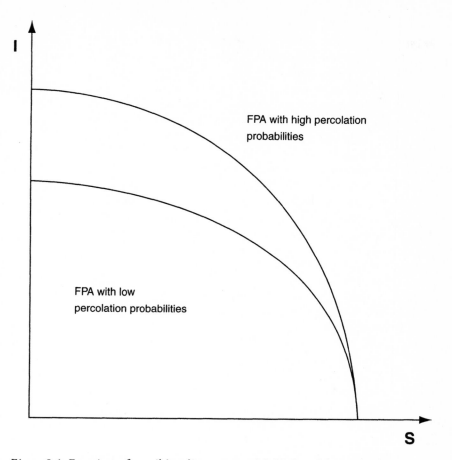

Figure 5.1 Frontiers of possible adjustments with high and low percolation
probabilities

institutions, takes place. Effective communication occurs when two
distinct events coincide, namely the emission of information, and the
reception of information.

At the innovation system level, this relationship with interaction probability becomes even more important. We are now able to fully articulate
our hypothesis, defining the maximum attainable efficiency of innovation
systems as follows:

$$\text{LTK}_\text{S} = f(\text{R\&D}_\text{S}, \text{LEARNING}_\text{S})^{(g\text{IP})} \tag{9}$$

where LTK_S is the amount of localised technological knowledge produced
in the innovation system, $\text{R\&D}_\text{S}$ and LEARNING_S are the aggregate
amounts of R&D expenditures and learning activities conducted in the

system, *g* is the average effect of external technological knowledge actually communicated, that is delivered and received by each firm in the innovation system, on its own innovative efficiency, and IP the communication capability as measured by the interaction probability of the system.

Clearly the probability of effective technological communication has a strong effect on the productivity of the total amount of resources devoted to research and learning activities. Specifically, we see that, the greater the receptivity of the research agenda of each firm to the information transmitted and the greater the connectivity among firms, therefore the larger the general interaction probability and the larger the productivity of resources invested in research and learning.

We also note that this relationship is non-linear: some regions can experience connectivity and receptivity levels that are just below certain key values, resulting in innovation networks which experience lower levels of productivity of R&D activities. Other regions with slightly larger connectivity and receptivity parameters can experience far larger values of overall communication probability and hence innovation activity. When time is accounted for the picture becomes even more interesting: all changes in the basic parameters of the interaction system around the critical values are likely to exert strong effects. Changes which take place in values at a distance from the criticality thresholds are likely to have far smaller effects. Small historical accidents which take place close to criticality thresholds can have long-lasting consequences.

These properties have important implications for technology policy: all efforts to increase the communication probability of innovation systems are likely to have strong positive effects on innovative efficiency, for given levels of resources dedicated to learning and research activities. A new agenda for technology policy can actually be built on the basis of these results.

To fully articulate this point, however, time needs to be explicitly accounted for.

Feedbacks, learning to interact and path-dependence

Let us now further assume that the characteristics of the innovation system, as analysed by the methodology of spatial stochastic interactions, can reflect in a specific way the past behaviour of firms in terms of their technological conduct.[5]

We introduce here the notion of a sequence of spatial interactions where at the end of each period the structural characteristics of the system are allowed to change. Moreover, we model this structural change as the process of endogenous accumulation of knowledge and introduction of technological and organisational innovations, which is itself influenced by the results and effects of the stochastic interactions which have taken place in the previous time period(s).

At the end of each period new communication channels can be built, especially by innovative firms, new firms can enter, connectivity and receptivity probabilities can change. Firms with past experience of introduction of localised technological changes have higher probabilities of connectivity and receptivity, because they can build new links and activate new communication channels. We assume that economic regions and technologies with faster rates of introduction of technological innovations attract other innovative firms, so that not only the connectivity and receptivity probabilities, and the number of links, but also the density of communication networks is strengthened by past innovation capabilities.[6] This assumption implies that:

1   agents learn to interact and to make better use of the existing communication channels: innovative agents at time *t* are better able to implement their connectivity and receptivity parameters;
2   all communication channels among agents can be thought of as irreversible investment which become more and more valuable for their users, the better the conditions of use.

Hence, again, the number of communication links in place as well as receptivity and connectivity parameters, the aspects of communications networks we stress, are likely to increase after their use has proved to be fruitful.[7]

Within information networks, we can now establish a recursive relationship between the innovation capabilities and innovative choices of firms that have led to the actual introduction of localised technological changes at time $t - n$ and the structure of communication channels in place, the levels of receptivity and connectivity probabilities, within a communication network at time *t*. The structure of interactions at time $t - 1$ changes and, consequently, the stochastic outcome of the interactions at time *t*. The recursive character of the dynamics moreover is significantly affected by the criticality of the parameters involved: hence small changes in the receptivity and connectivity probabilities, determined by the rate and direction of technological changes introduced at time $t - n$, can bear important and even radical effects on the innovation system at time *t*. This dynamics of reinforcing feedbacks can have both positive and negative effects: within a maculated interaction system the agents located in empty spots introduce fewer and fewer innovations, while agents located in full spots experience faster and faster rates of introduction of innovations.

The density (G) of communication networks, measured in terms of the number of information channels in place in a given space, within an innovation system, is likely to increase, along with the rate of accumulation of localised technological knowledge (LTK) and the related introduction of localised technological changes in the previous periods of time. This time dynamics is likely to take place because of two distinct forces. The attraction exerted by the flow of local technological externalities on the entry of new firms, via either higher rates of natality or relocation in the technological district and diversification in the technological system, and the creation of new communication channels by incumbents, such as new joint-ventures, new memberships in a technological club, or the adoption of a new research standard shared with other innovators.[8] Hence we can write:

$$G_t = j(LTK_{t-n}) \tag{10}$$

The second step consists of assuming that the new communication channels in place and the increased number of firms, themselves associated with the amount of localised technological knowledge introduced, in turn affect the levels of connectivity probability (Pc_t) of each agent in any given communication network. Moreover, the levels of connectivity probability, that is the probability that each link is open, at the right time, is itself directly influenced by the amount of localised technological knowledge generated. This is because of the increased awareness of the economic value of the actual communication of external technological information. Once more the positive feedbacks stemming from the membership of technological co-operations and standardisation schemes, and the location into technological districts help firms to enhance their connectivity levels in order to make a better use of the external knowledge, both tacit and codified, available in the innovation system. Hence we can write:

$$Pc_t = z(G_{t-m}, LTK_{t-n}) \tag{11}$$

Finally, receptivity probability at time $t(Pr_t)$ is likely to be higher, for each agent, the higher the levels of accumulation of localised technological knowledge and the rates of introduction of localised technological change in a given information network experienced at time $t - n$. This is because of the positive effects of learning to learn from external sources, either by means of the socialisation of tacit knowledge or the recombination of codified, technological and scientific information, on the innovative capabilities of each firm and hence on their attention to the successful communication of the available information:

$$Pr_t = w(LTK_{t-n}) \tag{12}$$

Within a given communication system, conceived of as a network, a cumulative recursive process is likely to take place between the levels of localised technological knowledge accumulated and the rates of introduction of localised technological changes and the levels of interaction probability. At each point in time, the likelihood that firms choose to respond to given changes in their economic environment with the introduction of localised technological changes depends (also) on the levels of interaction probability. In turn however, the levels of interaction probability at each point in time depend upon the rates of introduction of localised technological changes at time $t - n$. Hence the levels and related criticality of the parameters of the spatial stochastic interactions context becomes endogenous. Specifically, here, path-dependence is obtained by the time stratification of a historic sequence of spatial interactions.

The interaction between changes in the economic environment and the evolution of the innovative conduct of firms now assumes all the characters of a path-dependent process. At each point in time within such a process, the topological structure, as it has emerged from the past, influences the future behaviour of the agents also via their effect on the transition probabilities to the following state; yet the dynamic characteristics, i.e. the values of the interaction probabilities, are not fully determined. The stochastic feature of the spatial interaction system does not allow deterministic interpretations about the effects of such changes to be made. Under such conditions, extreme reactions can take place at any moment in time, when the critical values are attained. Then the interaction probability can fluctuate for small changes in the parameters from one extreme to another. The path-dependent character of the process is now clearly established. The events at time $t - n$ have long lasting effects, but in a specific context. The state at time $t + 1$ depends on the states at time $t, t - 1, t - n$, together with the transition probabilities from each state to the next.

Conclusions

Economic topology is relevant to analysing the generation and the distribution of localised knowledge and hence the dynamics of localised technological change. Economic topology articulated in network analysis and spatial stochastic interactions models has important implications for both the economics of innovation and technology policy. First of all, it provides a theory and an interpretative framework to understand why local economic systems exposed to similar shocks, in terms of changes in relative prices of production factors and demand levels, may react by introducing either technological changes, which increase total factor productivity and enhance overall levels of welfare, or technical changes that are limited to re-adjusting input levels and combinations to the new levels of relative prices.

Second, we now have a theory about the dynamics of agglomeration within technological and regional innovation systems, based on clusters of innovative firms with a complementary knowledge base. The virtuous interaction between changes in the economic environment and the rates of introduction of localised technological changes, as shaped by the characteristics of local interactions, is such that in regional and technological systems, with effective communication systems in place, and hence, high interaction probability levels, spillovers and innovations reinforce each other, thus increasing their dynamic characteristics. The

dynamics of localised technological change and spatial stochastic interactions together can thereby explain the emergence of regional clusters of
innovative firms, especially around centres of academic excellence and the
clustering of innovative firms in technological systems characterised by the
introduction of a variety of complementary innovations (David, Foray and
Dalle, 1998; Cowan and Cowan, 1991; Carlsson, 1997; Swann and
Prevezer, 1996).

Third, we are now more able to appreciate how the characters of the
present wave of innovations in the new information and communication
technology system, itself a product of the clustering of localised and complementary technological changes, are likely to interact with the rate of
introduction of localised technological changes, enhancing the general
levels of innovation capability of firms coping with changes in their
economic environment. New information and communication technology
alters the very conditions of access, retrieval, processing and communication
of all types of information. Specifically, it increases the separability, tradeability and transportability of information, thus favouring exchanges of
technical information and enhancing the connectivity and receptivity of
information networks and their agents. Moreover, the diffusion of new
information and communication technologies can have an important structural impact, reconfiguring the position of service industries and making
the knowledge-based service sector, as the mediator of increasing interactions between tacit and codified knowledge, central to the innovative
capability and competitive advantage of an economic system (Antonelli,
1997b).

This approach also helps to understand the role of the characteristics of
industrial structures in terms of sectoral composition, with respect to the
generation of localised technological knowledge. The distribution and
quality of knowledge-intensive business service industries have important
effects on the economic system and its innovative capacity. An increase in
the exchange of tacit and codified knowledge, made possible by the services
of consultants and advisers, improves connectivity between agents, sharing
learning experiences and creating learning opportunities, and thus advances
receptivity. Similarly, improved business services, in terms of distribution,
capillarity, competence and access, in turn improves the interactions
between tacit and codified knowledge; and in so doing technological and
organisational innovations and solutions will be generated and will be
tailored to a firm's individual business environment. Small and medium-
sized firms in particular – where in-house R&D departments, which
formally evolve and implement tacit abilities into localised technological
knowledge, are unavailable – would benefit from such a dynamic situation.
Given such an influence on the exchange of knowledge, knowledge-
intensive business service firms, and their distribution in the architecture
of an economic system, obviously become a major factor in assessing a

system's innovative capability (Lundvall, 1992; Nelson, 1993; Antonelli, 1997b) (See Chapter 11).

Since the characteristics of an innovation system should not be considered given and/or exogeneous, we can assess the range of strategic actions which may be implemented by firms and governments to increase the interaction probabilities and hence the innovation capabilities of that system. Effective connections are the result of deliberate action and should rather be considered endogenous: an effort has to be made to establish each effective connection. The interaction probability at time t affects the behaviour of agents, not only with respect to the levels of their R&D expenditures, but also regarding the levels of deliberate action taken to build up connections and receptivity which enhance the efficiency of the very funds invested in R&D. Hence, the interaction probability at time t is influenced but because of its stochastic nature not determined by the conduct of the firms at time $t - n$. Thus, interaction probability may be thought of as endogenous in that the behaviour and strategy of agents at each point in time influence the values of the basic parameters.

In this context, technological co-operation plays an important role. Technological co-operation among agents affects the interaction probability and hence the innovative capability. It enhances a variety of factors: the circulation of tacit knowledge and its socialisation; the opportunities for external learning, that is learning from the specific knowledge generated by other co-operating firms; the opportunity for the accelerated recombination of the bits of codified knowledge generated by each co-operating firm; and finally, the scope for capitalising on potential complementarities among both the variety of firms and between the different R&D activities performed by each firm (See Chapter 9).

Standards and standard-setting procedures become particularly relevant here. Standards play a major role in enhancing compatibility and complementarity between technological innovations. They increase the connectivity and receptivity of information networks in making it possible to specify the conditions of inter-operability among new technologies and between old technologies and new ones. Furthermore, standards and standard-setting procedures increase the interfaces between the paths of localised technological change followed by each firm; and in so doing they improve the flow of technological externalities and ease the introduction of further technological innovations (See Chapter 10)

Finally, the implications for industrial and innovation policies are also far-reaching. In the traditional 'Arrovian' analysis, the production of knowledge and innovation as a public good was deemed to be sub-optimal because there was little incentive for potential innovators and it was difficult to correctly assess and assign property rights on the results of innovation processes. Fiscal allowances and public subsidies had become the standard, recommended way to sustain innovation levels.

When the localised technological knowledge is appreciated as the outcome of the blending of the four basic forms of knowledge: internal, external, tacit and codified, the characteristics of innovation systems, such as the regional clustering of learning firms, and technological systems of firms working in complementary technologies – where technological information is shared and percolates from one firm to another – become relevant and warrant greater attention. Appreciation and subsequent internalisation of local technological externalities among firms involved in complementary innovation activities becomes a potential strategy for firms and public intervention: indeed such activity leads to an increase in the productivity of resources invested in innovation activities (Metcalfe, 1995).

The cumulative outcome of local interactions is likely to be very sensitive to the critical values of connectivity and receptivity probabilities. Systems where successful complementarity in communication and, consequently, receptivity and connectivity, fall below these respective threshold levels are unlikely to be able to take advantage of the positive effects of spatial stochastic interactions on the generation of localised technological knowledge. Hence, architectural issues of innovation systems are important beyond understanding the long-term dynamics of innovation and growth: a system design capable of implementing the appropriate properties would be central to technology policy (Richardson, 1972; Sah and Stiglitz, 1986 and Mokyr, 1990).

Public subsidies aimed at encouraging technological co-operation among both firms and firms and universities, can offer the opportunity to internalise the spillover of localised technological knowledge. In such a context, the sponsoring of technological co-operation may be viewed as an intervention of institution-setting, favouring both the productivity of resources invested in research and the likelihood that firms will introduce localised technological change when coping with changes in the relative prices of production factors and demand levels.

All changes in relative prices and desired output levels can be accommodated by firms with either technical changes in a given map of isoquants or localised technological changes. When both the levels of producer switching costs and innovation opportunities are high, firms' adaptive responses to all changes in their economic environment will favour the introduction of localised technological change. The characters of the innovation system into which firms are embedded shape the attitude of firms in the trade off between technical change and technological innovations: the better the access conditions to the relevant technological externalities flowing within network systems and the better and more effective the communication flows, the higher the chances for the introduction of localised technological changes.

Part II

Applications

6 Localised technological changes in telecommunications and the network of networks

In this chapter we try to develop an economic and institutional rationale to explain the emergence of the new advanced telecommunications system as the outcome of the different and complementary localised innovative efforts of a variety of players.

New information and communication technologies may be considered a nascent technological system based upon a complex cluster of radical and complementary innovations. This system consists of a variety of applications of computer-based information-processing procedures. Increasing returns from the generation of new technologies are significant in the clustering in time of innovations in new information and communication technologies. The emergence of clustering appears to be the outcome of the introduction of interdependent innovations along a definable path shaped by a number of previously identified factors: complementarities and hence technological externalities; the advantages of learning to learn in this specific area of application; and the competence accumulated by means of the dynamics of learning to do and learning to use.

In this chapter, the first section briefly describes the current dynamics of the telecommunications industry, outlining the contrasting interactions in the generation of innovations. The specific nature of localised technological change within telecommunications is the subject of the second section, which considers the importance of data communication and the activity of users as vectors of future change. The major technological changes in telecommunications are itemised in the third section, and their classification and explanation in terms of innovation clusters illustrates the applicability of the models used so far. In the conclusion, the present situation is again outlined with a view to and an analysis of the regulatory implications of the network of networks, cited throughout the chapter as the potential resolution to the contradictory dynamic developments within the existing structure.

Innovation and the evolution of telecommunications

Telecommunications constitutes an essential component of the emerging information and communication technological system. New uses of telecommunication services are strongly associated with the introduction and diffusion of new information and communication technologies. Innovative uses of information technologies are increasingly associated with systematic networking of computers by means of telecommunication services, paving the way for the dynamics of learning to learn based upon learning to use. In turn, the new uses of telecommunication services appear to be significantly associated with increases in total factor productivity. The telecommunication services industry thus increasingly assumes the characteristics of a key industry, that is an industry which provides the rest of the economic system with important pecuniary and technological externalities affecting overall levels of output and productivity.

Within this process, different forms of positive feedbacks and increasing returns in the generation of localised technological changes are at play, contrasting each other. The search for complementarities pushes incumbent telecommunication carriers to generate technological innovations that are complementary to existing technologies in order to increase their scope of application and take advantage of the competence already acquired from learning to do. Users, however, have different incentives and opportunities: the dynamics of learning to learn and the search for technological externalities push them to generate new technologies complementary to their own needs.

Such a division has important implications with respect to the organisation of the innovation process within the telecommunication services industry. In recent years, users have been introducing an increasing share of the overall flow of innovations. Technological change in the telecommunications industry, traditionally determined by the interaction of telecommunication equipment manufacturers and telecommunication network operators, is now increasingly characterised by the triangular interaction between large users, equipment manufacturers and network operators.

Localised technological changes and telecommunications

New information technology and industrial change

A large amount of empirical evidence is available on the characteristics of the introduction of new information technologies by firms, and the dramatic changes in the organisation of firms and productivity growth that parallel their diffusion (Beniger, 1986; Bresnahan 1986; Antonelli, 1988 and 1995b; Scott Morton, 1991; Chandler, 1992; Allen and Scott Morton, 1994; Brynjolfsson and Hitt, 1995; Loveman, 1994). The use of telecommunication services as an instrument to integrate a variety of computers into a network emerges as the distinctive feature of the effective adoption and implementation of the new technological system.

The productivity effects of the adoption of new information technologies are likely to become more evident when attention is paid to the capability of firms to use telecommunication services to enable the interconnection and inter-operability of information systems of different units. New, innovative uses of telecommunication services, based on an array of innovations introduced since the mid-1980s, denote an important step in the evolution of information technology towards what may be considered a technological system. New technological systems emerge when new technologies, which are individually more effective and productive than their direct substitutes, offer scope for further improvements of productivity levels when associated with other technologies, new organisational structures, new skills and new intermediary inputs. The introduction and adoption of complementary innovations in telecommunications, especially when emerging from a bottom-up process that reflects the needs and constraints of users, is itself a factor in the implementation of the broader information and communication technological system, including important organisational changes, and consequently, is an essential factor in the additional growth of productivity (David, 1987).

The coupling of new uses of telecommunications services with information technologies involves the systematic use of the telecommunication infrastructure, originally conceived to carry voice messages, as a vector of data communications that make networking among computers possible. The networking of computers in different locations, both within the same multi-site organisation and between different organisations, has generated important positive effects on the conduct and performance of firms, and subsequently on their overall productivity levels. However, in order to be successfully implemented and embedded into the behaviour of firms, networking generally has very high requirements with regard to interrelatedness and complementarity, in terms of communication standards, information processing procedures, and organisational structure. As a result, networking is only likely to display its full effects when the entire set of complementary and interrelated organisational and manufacturing changes has been made (Antonelli and Marchionatti, 1998).

Empirical evidence confirms that the adoption of new networking technology has significant effects on the organisation of productive processes, radically modifying the sequence of the various productive phases, the length of the productive processes, and the quantitative and temporal relationships between the stocks of intermediate and final goods. In this way, new networking technologies enable the economies of scale at batch, department and plant levels to be modified. The adoption of new networking technology makes it possible to modify the organisational relationships between phases of the productive process, so that market relations can be strengthened by systems of electronic communications and bureaucratic coordination can be replaced by a mix of co-operative relationships implemented by on-line communication systems. More generally, based on case studies and industrial history, much qualitative evidence shows that within the ongoing process of introduction and diffusion of the new technological system, the introduction and implementation of new networking technologies marks a real discontinuity, a quantum jump, enabling sharp increases in overall productivity levels. This jump is based precisely on the high intensity usage of telecommunication services for data communication.

The role of innovative users

The important effects on users of telecommunication services, stemming from the introduction and implementation of new information and communication technologies, hold major implications for technological change in telecommunications. As we have seen, technological change cannot be considered the neutral outcome of exogenous forces, but should rather be defined in terms of a wide variety of factors: the intentional strategies of agents embedded in the circumstances of place and time, which constrain their behaviour; innovative conducts based on the opportunities to generate technologies appropriate to existing local circumstances; the accumulation of localised knowledge built upon tacit learning processes that are both internal and external to firms; the consequence of the interaction between users and producers; and a factor which asymmetrically affects the cost conditions and the market conduct of agents (Antonelli, 1995a and 1995c).

Considering technological change in this way, we can articulate our hypotheses specifically. The strong positive effects that the adoption of information and communications services for users have on productivity has forced the pace of technological change in telecommunications. Large users discovered new, important technological and innovative opportunities based on the blending of telecommunications with already operational information and communication technologies. Technological change in telecommunications is more and more the result of the technological strategies of different groups of firms, each pursuing their own market strategy and building upon their localised, specific technological capability. This new trend has drastically altered the traditional centripetal direction of innovations, adding a strong centrifugal effect.

Recently a new phase has characterised technological change in telecommunications. Users themselves have been able to introduce an increasing share of the overall flow of innovations and, as a result, technological change is increasingly generated by a triangular interaction involving those large users, equipment manufacturers and network operators. Previously, the latter two agents had mainly been responsible for the actual innovation, rate and direction of technological change. Interdependence between the process of the introduction of new technologies and the technological and market strategies of innovating companies is also an important consideration. Much recent literature contains empirical evidence of an interactive process consisting of the introduction of alternative and competing innovations, their selection and implementation, increasing complementarity and user value and hence their diffusion (Arthur, 1989, 1994). Technological convergence now appears to be the outcome of a collective effort to build a new technological system made up of complementary and compatible innovations deliberately introduced by innovators drawing on localised competencies and capitalising on potential technological externalities spilling from a common knowledge base.

In conclusion, two strategies of collective innovation seem to be at work. On one side, centripetal forces push technological change towards higher levels of integration within the centralised network structure, finding and building new complementary uses from the existing infrastructure. On the other, new complementarities, mainly based on large user needs, are implemented creating an alternative technological system. In the convergence of telecommunications and new information technology a battle appears to be taking place between technological systems. Given our analysis, the outcome is likely to be shaped by the dynamics of lock-in and path-dependence.

The traditional structure of networks is under increasing pressure, and serious risks exist of undermining its coherence in terms of inter-operability and interconnectivity. The inflow of centrifugal innovations, mainly generated by large users, is threatening the strong centralised and coherent character of the networks. As a potential resolution to this situation, the network of networks, as it is emerging in the European Union, seems an organisational architecture especially conducive to fostering the rate of introduction of innovations and accommodating the different directions, whether introduced by users or network operators.

Major technological changes in telecommunications

Each major technological innovation introduced in telecommunications has changed the shape of the factors determining the role of increasing returns and complementarity among the different components of the network. Technological change has affected in depth, not only the market position of each operator in the network, but also the technical and organisational features of the architecture of the network. Each of these innovations deserves to be analysed as the outcome of the localised effort of well defined groups of actors, changing their technology and consequently their role within the network, their markets and their profitability.

Analysis of the most important technological innovations introduced in the telecommunications industry in the last twenty years enables the identification of two clusters:

1   centripetal technologies that enhance the relevance of economies of scale, scope and density, mainly introduced by network operators;

2   centrifugal technologies that reduce the relevance of technical economies of scale and density; specialising technologies that reduce the role of inter-functional telecommunications economies of scope, and segmental technologies that reduce the role of network externalities, all mainly introduced by large users.

Centripetal technologies that enhance the relevance of economies of scale, scope and density, mainly introduced by network operators

1   Coaxial cable systems, introduced in 1946. These consisted of four pairs of coaxial cables and had a total capacity of 1800 two-way voice circuits. Coaxial cable technology considerably reduced transmission costs and had important effects on increasing returns, both in terms of economies of density and economies of scope, with respect to switching activity. The capacity of switching centres could be better exploited with the new transmission capacity of cables.

2   L4 transistor systems in repeaters, introduced in 1967. These made it possible to increase the transmission capacity of coaxial cables and carried 32,400 two-way voice circuits over eleven pairs of coaxial. The last generation of repeaters, L5, introduced in 1978, enhanced the transmission capacity to 132,000 two-way voice circuits and used integrated circuits. The centripetal effects were even stronger than the ones exerted by L4 technology.

3   Digital switching, introduced in 1968. Digital switching made it possible to share the transmission capacity with many different users, converting each signal to a digital format and then combining the digital signals in time (time-division multiplexing) adding on to the centralising role of the switching system.

4   Optical fibres, introduced in the late 1970s. A strand of optical fibre carries 2 gigabits, which is equivalent to 30,000 telephone circuits. Each fibre transmission system has dozens of fibre strands in each cable. Plummeting costs and above all the enormous increase in optical fibre capacity means that there were economies of scale to be gained. Once a network has been set up, the incentive to increase the volume of traffic is very strong: average costs continue to fall, and marginal costs continue to be lower than average costs with a higher negative trend.

5   The intelligent network, introduced in the late 1980s. The intelligent network can be considered a radical innovation in signalling which, together with switching, transmission, distribution and billing, is one of the most relevant functions within a network. It deeply affects the features of the production process and leads to important economies of scale, density and scope. Intelligent networks consist of compact and inseparable systems of advanced computers and software capacity,

which perform three distinct yet interdependent functions: they shape the flow of the traffic within the network; at the same time, they take track of the billing, an essential issue for telecommunication carriers; and they provide a variety of advanced services such as the 'follow me' or 'voice messages'. The intelligent network is capable of providing centrally the whole array of services available on virtual and local networks by private branch exchange equipment located on the customers' premises. It thus enables centralised network operators to 'strike back' at specialised and virtual networks, offering the same range of new innovative services throughout the network at much lower costs. Because it relies on a strong know-how and software content the average costs of the intelligent network are deeply affected by advanced sunk costs: hence the larger the numbers of systems delivered, the lower the costs. Consequently, the operators of large networks have lower costs than the operators of small ones.

6 Digital time division switching introduced in the early 1980s. Digital time division technology enhances switching capability, increasing capacity and speed, and enables the use of both voice and data-communication.

7 Integrated Services Data Network and Broadband Integrated Service Data Network (ISDN and BISDN), introduced in the late 1980s. ISDN and BISDN are integrated multiservice and multipurpose networks that provide a wide range of services including voice, data and images (BISDN), which, within the framework provided by ATM switching technology and intelligent network signalling systems, would make it possible to reconcile within one large, unified, centrally-managed and planned network the provision of different services to different groups of customers.

8 Asynchronous Transfer Mode (ATM), introduced in the early 1990s. ATM is a new switching and multiplexing technology designed for broadband multiservice telecommunications.

9 Digital Extended Cordless Telephony (DECT), introduced in the early 1990s. DECT is a new cellular telecommunication technology which relies on microwave cells; it is tightly linked to the fixed network and operates with a limited ray of autonomy. As such, DECT seems designed to maximise the potential economies of scope of the large communication capacity of the fixed network.

10 Asymmetrical Digital Subscriber Line (ADSL), introduced in the mid-1990s. ADSL is a technology that allows multiple, simultaneous high-speed services to be carried over existing twisted pairs, thus dramatically increasing the potential of already installed copper networks.

*Centrifugal technologies that reduce the relevance of technical
economies of scale and density; specialising technologies that
reduce the role of inter-functional telecommunication economies
of scope; and segmental technologies that reduce the role of
network externalities: mainly introduced by large users*

1   Computer-to-computer communication, introduced in the early
    1960s. Computer-to-computer communications were initiated by
    IBM to enable remote maintenance of large computers. Particularly
    in the early stages, data communications especially were mainly used
    for linking plants and headquarters in order to streamline the produc-
    tion process and increase the co-ordination capacity of large bureau-
    cracies. They had two significant effects. First, network externalities
    were not relevant at all for intra-corporate data communications.
    Second, firms' derived demand for telecommunication services increased
    many times. This segment of demand had a very low price elasticity
    because in many instances the opportunity cost of not using the service
    was already technologically unacceptable, and the effects of advanced
    telecommunications on the competitivity and market share of firms,
    and consequently on output, were very great. Moreover, revenue
    elasticity was very high because of the effects of the diffusion of
    information and communication technology already underway.

2   Microwave radio systems, first introduced in 1950. Microwave systems
    had a limited capacity and drastically reduced the levels of fixed
    investments, sunk costs and density economies. Microwave systems
    are the technology that enabled the entry of Microwave Communica-
    tions Inc. (MCI)[1] on the famous St Louis–Chicago route in 1972.

3   Advanced Customer Premises Equipment (CPE), introduced in the
    early 1970s. CPE made it possible to locate large portions of the
    intelligent capacity of switching services on the customers' premises
    so as to segment the network and enable specialised access.

4   Centrex, introduced in the early 1980s. A modularisation of switching
    centres that made it possible to customise and dedicate switching
    capacity to large users, by-passing the general network.

5   Geostationary satellites, introduced in the mid-1970s. The technology
    of geostationary satellites had a major cost advantage over coaxial cables
    because of larger capability, in terms of volume, with lower fixed costs.
    On top of this, however, geostationary technology made it possible to
    reduce the effects of economies of scale and density in transmission.
    Finally, in low-density regions, satellites provided a radical opportunity
    to completely by-pass the terrestrial infrastructure. Geostationary
    satellites are now used mainly for long-distance broadcasting.

6   Cellular telephony. A wireless telecommunications system used exten-
    sively for mobile communications, which divides a geographical region
    into cells, uses low-power transmitters within each cell and reuses

transmission frequencies in cells that are not contiguous. Cellular telephony requires a new network of cells to be built and hence drastically reduces the economies of scope for existing infrastructure. The rapid growth of cellular technology, especially in terms of more efficient uses of frequencies, has created concrete possibilities of replacing the fixed network by a cellular one. In many OECD countries in the early 1990s, the cellular network covered 100% of the geographical area and with such a density of subscribers the network's average fixed costs may be considered negligible.

7   Low Orbit Satellites (LEO), introduced in the mid-1990s. LEO are satellites designed for fixed-point connections that are especially suited for communication with mobiles. It can be said that communication between mobiles will not be subject to technological rivalry from optical fibres.

8   Personal Communication Networks (PCN), introduced in the mid-1990s. PCN provide direct wireless access by means of low-power cells analogous to those used in cellular telephony. Their effect however is mixed: on the one hand, they by-pass the terrestrial distribution system so that they can be thought of as a new generation of advanced customer-premises equipment; on the other, they reduce the size of the cells, so enhancing economies of scope and density with existing terrestrial switching and transmission infrastructure.

9   Video communication, introduced in the mid-1980s. Video communication and interactive TV encourage the merging of broadcasting and telecommunications. In fact, they may be considered a complementary technology to optical fibres. Because of the huge transmission capability, both in terms of capacity and speed, optical fibres can carry a wide variety of different communication services including data communication and images. Enormous progress in optical fibre technology has brought together the television and the telecommunication industries. The actual traffic which optical fibres can carry is such (hundreds of high-speed television channels and thousands of high-speed telephone lines) that the distinction between telecommunications and television has been radically blurred.

Classifying technological changes

The cluster of technological changes introduced in the 1950s and 1960s perfectly mirrored the technological conditions of the telephone industry from the 1920s until the late 1960s, i.e. the 'perfect' natural monopoly, and clearly reflects the 'centripetal' efforts of the natural monopolist to reproduce and extend the conditions of the monopoly by the introduction of innovations that reinforce the dynamics of increasing returns.

In the early 1970s, along with the emergence of new information and communication technologies, the direction of technological change in telecommunication services entered a new phase, fuelled by the emerging relevance of such services for users and the opportunity they offered to earn significant quasi-rents. This new phase made the institutional set-up and the established organisation of the industry progressively out of date. The new cluster of technological changes introduced in the telecommunications service industry from the late-1960s and until the mid-1980s had, rather, all the characteristics of a localised process of innovation led by large, advanced users.

Data communication has played a key role in this context. Initially, data communication was concerned with limited groups of very large users that had low levels of network externalities. These were very sensitive to the high levels of long distance tariffs for their large quantities of communication. The focusing device here was on the intrinsic opportunities for cream-skimming that are almost necessarily built into markets characterised by network externalities. The segmentation of the overall demand into niches and the identification of classes of customers with low levels of demand externalities *per se*, without any effects on the cost side, offered important market opportunities. New communication media, such as dedicated data-communication systems, actually made it possible to better identify the needs of some important and growing groups of customers.

The pressure of large customers, stirred by the high levels of tariffs paid to telecommunication carriers for their increasing levels of data communication and, more importantly, the opportunity to reap the important quasi-rents associated with the innovative usage of telecommunication services, may be considered one of the strongest factors influencing both the enhanced rate of introduction of technological innovations since the late 1960s, and the shift in the direction of technological change following the introduction of centrifugal innovations which eventually led, at least in the United States, to the segmentation and specialisation of the centralised network into a web of special-purpose networks.

Since the mid-1980s, a third cluster of new technologies has been progressively emerging around such centripetal and integrating technological innovations as ISDN and BISDN, ATM, DECT and intelligent network. These new applications of digital technology make it easier to find centralised solutions, not only to the management of administrative problems (essentially billing), but also to technical problems related to traffic management (switching, routing, etc.), and the supply of increasingly advanced services (follow me or answering phone networks).

As has been said, innovation in the telecommunications industry today features a three-way interaction that now involves large users: the original vertical quasi-integration between equipment manufacturers and network operators has come under question and the centralised network structure is now at risk. This is the situation within which the network of networks is emerging. Under this notion, the actual innovator, whether user, manufacturer or operator, is unimportant: the larger the variety of independent players, the larger the opportunities to generate new technologies. Within the European Union, the notion of the network of networks represents an instrument to preserve technical pluralism, the target of regulatory decision-making that properly values dynamic efficiency.

A regulatory regime for innovation in communication industries

The network of networks provides important advantages from a dynamic point of view at a time when technological change is very rapid. The network of networks is also a multitechnological network which incorporates a variety of alternative technologies such as cables, satellites, fibres and signalling technologies based on intelligent networks. Innovative entry into a network of networks should prevent dominant positions from being formed and a return to an unnatural monopoly, while introducing elements of technological variety, flexibility and competition into a system of traditional networks which have long been characterised by a monotechnological monopoly. Moreover, the technological pluralism made possible by a network of networks reduces the risk of the technological lock-in of inferior technologies, which are diffuse only because they were chosen first. The wide variety of technological choice means that it is possible to experiment more than when there is a limited number of technological alternatives, with the result that the increasing returns of adoption and positive feedback can affect a broader spectrum of competing technologies.

In this context, the distinction between structural regulation and price regulation seems relevant. Structural regulation is aimed at the definition of the wide range of non-price relations among firms in the market place; price-regulation focuses on the price strategies of firms. Regulation of the network of networks should be based on a mix of interventions where structural regulation plays a much larger role than price regulation. Structural regulation should apply to the conditions of interconnection, entry, standardisation, and licensing. Price regulation should focus mainly on interconnection prices. The levels of tariffs for final services could eventually be left to market forces.

The key characteristics of a regulatory mechanism designed to foster both upstream and downstream innovation would seem to be:

1   non-exclusive ownership of the network's infrastructure and consequently mandatory interconnection;
2   regulated entry into the hard-network, so as to avoid cream-skimming ventures, which means entry can take place only when market contestability is proved, i.e. when a newcomer's actual average costs are shown to be lower than the marginal or incremental costs of the incumbents. In this way new technologies can be assessed in a multi-technological

context and a market for the access to different bundles of alternative infrastructure can be generated;

3   free entry into the virtual network, so as to facilitate the competitive supply of a wide range of unbundled services, e.g. different kinds of voice communication, data and video services, which can exploit the access to alternative media such as fibres, coaxial cables and satellite links, and so free of the negative effects which sunk costs and increasing returns have on competition. As these are mainly linked to the operation of the hard-network, the competitive process can bring down tariffs so that they are as close as possible to the actual costs incurred through access charges and specific service delivery costs;

4   search for *ex-ante* technical compatibility, based either on mandatory or voluntary standards, while, at the same time, regulatory authorities should try to reduce the negative effects of *de-facto* standards which emerge from a market in which there is a multiplicity of actors due to bandwagon effects, network externalities and technological lock-in;

5   mandatory licensing of intellectual property rights over network software so as to avoid barriers to entry and duplication costs for potential competitors, based on proprietary knowledge;

6   regulation of access costs based on access deficit charges. However, such costs should incorporate a correct application of Ramsey-pricing which would take account of the effects and implications of the dynamically-derived demand for telecommunication services associated with the diffusion of new information and communication services. Access charges for the delivery of services to business users, in other words, should be calculated in such a way that some cross-subsidies from the access charges for the delivery of services to households can be incorporated and yet be set at the overall levels which are necessary to ensure fairness;

7   tight regulation to achieve the maximum unbundling of access services so that the firms using access as an intermediary product can adopt high levels of 'mix and match' production strategies;

8   universal access to an advanced infrastructure; necessary in order to encourage the diffusion of new information and communication technologies among marginal users, too, and to accelerate diffusion among core adopters. This would be achieved through larger numbers of prospective adopters and hence would lead to higher levels of increasing returns to adoption and stronger epidemic contagion.

Conclusions

New information technologies may actually be regarded as an emerging technological system. Such a system is characterised by high levels of complementarity and interrelatedness among different technologies that represent at the same time product, process and organisational innovations, as well as innovations that change the production mix of firms and their markets. This array of technological innovations is itself characterised by the complementarity of innovative efforts of a variety of players, each embedded in its own localised field of activity. In this chapter, we have shown how the emergence of the new advanced telecommunication subsystem, an important component of the new information and communication system, can be viewed as the result of the convergence of the innovative efforts of traditional manufacturers of telecommunication hardware, telecommunication service providers and telecommunication service users. Two alternative paths are being created, one centred upon the search for complementarities between the new technologies and the existing infrastructure; and a rival one, mainly based upon the search for new complementarities between the current needs of large users.

Given this context, we are far from ensuring that the necessary conditions of dynamic efficiency within telecommunication networks are actually in place, ready to respond to the little scope that is available for the centrifugal innovations of large users. At present, the market structure of the telecommunication network in most European countries is based on high levels of horizontal and vertical integration, among switching, transmission and distribution, for data and voice communication and state-owned monopolies respectively, In the United States instead, the centralised structure of networks, in terms of inter-operability and interconnectivity and the related advantages stemming from network externalities, is under threat from the increasing plurality and variety of operators.

Within the blending of these two extremes may lie a new network: 'the network of networks'. This will be possible when plurality and entry in the network are enforced, yet the conditions of interconnection and inter-operability, both between and within networks are clearly defined. The network of networks can accommodate both the centrifugal and the centripetal forces which we have identified and analysed by allowing a variety of sources of innovation while still preserving their coherence. The adoption of a network of networks approach can enhance the implementation and diffusion of further technological and organisational innovations in telecommunication networks.

The model of the network of networks is based on the entry of a number of firms which are technically and organisationally complementary and compatible in both horizontal and vertical terms. Within the network of networks, firms operate in a variety of markets, which have no entry barriers in terms of differentiated access to the basic intermediary input, such as basic infrastructure services. Ownership of the network infrastructure is characterised by non-exclusiveness.

The network of networks can be considered an integrated and pluralistic structure of specialised and complementary networks, which are virtual and/ or infrastructural. As ownership rights in every section of the network are not exclusive, transfers and access and use may be considered intermediate productive factors, supplied to any service provider either in final or intermediary markets. Some customers could therefore be service firms which may be directly competing with their own suppliers of intermediary services.

The principle of non-exclusive ownership and mandated interconnection (see Antonelli 1995c), together with organisational compatibility based on mandatory standardisation (see Antonelli 1994a and Chapter 10), should encourage the bottom-up formation of an advanced multi-technological network containing a variety of local multipurpose distribution systems, transmission systems using cables, satellites and fibres, and signalling technologies based upon intelligent network. The combination of regulated entry into the infrastructure, to avoid the price-skimming creation of new portions of fixed network, and freedom of entry into the virtual network, should avoid both the formation of dominant positions and the renewal of unnatural monopoly. Regulatory agencies would concentrate their actions on the definition of interconnection conditions and prices, while the levels of tariffs for the actual communication services could be increasingly left to market forces.

Because it values complementarity and compatibility between sections of the network, and guarantees the right to interconnection between and within networks, the model of the network of networks seems to provide the best way forward, introducing elements of technological variety, flexibility and competition into the system of traditional networks which have long been characterised by a monotechnological monopoly.

The implementation of such a model can lead to the transformation of the structure of the present telecommunication system, enabling it to be more flexible and adjust from time to time to the stimuli from the evolution of demand and technology. It represents the institutional outcome of an intensive search for compromise between three features: the overwhelming pressure of network operators that are traditionally strong, state-owned corporations; the attempt of large information equipment manufacturers to grab a share of a promising new market; and the increasing sensitivity of users to large and fast-increasing telecommunication bills based on tariffs far above unit costs.

In such a context, a network of networks emerges as an organisational architecture of specialised and complementary networks, based on two quite distinct industries: the hard-network industry, which is responsible for the transportation infrastructure, and the soft-network which provides the communication services. Access to the hard-network can be considered an intermediate productive factor which should be supplied to any service provider in both final and intermediary markets. The network of networks should be based on co-operation among the plurality of specialised firms and this can be established both *ex-post* by means of market exchanges and *ex-ante* by means of suitable regulations. Furthermore, such a network should be based upon competition among different networks as well as competition within networks themselves, so as to ensure both a plurality of complementary firms which operate complementary components of the network, and a plurality of rival firms which either operate alternative segments of the network or use the networks to supply services to third parties.

Finally, it appears possible to assert that the model of the network of networks offers the best conditions in which the transformation of the present structure of the European telecommunications system, which is still based on vertically integrated oligopolies, can be carried out, becoming a more flexible structure based on a complementary variety of competing firms able to handle the evolution of demand and technology. A regulatory design to implement the network of networks should be built upon structural interventions rather than price controls. In the European Union, a network of networks could become a tool to ensure technological pluralism and could be the key to a system of regulatory decision-making that properly takes into account the notion of dynamic efficiency.

7 Localised technological change and unemployment in the global economy

A Schumpeterian approach

The persistence of high levels of unemployment over business cycles since the late 1970s, especially in continental Europe, demands special attention in order to try to understand its causes and possible remedies. Unemployment has been increasing steadily through all the OECD countries in the 1980s and at each successive downturn of the business cycle it has reached larger and larger levels. In the early 1990s it was still increasing in continental Europe, approaching levels that paralleled those reached in the 1930s (Bean, 1994). The traditional debate on the determinants of unemployment alternates between the 'classical unemployment hypothesis', due to excessive real wages and 'Keynesian unemployment', attributed to lack of demand. Little attention in this regard has been paid to the Schumpeterian analysis about the effects of technological rivalry (Schumpeter, 1934, 1939).

This chapter provides an empirical analysis of the relationship between the innovation capability of an economic system, open to global competition, and its levels of unemployment. According to the hypothesis put forward, the higher the innovation capabilities of each economic system, the lower should be the unemployment. Innovation capabilities of each economic system should be measured by the total levels of R&D activities, learning and investments. Special attention has been given in this context to measure the contribution of technological externalities available to each firm, within its own national innovation system, with respect to the general levels of innovation capabilities.

The chapter is articulated as follows: the first section briefly considers theories of unemployment, concluding on the somewhat neglected relevance of technological change. With reference to the new information and communication technologies, the second section assesses their effects on the economic structure identifying their localised character and the globalisation of their imitation as the most salient features, with efficiency wages also significant. Based on this picture, a Schumpeterian model is elaborated and formalised, with the replicator dynamics, in the third section, to explain the dynamics of modern-day unemployment. The results of the empirical analysis, carried out in the fourth section and based on OECD countries and their investment in innovation and R&D, both internal and external to firms, confirm assumptions about the relation between innovation capability, external sources of technological knowledge and employment levels in a global context; and the conclusion outlines the combination of causes of unemployment and possible industrial-policy remedies.

Theories of unemployment

Within the neoclassical approach to unemployment, a large amount of literature has explored the determinants of wage rigidity. Wages are rigid for a variety of reasons, such as union bargaining power, unemployment benefits, insider membership and efficiency wages. Within the Keynesian framework, instead, much attention has been paid to the types of demand that can contribute to an increase in employment. These traditional schools of thought seem unable to provide a consistent explanation for the dramatic change in European economies. It is not explained why real wages are rigid and excessive in the long term; nor is a rationale provided to explain the repeated failure of both Keynesian demand-pulls and business-cycle upswings to sufficiently reduce unemployment; as happened in a number of European countries in the 1980s. Moreover, the traditional notion of an 'equilibrium level of unemployment', as defined by the wage-price spiral, would appear to indicate a continuous increase in the levels of unemployment in order for inflation to stabilise.

Recently a flexibility argument has been proposed according to which the microeconomic rigidity of labour markets, defined in terms of the lack of flexibility of entry and exit conditions from jobs to unemployment and *vice versa*, is the real cause of stubborn unemployment levels rather than wages: firing and hiring costs become the culprit. As a result, countries with high levels of labour-market flexibility should experience lower levels of unemployment. However, the international empirical evidence provides little support for such a hypothesis: Japan and Switzerland are the best examples of rigid labour markets with low levels of flexibility and yet they are characterised by very low levels of unemployment (Layard, Nickell and Jackman, 1994).

While the flexibility argument *per se* does not seem able to offer a consistent account of the long-term mass unemployment, it does provide interesting clues when combined with the technological approach. Many authors have stressed the role of technological change in reducing employment below full employment levels, because of lack of flexibility in labour markets. The mis-match between the skills, regions and industrial sectors which new technology would privilege and those actually available within economies, especially in Europe, is considered a plausible factor of unemployment by Lilien (1982) and Ducatel (1994).

Freeman and Soete (1994) stress the implications for employment of the specific characters of new information and communication technology, in terms of skills and organisations, as well as the strong potential productivity growth they generate. Although it is only with an appropriate mix of active labour policies, focused on training, learning and Keynesian aggregate demand policies, that new information and communication technology can actually deliver their promises. When the general effects of the new cluster of information and communication technologies are taken into account, it does seem that technological change is highly relevant to a consistent explanation of mass unemployment.

Technological change and new information and communication technologies

The generation, introduction and diffusion of new information and communication technologies define the present rate and direction of technological change. Such technologies are the dynamic core of a newly emerging technological system shaped by strong complementarities between single, specific innovations and applications. The dynamics of positive feedbacks and increasing returns in the generation of new technologies is at the origin of the clustering in time of innovations in the information and communication technological system. A range of complementary innovations is being introduced along a path shaped by complementarities among new technologies, and, hence, technological externalities spilling among firms which take advantage of learning to learn in this specific area of application and the accumulated competence.

The cluster of new information and communication technologies that has shaped the rate and direction of technological change since the late 1970s, appears to have had two important effects. It has resulted in a growing 'localisation' of the production processes in terms of skills, capital intensity, complexity of industrial systems. At the same time, we have also witnessed a growing 'globalisation' of economic activity, with increased opportunities for independent imitators and the 'footloose' geographic localisation of manufacturing and service activities by multinational, global corporations, with major consequences in terms of trade flows on international markets.

The hypothesis we wish to articulate and put forward in this section elaborates upon the 'technologically induced mismatch approach' and is based on these two effects of the new cluster of information and communication technology, where imitation and application is irrespective of geographic location (Antonelli, 1992), i.e. the implications for adoption of the localised character of technological change and the new context of the global economy.

The adoption of new information and communication technology: efficiency wages

New information and communication technologies are localised because their use requires:

1 labour with high levels of human capital and dedicated skills, acquired by means of lengthy on-the-job training and learning processes;

2 high levels of capital intensity at the system level because of the enormous requirements in terms of dedicated infrastructures accessible to the largest possible number of users, for the important role of network externalities;

3 high levels of complementarity and interrelatedness between the production processes of different firms in different industries, because of the enhanced levels of division of labour and speed of production flows made possible by the successful adoption of such processes (Antonelli, 1992);

4 specific models of network organisation within firms, that make it possible to command and valorise the enhanced speed of information flows, so that firms can build their competitive advantage on procedures of decision-making which integrate the different functions of the firm more systematically (Antonelli, 1988);

5 active participation of the workforce in implementing learning processes and elaborating new applications and incremental innovations, in products, processes and especially organisation, necessary to adopt the new technologies successfully and adapt them to the specific context of operation of each firm.

As localised technologies, they are characterised by technical coefficients which limit the possibility of substituting factors according to relative cost. Nowadays, an enormous variety of goods can only be produced using almost fixed production coefficients. In a global economy, substitution is far more limited than the huge differences in factor costs would actually suggest, with 'well-behaved' production functions. New information and communication technologies provide a clear and strong example of the localised character of new technologies in general, in terms of technical coefficients, capital intensity, skill requirements, industrial structure and organisation (Antonelli, 1995b, 1996a).

The role of localised technological knowledge in the introduction of new information and communication technologies, and the active demand it makes on the workforce, means that efficiency wages become relevant. Efficiency wages are most important for adopting firms, who rely on the tacit knowledge of the workforce to de-code, then integrate localised technological knowledge embedded and embodied in the innovations generated by other firms. By means of efficiency wages, adopting firms can reduce the time lags between the initial introduction of new technologies and their successful adoption.

New information and communication technology and globalisation

New information and communication technologies are global because the lags between the generation, the first introduction and the imitation and adoption by third parties can be extremely short. Specifically, the characteristics of new information and communication technologies enable:

1   multinational companies to spread such technologies over a large variety of plants and offices worldwide, taking global advantage of a more efficient use of information. By means of new technology applications, multinational companies can reorganise as global corporations, maximising the mix of locational advantages stemming from the factor market conditions of each country, and firm-specific advantages in terms of the rates of introduction of product and process innovations. Global corporations can systematically rely on new information and communication technologies to increase international integration and the division of labour between affiliates and local suppliers for specialised intermediary products and services, generating unparalleled flows of international exchanges and exports from low-wage countries (Dunning, 1992).

2   increases in the amount and the quality of information, its accessibility and the capability of users to retrieve and process it. The introduction of new technologies seems parallel with a sharp decline in the time windows of monopolistic advantage of innovators. The imitation opportunities of new products and processes, introduced by innovators in any technological field, for firms located abroad and, in particular, in lower wage countries, appear to be sharply increased. Hence, the general proposition that new information and communication technologies are likely to increase the international spillover of productivity growth and the international leakage of technological know-how. Transient monopolies based on innovation lead-times are reduced: barriers to entry in the rich markets of high-wage countries are likely to become lower and lower for imitating firms located in lower-wage countries (Antonelli, 1991).

Given this overall picture, a return to our initial Schumpeterian approach would seem useful.

A Schumpeterian model

In the Schumpeterian conception, successful innovators enjoy extra profits which repay them for their willingness to accept high levels of risk and to manage a complex and risky productive process, such as the one which leads to the creation and adoption of technological and organisational innovation, after investing resources and generating appropriate levels of knowledge. Profit is, however, transitory. Imitators are ready to copy innovation and the levels of return on income flows associated with the introduction of successful innovations fall rapidly (Sylos Labini, 1984).[1]

According to the augmented replicator dynamics, (See Chapter 3), innovating firms can translate their competitive advantage not only into high levels of extra profit but also, and above all, into high levels of internal liquidity, based upon retained earnings, higher propensity to fund search and research activities, higher investment, higher rates of introduction of localised technological changes, and consequently more rapid growth in size.

In the initial stages, immediately after the introduction of an innovation, non-innovating firms find it difficult to survive and run the risk of being forced out of the market. They are only able to survive if they have a substantial competitive advantage based for example on access to favourable factor markets. Innovators themselves can increase their market share and their output. After the initial innovation however, innovative firms are unable to maintain their technological lead and are exposed to the 'drawbacks' of imitation. Other firms acquire the information and technological knowledge on which the innovation is based, so the supply curve moves to the right and prices fall together with the level of extra profit and the size of the innovating firm.

According to this Schumpeterian framework, at the country level, market shares and employment depend on two factors: available technology and the cost of the factors of production, especially labour.[2] With given rigid levels of wages in the labour markets, of both innovating and imitating countries, employment levels will be directly determined by the intensity of innovation flow. Employment will be higher in the innovative country only when it has the ability to offset higher wage costs with higher rates of innovation.

The case of intermediate countries, characterised by weak technological capabilities with low levels of technological externalities in loose innovation systems, but exposed to strong global competitive pressures, appears particularly interesting. These countries have high labour costs compared to those of developing countries and are unable to make a suitable contribution to the process of generating localised innovation with a factor mix appropriate to their own factor markets. The pressures of international competition affect the domestic level of employment in these countries in two ways: if the rate of indigenous generation of innovation is too low, technology is borrowed from more advanced countries where the factor mix is different and consequently there will be a lower 'natural' level of employment; the high level of wages exposes domestic firms to strong and growing competitive pressure from firms situated in countries with lower labour costs. Innovation therefore offers only a weak defence against competition.

Our Schumpeterian approach, following Metcalfe (1997), can easily take into account the Fisher-Pry formalisation. In this case there are two 'species', the innovators operating in conditions of high wages and the imitators who can pay modest wages. The difference between the average unit cost levels determine the size of the two populations, which are competing for market shares of total world demand. For a given variance in competitive advantage, the population with the larger advantage will increase in size over time with the entry of new firms and the growth of incumbents.

With wage levels given and rigid in both countries, the number and size of the firms, and therefore the level of employment (population density) in the two countries is directly dependent on the difference in innovation flow. If an innovative country with high wages reduces the flow of innovations which gives it a competitive edge over an imitating country with modest wages, its market share will diminish and the level of employment will fall. The rise in the share of total world demand is therefore a direct function of innovative capacity. Moreover, aggregate demand in an innovative country with high wages cannot grow if the rate of innovation is insufficient to offset the loss of competitive advantage caused by the imitation of previous innovations. If the world market share of the innovation species with rigid wages diminishes, the number and the size of the firms, as well as employment, diminishes. For a given difference in innovative 'fitness' in the population of innovators, a fall in the world market share and therefore in total domestic demand will force the less efficient firms to leave the market, and unemployment will increase.

In short, in global markets the level of unemployment of each country is directly and positively related to the rate at which competitive advantage based on a country's innovative capacity, declines; it is therefore negatively linked to the amount of effort made to renew the stock of technical and organisational knowledge on which a high-wage country's international competitiveness is based.

A simple model would enable its characteristics to be established. In the first place, we may say that the market share of country i depends on the relative levels of wages W_i and technological capacity T_i with respect to the average (A) of competitors:

$$X_i = f(T_i/T_A, W_i/W_A) \tag{1}$$

where X_i represents the share of world demand. Given a world demand Y and an aggregate production function, then employment N in the ith country will be directly determined by:

$$N_i = f(Y, T_i/T_A, W_i/W_A) \tag{2}$$

Applying the Fisher-Pry formalisation, we see that the share of world demand gained by the country changes over time in relation to the difference in competitiveness:

$$X_{i(t)} - X_{i(t-1)} = f(g(T_i, W_i)_{(t-1)} - h(T_A, W_A)_{(t-1)}) / h(T_A, W_A)_{(t-1)} \qquad (3)$$

The substitution of (2) in (3) leads to (4), where we see that the evolution of employment in the *i*th country depends directly on the evolution of competitiveness:

$$(N_i)_{(t)} - (N_i)_{(t-1)} = f(g(T_i, W_i)_{(t-1)} - h(T_A, W_A)_{(t-1)}) / h(T_A, W_A)_{(t-1)} \qquad (4)$$

It is clear in (4) that for given levels of total world demand in the *i*th country, the evolution of the effective employment in each country with respect to full employment (N*) directly depends on the relative evolution of the state of technology and factor costs. Within a given time interval, growing pockets of unemployment are formed in the *i*th country when the function (*g*), which relates the factors of a country's international competitiveness to its market share and hence employment, is lower than that of the average of its competitors (*h*).

Within this context, attention should be paid to the positive effects of efficiency wages, stimulating the learning processes of firm and workforce into the accumulation of localised technological knowledge and the creative adoption and implementation of new technologies. As we have just seen, employment levels, via the evolution of competitivity, are themselves related to the state of technological advance. The latter is determined, not only by the long-term efforts made by innovating countries to increase innovative capacity, in terms of R&D expenditure and investment, but also the immediate incentive structure, based on efficiency wages, encouraging the actual accumulation of that capacity. Our model enables a direct structural relationship to be established between the level of unemployment and the evolution of the variables on which technological competitiveness in the global economic system depends.

Empirical verification

A simple empirical test of this hypothesis about the structural relationship between unemployment and the state of technology, as approximated by the levels of long-term innovative efforts under the control of labour costs, can be made using data from the main OECD countries. The econometric model may be expressed in the following reduced form:

$$UE = a + b(R\&D) + c(INV) + d(W) + e \qquad (5)$$

where UE measures the average level of unemployment in twenty-two OECD countries in the years 1990—92 (OECD, 1992a, 1994); R&D measures the average level of relative efforts made to generate innovations, in terms of the share of R&D expenditure on GNP in the years 1988, 1989 and 1990 (OECD 1992b); INV measures the average efforts to adopt innovation measured by investments as a percentage of GNP in the same three years (IMF, 1992); and W measures the average labour costs experienced in those years (OECD, 1992b). All independent variables are specified with a two-year time lag with respect to the dependent variable UE. The structure of the lags and the average values over a three-year time span, used to build the variables, appear sufficient to appreciate the structural relationship between the variables considered.[3]

Close inspection of the data confirms the strong negative relationship between unemployment and the intensity of R&D expenditures with respect to gross national product (GNP). In countries where in 1990 unemployment was below 6% of the total workforce, investment in R&D was almost 1.9% of GNP. This is the case in countries like Japan (unemployment 2.1% and R&D 3.08%), Switzerland (unemployment 0.6% and R&D 2.86%), Sweden (unemployment 1.5% and R&D 2.90%), US (unemployment 5.4% and R&D 2.74%), Finland (unemployment 3.4% and R&D 1.91%), Norway (unemployment 5.2% and R&D 1.85%), and the UK (unemployment 5.5% and R&D 2.19%). At the other extreme of the distribution we see that in all countries where unemployment is over 9%, the ratio of R&D expenditure to GNP is very low. This is the case in Spain (unemployment 15.9% and R&D 0.85%), Ireland (unemployment 13.7% and R&D 0.91%), Italy (unemployment 11.2% and R&D 1.3%), Belgium (unemployment 8.7% and R&D 1.69%), and Denmark (unemployment 8.3% and R&D 1.62%). A few exceptions are found in countries like Portugal (unemployment 4.6% and R&D 0.61%), Greece (unemployment 7% and R&D 0.46%), and Austria (unemployment 3.2% and R&D 1.42%), where unemployment is 'too low'; and in countries where it is 'too high' such as France (unemployment 8.9% and R&D 2.42%).

The econometric test was carried out using a logarithmic specification for R&D so as to value the multiplicative effect of research activity on a country's competitiveness and hence employment. A simple OLS estimate of the data gives the following results:

$$UE = 3.324 - 1.817 \, (\ln R\&D) - 0.196 \, (INV) - 0.115 \, (W)$$
$$ (2.827) (2.414) (0.972)$$

$R^2 = 0.47; F_{(1-22)} = 69.159$
(Student t-values in parentheses)

As can be seen, the results are reassuring both in terms of total explained variance and, above all, the significance of the independent variables. The variables which directly measure technological capacity in terms of adoption capability, e.g. investment, and innovation capability, e.g. R&D expenditures, are significant at a 99 per cent level of confidence. The variable which expresses the effects of labour costs instead, is not significant: this result can be understood if we consider the positive effects of efficiency wages on innovation capacity. Labour costs do have a (negative) role in the overall levels of unit costs and thus international market shares and employment levels; *but* efficiency wages have a positive effect in that their levels help sustain the innovation capacity of a country, mobilising the processes of tacit learning in order to implement the introduction and adoption of new (information and communication) technologies.

A 'panel' estimate with the same annual observations would seem legitimate considering the 'structural' interpretation of the relationships between the variables. The substantial stability of the series analysed enables us to consider the annual observations of R&D expenditure and investment respectively, as reliable proxies for the *structural capability* to generate and adopt innovative technology. Consequently, investment, R&D expenditure and wages are expressed for each of the three years considered. The model is specified with the same lag structure as equation (6). In the panel estimate, Turkey is excluded because of insufficient data. In terms of total variance, the panel estimate gives even better results than the previous estimate: while confirming the absolute validity of the partial estimate coefficients it concentrates on the relative anomalies of Greece (G) and Portugal (P), whose levels of unemployment are 'too' low.[4] The test[5] provides satisfactory results:

$$UE = 18.043 - 6.911\,(\ln R\&D) - 0.346\,(INV) + 0.074\,(W) - 9.72\,(G) - 8.382\,(P) \qquad (8)$$
$$ (7.969) \qquad\quad (2.567) \qquad (0.691) \qquad (5.583) \qquad (6.234)$$

$R^2 = 0.643$; F (1–63) = 23.341

(Student t-values in parentheses)

Such results are important because they illustrate the strong and significant negative correlation, which in the light of the Schumpeterian model adopted represents a real and significant causal relationship, between R&D levels and investment intensity in relation to GNP and unemployment. The levels of pay per capita used as a proxy for labour costs turn out not to be significant. This further confirms our hypothesis about the double effect built into such a variable: the positive role of efficiency wages on innovation capacity and hence employment, together with the negative effect on unit cost and hence again on employment. The evidence actually shows that market shares, and therefore levels of total demand and employment, at least in advanced countries such as those in the OECD area are not significantly influenced by labour costs. Employment levels cannot be protected by reducing wages, without risking reduction in innovation capacity. Instead, it is necessary to innovate at a faster rate than the closest competitors; at a rate which enables the innovating country to face the competition of developing countries, which have low labour costs and fast imitation rates. Innovation generated elsewhere is increasingly rapidly adopted in the productive process by imitating countries (Nelson and Wright, 1992).

Given the relevance of R&D in maintaining the level of employment, it would seem useful to investigate in more detail the effects of the different patterns of R&D, which up to now has been considered an aggregate figure. In order to appreciate the distinctive role of both internal R&D activities and external knowledge, and technological externalities (made available to each firm by the R&D activities conducted within universities and other public research institutions), the analysis concentrated on R&D within firms (BERD) and R&D in the field of higher education (HERD) (OECD, 1994). The correlation matrix shows strong colinearity for the two components, which means that they cannot be introduced simultaneously in our regression equation. They have therefore been introduced separately, and the results have been compared. The results are as follows:

$$UE = 13.295 - 5.187\,(\text{InBERD}) - 0.361\,(\text{INV}) + 0.84\,(W) - 10.973\,(G) - 0.675\,(P) \quad (9)$$
$$ (6.297) \qquad\qquad (3.642) \qquad (1.158) \qquad (5.283) \qquad (4.485)$$

$R^2 = 0.553;\ F(1\text{--}63) = 16.355$
(Student t-values in parentheses)

$$UE = 3.556 - 7.936\,(\text{InHERD}) - 0.259\,(\text{INV}) + 0.55\,(W) - 8.674\,(G) - 6.38\,(P) \quad (10)$$
$$ (10.036) \qquad\qquad (3.436) \qquad (1.108) \qquad (3.71) \qquad (5.894)$$

$R^2 = 0.727;\ F(1\text{--}63) = 34.069$
(Student t-values in parentheses)

The results clearly demonstrate that R&D in higher education is particularly useful in maintaining a country's innovative capacity, thus limiting unemployment. The contribution made by R&D in higher education institutions is actually greater than that carried out by firms themselves. Total explained variance due to the substitution of R&D with BERD and HERD increases considerably, as does the significance of the variable itself. Thus, R&D, especially when performed in the higher education sector, as a proxy of the efforts invested in the generation of new non-proprietary technologies, exerts a positive effect on the competitive advantage of countries and *hence* on their employment levels. This result confirms once more the strategic importance of the scientific and technological knowledge pool made available to firms by the public research system, percolating by means of technological spillovers, and the role of education in general in sustaining the performances of countries in global markets.

Conclusions

Once the analysis of static equilibrium is abandoned and the characteristics of international rivalry in global markets, based on the process of generation, adoption and imitation of technology, are considered, it is clear that economic analysis has to concentrate on the dynamics of structural change. Competition is above all a process of adjustment towards a hypothetical equilibrium continually upset by structural changes associated mainly with new cycles of generation, adoption and imitation of innovative technology.

Within such an approach, unemployment increases where economic systems are unable to maintain suitable rates of technological advance. When the rate of technological advance in relative terms declines, selective processes are set off which lead to the exclusion of the labour force employed in marginal firms. With rigid wage levels the labour force cannot find alternative jobs. It is evident that total demand in an open economy exposed to international competition grows more slowly than the productivity of labour *only when* the latter grows too slowly.

The results of empirical analysis suggest that a country's competitiveness and therefore its share of total world demand is mostly, if not exclusively, determined by its innovative capacity. Wage levels alone, even when they fall in relative terms, cannot re-establish conditions of full employment. Efficiency wages are an important complementary factor in actually building the innovation capacity of a country. On the basis of these considerations, it seems plausible to argue that present day unemployment, a major characteristic of numerous European countries at the end of the twentieth century, is caused by a combination of four factors:

1   the localised character of the new wave of information and communication technology generated in the more advanced countries and characterised by a factor mix appropriate to economic systems, in which there is an abundance of capital and a relative scarcity of labour;
2   the strong and rapid dynamic decline in competitive advantages and quasi-rents based on the introduction of new information and communication technology;
3   the strong, international competitive pressure from countries with lower wage levels and a greater capability to host the affiliates of multinational companies and imitate the applications of new information and communication technologies developed in the innovative countries;
4   the role of external knowledge and technological externalities percolating in the economic system as they relate to innovative capability.

The policy implications of this conclusion are clear enough. In order to increase the share of total world demand and contribute to the general process of improving the standard of living in the global economy, it is necessary to increase a country's technological capacity and its ability to develop localised innovative technology within its own system of factor prices. Only in this way, for given efficiency wage levels – which, as has already been noted, it does not seem opportune to raise due to their positive effects on learning processes and, hence, innovation capability – can the employed labour force be increased with a resultant fall in unemployment. To conclude, an industrial policy geared towards both innovative investment – encouraging innovation, adoption and R&D – increasing the generation and effective transmission and reception of technological externalities, can also be a very effective employment policy, especially when carried out in universities and public laboratories.

8 New information technology and the evolution of the organisation of knowledge production

This chapter considers the emergence of the new knowledge industry as the result of the institutional formation of an actual market for knowledge. This formation is seen to be based on a three-pronged process consisting of the deverticalisation of knowledge-production activities from the boundaries of corporations, the specification of a real demand for technological competence, and the specialisation of independent firms in the production of knowledge and technological competence. Information and communication technologies are the enabling engine of such a process, which in turn increases the rate of further technological innovations. Within this evolution, the various organisational modes of knowledge-production have illustrated the contrasting effects in terms of innovation incentive, resource allocation, dissemination capability and private efficiency. The most recent growth of specialisation in the context of the new knowledge economy offers a potential solution to the knowledge trade off and an enhanced role for knowledge-intensive business services.

The significance of the new information and communication technology on the production and use of knowledge is explained in the first section; then the historical evolution of the organisation of knowledge production is analysed via various models. With regard to the productivity and subsequent efficiency of knowledge, the merits of each model are assessed under established criteria in the second section. The third section considers the development towards the knowledge industry enabled by new information and communication technologies and anticipated by multinational corporations and technological clubs.

The organisation of knowledge production

The key role of knowledge in the economy has long been understood. However standard economics has dealt much more with the problems associated with the distribution of knowledge rather than its production. The production of knowledge appears to have an increasingly strategic position in the economy as the engine of growth. In this context the organisation of the knowledge production becomes central in assessing the performance of activities involving the production and use of knowledge within the economic system. The tools of the economics of organisation, based on the economics of information and learning, can be used to analyse the relationship between the production of knowledge and the production of other goods (Williamson, 1985; Langlois and Robertson, 1995; Loasby 1994 and 1995).

In assessing the organisation of knowledge production the knowledge trade off between the contrasting effects of property rights on innovation incentive and information dissemination, respectively, plays a crucial role. Protection measures for inventors, like patents or lead times, obstruct or delay both the disclosure of the information and the reduction of quasi-rents associated with the successful technology which depends on it. As such, they represent prospective revenue for innovators and thus are a fundamental incentive for agents to innovate and undertake inventive activity and for funders to invest their money in research and search activities. They exert a positive influence on the allocation of appropriate resources to the generation of knowledge. At the same time however, property rights on scientific and technological knowledge, of both the *ex-ante* patent and *ex-post* market-power type, have a significant negative effect with regard to social welfare. First, the exclusive and proprietary character of the new knowledge, and the related delay in its imitation by competitors, is associated with monopoly rents. Second, price-elastic adopters delay the diffusion of product and process innovations, subsequently embodying the new knowledge. There is also a duplication of efforts, and therefore a waste of resources, in re-inventing knowledge which is already available but proprietary. Finally, the possibilities for the dissemination, recombination and cumulative usage of the new knowledge are also reduced for third parties who, moreover, are not necessarily direct competitors of the innovating firm (Arrow, 1962b; Dasgupta, 1987; Dasgupta and David, 1987 and 1994).

The evolution and articulation of the organisation of knowledge production has been profound in recent economic history. According to most authors, entrepreneurship originally dominated and was the sole mode during the industrial revolution when scientific entrepreneurs constituted the norm; statistics confirm that a large majority of scientific discoveries and technological applications were patented by individuals in that period (Schmookler, 1957). At the end of the nineteenth century, the organisation of the production of knowledge in most countries evolved towards the enforcement of institutional variety, with an increasing role for universities. In the early twentieth century vertical integration was introduced (Mowery, 1983; Wright, 1990). In this century, the United States, and eventually Great Britain, took the lead in the choice of vertical integration, while France and Italy seemed to rely more systematically on institutional variety; Germany relied for a long time on universities (Noble, 1977; Reich, 1985).

After the Second World War vertical integration became the dominant mode of organisation in knowledge production (Mowery, 1995). Recently, the systematic use of technological co-operation has emerged as the dominant design, particularly in industries and technologies where both rising absolute costs, associated with efficient research programmes, and increasing technological complexity, based on the convergence of different skills and competences, have demanded larger research laboratories and generated a larger range of both competences and potential uses of new knowledge. Such co-operation between firms, especially firms active in different markets, can help spread the high levels of average costs and, as has been said, provide better opportunities for exploiting unforeseen research results. When and where the appropriability, tradeability, divisibility and transportability of information is higher, and the separability, between the competence that generates knowledge and the bits of information that use it, is more distinct, there has been an increasing specialisation in the production of knowledge.

The actual characteristics of the organisation of the knowledge production can be analysed with the aid of the following four stylised modes.

Entrepreneurship

The traditional Schumpeter Mark 1 model sees the creation of new firms and their entry into the market as the fundamental mode of introduction of technological knowledge into the economic system. The acquisition of technological knowledge in this model takes place by means of learning processes and the personal creativity of entrepreneurs; conceiving of new ways of producing old goods, new intermediary inputs, new goods and new markets, and evaluating the scope of application of such products to current business via entry. The market selection process reveals to what extent the new knowledge is actually relevant and successful innovations are sorted out from tentative ones. Here, the market works as an information-processing device, enabling the testing of relevance of new knowledge along the traditional lines of competition as a process of discovery at the core of Hayek's analysis on the role of the market. Entrepreneurs are new agents who have acquired technological knowledge by means of personal application in either other business activities or academic studies. The translation of scientific and technological knowledge gained by formal learning and tacit learning by doing and by using respectively, is left to individual efforts. Innovators mainly learn on-the job so that existing firms are incubators of new innovative firms. The rate and direction of technological change hence depends on the supply of such innovative entrepreneurs who are able to spot the commercial and economic value of existing ideas floating around in the system (Antonelli, 1982).

Institutional variety

The division of labour between universities and firms is crucial here. The market exchange of knowledge is affected by its characters as a public good.

The co-ordination of the demand and supply of knowledge in the market place is put at risk by its low appropriability: when sellers make their knowledge explicit, potential buyers have no incentive to purchase what is *de facto* a public good; yet at the same time, buyers are seldom ready to buy a piece of information without any details. In such a context the funding of universities, via resources collected from taxation, can solve the intrinsic risk of the underproduction of knowledge. Universities are institutions where the accumulation and publication of new knowledge represents the basic function and assessment of performance: the objective function of academic personnel is to research and publish, and the longer the publication list, the more qualified an academic researcher, and the better the chances of attracting research funds and new research assistants. At the same time, the academic system generates technological externalities for the rest of the economic system, which receives, at low marginal costs, the flow of technological and scientific information, both via new publications and trained labour exposed to the scientific undertakings of researchers and consequently able to overcome the natural excludability of much codified knowledge. Hence, the circulation of new knowledge is maximised without any harm to the incentives for its production. Firms can benefit from the externalities and are left with the task of transforming this new knowledge into new processes and new products of effective use and actual economic value. In this model, the division of labour between the two institutions is quite clear: universities generate technological externalities which firms absorb and translate into economic value (Rosenberg and Nelson, 1992).

Vertical integration

Firms develop their own research centres and produce internally, within their own boundaries, the new scientific and technological knowledge necessary to generate new product and process technologies. The economic rationale for the vertical integration of the knowledge production within the firm is complex and is based on a variety of market failures. Transaction costs reduce the scope for market exchanges; credit rationing by sceptical bankers limits the provision of the financial resources necessary to undertake risky investments, such as those in scientific and technological research. Thus, only large firms, able to extract some extra profits from their current business, can fund research activities with their own money. Vertical integration is justified on the grounds of the secure internal provision of finance for research activities and the reduction of information asymmetries between bankers and skilled experts, who are better able to assess the actual technological perspectives of each research investment. The issue of inseparability between the production of knowledge and the production of goods arises. The interaction between the actual production process, the accumulation of tacit knowledge and the production of new technological knowledge, implemented by R&D activities, is essential to increase the productivity of research activities. Consequently, relevant economies of scope would characterise the production of knowledge and the production of goods.

Technological co-operation

The characters of the production process of new technological knowledge, such as significant economies of scale and scope, encourage firms to join forces and establish different forms of technological co-operation, as a way of benefiting from increasing returns yet avoiding the transaction costs associated with the market exchange of new knowledge. Research processes are denoted by high levels of fixed costs and minimum thresholds of activity: it is difficult for small firms to operate an independent research laboratory. Classical economies of scale apply to the production of knowledge, such as the sharing of multipurpose expensive tools and skills over a large number of projects. Moreover, the larger the size of the laboratory, the smaller the unit cost, because of the great variety of research programmes which can be developed in parallel and the greater possibility of cross-fertilisation among them. More importantly, technological co-operation enables the socialisation of tacit and codified knowledge accumulated in different firms and the recombination of codified knowledge relevant in different fields, but potentially complementary with respect to a new technological field. Finally, relevant *ex-post* economies of scope also apply because of the uncertainty which characterises the outcome of research activities: the wider the scope of operation of the firms involved in funding and orienting the activities of each lab, the greater the possibility of finding an appropriate use for the unintended range of outcomes of each research project.

Assessment and interpretation

Although these basic modes emerged through time and replaced each other, as the dominant organisational design, they are all still in use across countries and industries. Entrepreneurship is relevant in industrial districts of small firms co-localised in close proximity and specialising in skill-based industries (Antonelli, 1986; Becattini, 1987). Institutional variety is very important in new emerging radical technologies such as biotechnology, where scientific entrepreneurship flourishes in science parks nearby large universities (Jaffe, Trajtenberg and Henderson, 1993; Clarysse, Debackere and Van Dierdonck, 1995; Swann and Prevezer, 1996; Swann, Prevezer and Stout, 1998). Vertical integration is still the dominant design, yet characterising mainly large firms (Foray and Mowery, 1990). Technological co-operation is now deeply rooted especially in new information and communication technologies (Duysters, 1996). This makes their assessment all the more interesting.

The analysis of knowledge trade off has shown that the main factors at play in assessing the organisation of knowledge production are: the structure of incentives and the availability of resources to actually produce knowledge; the efficiency in its production at the firm level and its dissemination capability at the system level – as measured in terms of technological communication consisting of the outcome of connectivity and receptivity of levels, stemming from the intellectual property rights regime; the duration of monopolistic rents; and, most importantly, the social division of labour that generates new technological knowledge. Let us consider each of the four models in these specific terms (See Table 8.1).

The entrepreneurial mode of organisation is clearly very strong in terms of incentives, because each successful entrepreneur will establish a monopoly and extract important rents. However, it is weak in terms of availability of resources to produce knowledge because bankers are often reluctant to lend the necessary funds to initiate a new activity. It is also very weak regarding the efficiency of the production of knowledge, which is left to personal competence and creativity with low levels of structured activity. Communication capability in terms of connectivity and receptivity is very low since knowledge production relies on individual efforts and craftsmanship. The natural excludability of tacit knowledge reduces the spillover of technological externalities. Under entrepreneurship, and weak intellectual property rights regimes, however, innovations are readily diffused through the system by the inflow of imitators; this means that the duration of monopolistic rents is small. The shorter the duration of monopolistic rents, the higher such dissemination capability is; but at the same time, the shorter the time lag between innovative entry and competitive imitation, the lower the incentives and the amount of resources made available (by the financial markets) to innovate.

Institutional variety and the interaction between universities and firms ranks very high in terms of the structure of incentives to produce codified

Table 8.1 The organisation of knowledge production and the knowledge trade off

	Incentives	Resource availability	Private efficiency	Communication: receptivity and connectivity	Dissemination: duration of monopolistic rents
Entrepreneurship	*****	*	*	***	**
Institutional variety	*****	*	*	***	*
Vertical integration	****	****	*****	**	***
Technical co-operation	***	****	*****	***	**
Specialisation	****	****	****	*****	*

* measures the relative weight

knowledge. Two different incentives are actually at work: academics think of publications as a list of honours while they are a means of knowledge dissemination; firms regard academic products as potential sources of technological externalities and, hence, increased profitability. The transfer of academically-produced knowledge to firms is poorly served, based on the assumption that the sharp difference between such heterogeneous institutions, in terms of conduct and objectives, does not affect the receptivity of externalities. The dissemination of scientific and technological information is based on the assumption that the receptivity of externalities between heterogeneous institutions is not harmed by the sharp differences in terms of codes of conduct, goals and objectives. Moreover, because the actual implementation of the new knowledge produced in universities into technological innovations is left to the dynamics of externalities and spillover, the allocation of 'rational amounts' of resources to universities and research activities is difficult to assess and determine. In terms of the communication capability, the missing link between academic output and effective usage by firms makes it difficult to evaluate the contribution of universities to the real production of new technological knowledge readily available for subsequent technological innovations; in other words, the social efficiency of this mode is unclear. Similarly, most resources to innovate are provided to universities on an absolute fixed cost basis by the tax-payer, with little chance to assess effective rates of return. When and where firms have developed high levels of receptivity and absorptive capability, the model of institutional variety can be strong in terms of communication efficiency, and hence in the social use of the new knowledge. Indeed, the academic publication of new ideas and concepts, and the training of skilled labour, associated with a steady flow of production of new knowledge in receptive business firms, can fetch high levels of social welfare.

The incentive for firms to integrate vertically and produce their own knowledge within the borders of the corporation clearly rests on the levels of transaction costs associated with knowledge appropriability and the limits of external financial markets in terms of credit rationing for research activities. The lower the appropriability conditions, and hence the lower the protection secured by property rights, the lower the imitation costs for followers. Consequently, the higher the codified content of the knowledge produced, and the reluctance of financial markets to provide funds to independent innovators, the higher the incentives to invest the quasi-rents, made available by market power, in research activities and to integrate them vertically into the production of knowledge. The efficiency of research activities conducted within the corporation is enhanced by close interaction with the production process of goods, that is the firm's core activity, and hence, cross-fertilisation between tacit and codified knowledge, on-the-job and formal training, scientific, top-down procedures of discovery and bottom-up procedures of induction. Within the corporation, the allocation of resources to innovate is also more effective: scrutiny and selection of new research projects are often better performed internally than by the external assessments of financial investors. The serendipity of long-term research can be harmed, though, by the profit-oriented decision-making of firms, unable to foresee the eventual benefit of new research ventures. Particularly since the Second World War, many countries have sought to integrate the long-term production of knowledge conducted in universities with the short-term projects carried out in industrial R&D labs by means of a combination of vertical integration and institutional variety models. Knowledge, generated by research activities conducted within firms, tends to become proprietary; property rights are enforced so as to prevent imitation by competitors and dissipation. The recombination of knowledge and its application in new fields is also limited, and the possibility that unrelated third parties, active in other industries and regions, might benefit is needlessly restricted. Hence, the dissemination capability of this mode is very low and the duration of monopolistic rents often too long.

The technological co-operation mode has many advantages in terms of incentives because firms can share the costs of research activities yet retain appropriability of the output. This is especially so when the firms that are partners in the club are active in different industries, minimising the risk of eventual technological rivalry in marketing the application of the new collectively produced knowledge. The availability of resources is favoured by the pooling of funds and competencies, and the efficiency of the production process similarly enhanced by the many advantages of the economies of size offered by the club. This mode also reduces the costs of absorption of the new knowledge because each partner is involved in its production. In the same way, it also reduces the duplication of research projects: internal connectivity and receptivity are high. Obstacles to the socialisation of the knowledge and its positive effects to unrelated parties constitute the major limitation of technological co-operation. Moreover, partners in the club tend to become strong monopolies in their own market niche, with little possibility of information leakage and imitative entry. Technological co-operation also reduces the scope for application, dissemination and cross-fertilisation of new knowledge to new unrelated fields and technologies, even with a membership characterised by variety, in terms of industrial and technological activity, because of negative effects from the creation of new oligopolies.

The diffusion of new information and communication technologies seems to open a completely new direction to the economics of the organisation of knowledge production. Such technology enables the increasing separation of the provision of technological information from the accumulation of technological competence, via specific question-and-answer interaction between the producers and users of knowledge. This mode of delivering and marketing technological competence, implemented by the design of appropriate long-term research contracts, is likely to strengthen the interaction between the specific, localised characters of the problems and competence of firms and the generic competence and codified knowledge made available by knowledge producers. Moreover, the diffusion of this new technology greatly reduces both the division between the production and absorption of knowledge and related high social costs.

New information technology and the knowledge industry

We have seen how the generation, introduction and diffusion of new information and communication technologies characterise the present rate and direction of technological change. Such technologies represent the centre of the new technological system, radically affecting the conditions under which knowledge is produced, namely the separability, tradeability, divisibility and transportability of information (Antonelli, 1992; Metcalfe, 1995). Subsequently, the delivery conditions of information-intensive products in the economic system are also affected. Products can be differentiated according to the content and role of the information they contain. Products such as banking services, airline reservations, logistic services and knowledge-intensive business services have high levels of information intensity; indeed information directly concerns the specification of the product itself (Preissl, 1995; Von Tunzelmann, 1995).

The diffusion of new information and communication technologies is a powerful factor in the institutional evolution of the organisation of knowledge production. The larger the penetration of computer networks and the volumes of electronic communication, the larger the scope for more effective communication links among firms and the more systematic the exchanges of tacit and codified knowledge in the system. In this context new information and communication technologies favour the diffusion of the demand for knowledge-intensive business services, the supply of knowledge-intensive business services and the creation of a proper market for such services.

At present, the organisation of knowledge production is moving away from the high levels of vertical integration that became the dominant mode of organisation after the Second World War and is now directed towards the progressive unbundling of the production of knowledge (Veugelers, 1997). Specialisation, based upon the notion of competence is now becoming the leading organisational mode, engendered and implemented by the institutional creation of markets for knowledge; and all emerging from the extensive use of new information technologies and *ex-ante* contractual agreements.

Both business firms and knowledge-intensive service firms can benefit from the diffusion of new information and communication technology via the increased social division of labour and the emergence of new markets for the supply and demand of competence and expertise. The diffusion of new information technology enables higher levels of appropriability of specific, problem-solving methodologies, and easier interface between the tacit knowledge embedded in learning customers and the 'quasi-generic' knowledge stored by service firms, acquired by means of repeated contacts with competent users in universities and research laboratories.

In this context, the key institutional and technological change is the possibility of on-line interaction between customers and producers of knowledge; the opportunity for customers to access the competences of the seller. In other words, the market exchange of information takes place in terms of the demand for advice and problem-solving capabilities and the supply of competence. This interaction between demand and supply is thus a process of market co-operation among customers and suppliers, taking place in time and on-line. The economics of the exchange of knowledge thus relies heavily on the design of research contracts (Wright, 1983). While the exchange of goods is a punctual event, that is an actual exchange, the trading of information made possible by new information and communication technologies consists instead of the contractual possibility of using the competencies of the suppliers and the application of their problem-solving capabilities in a project or problem which the customer is willing to undertake and solve (Loasby, 1994).

Multinational corporations and technological specialisation

In many respects the growth of the multinational corporation has paved the way towards such changes. Multinational corporations have proved the most efficient in taking advantage of the scope of application of new information and communication technologies, managing the flow of information and organising the production of knowledge. In fact, new information technologies enable the headquarters of multinational companies to specialise in the production of knowledge and to spread the use of such knowledge to a large variety of plants and offices all over the world, proliferating, via their global organisations, the advantages of more efficient uses of technological information. In fact, such technologies are one of the founding elements enabling the global mode of production and distribution. By means of their applications, manufacturing and commercial processes can be organised worldwide, maximising the mix of locational advantages stemming from the factor market conditions of each country, and firm-specific advantages, in terms of the competence to generate technological knowledge to feed the process of introduction of product and process innovations (Cantwell, 1989).

Global multinational companies systematically rely on new information and communication technologies to achieve high levels of international integration, both horizontal and vertical. The subsequently enhanced division of labour between affiliates and local suppliers, and international outsourcing for specialised intermediary products and services, generate unparalleled flows of international exchanges. This situation is characterised by exports from low-wage countries of intermediary products, such as components or semi-finished high-tech products, to rich markets, in countries increasingly involved in the production and exchange of technological knowledge.

The production of knowledge is at the core of the new global telematic corporation whose headquarters act as the producer and synthesiser of core competencies and technological knowledge, which is then applied to manufacturing processes located in remote sites. The technological interaction between affiliates and headquarters takes place within internal markets and is increasingly characterised by a two-way flow of generic competencies and codified knowledge located at the headquarters and specific competencies in the manufacturing and commercial units. Peripheral units request the technological competence of headquarters to solve specific problems, that is to apply the generic competencies and codified knowledge which have been elaborated centrally. At the same time, headquarters can provide answers to questions raised by the affiliates and learns from the tacit knowledge emerging through the communication process. The technological heart of multinational companies acts as a problem-solving centre that is also able to learn and hence provide continually-improved technological information. Here, specialisation in the production of knowledge is implemented by internal markets, reducing both the risks of leakage and the cost of absorption at the same time. Common ownership is the institutional tool organising internal markets and providing connectivity and receptivity in order to enable the exchange and trading of information to take place (Antonelli, 1988; Pavitt, 1987).

The diffusion of new information and communication technologies has been an important factor in the spread of the technological mode of co-operation among firms in order to undertake complex research programmes. Indeed it seems to be an important step forward in the attempt to combine proper levels of incentives to innovate and to make the best social use of new knowledge produced. Within technological clubs, enforced by on-line communication systems, firms can maximise the efficiency of the production of knowledge when economies of size matter, spreading the benefits to a large number of complementary users, yet keeping control over the conditions of appropriability implemented by *ex-ante* contractual agreements and enforced by reputation-building and signalling. In this context, applications of new information and communication technology, enforced by a rich array of contractual devices, seem relevant to the creation of effective quasi-internal markets for actual technological information and technological knowledge. The opportunistic behaviour of partners can be sanctioned not only by the decline of reputation as faithful members, hence difficulty in joining other clubs, but also and, most importantly, by exclusion from the intra-corporate networks of communication and exchange on which technological co-operation is based, i.e. mutual access to data banks, proprietary software, electronic archives and such like.

The evidence of both multinational corporations and technological co-operative clubs shows how important it is to combine the production and use of knowledge in order to resolve the knowledge trade off between the need to enforce appropriability to encourage the production of knowledge and the failure to disseminate the application of that new knowledge to the rest of the system. The development of knowledge within industries is strongly influenced by the network structure of relations among firms. Firms relying on localised knowledge implement their technological capabilities not only by means of R&D expenditure and internal learning but also through the systematic absorption of the technological and scientific competencies available in their environment.

The development of specialisation

The introduction of new information and communication technologies offers increasing opportunities for firms to shift towards specialisation in knowledge production. The result of the tradeability and exchangeability of technological information and technological know-how is the emergence of a veritable industry for the production of knowledge. Specifically, there are important positive effects in terms of accrued capability to separate the bits of information from the know-how which generated them. The procedures originally implemented for the on-line use of software packages located in the premises of independent software-houses (knowledge producers) find important applications in a variety of contexts. All competence and tacit knowledge, acquired by means of learning processes, can be better cumulated, monitored, converted into codified knowledge, and made available at a distance via telematic applications via new information and communication technologies. Subsequently it can be replicated and applied in different contexts and conditions.

The introduction of these technologies creates a highly idiosyncratic mode of market interaction between supply and demand based on question and answer. Customers make specific requests according to their own research needs, and increasingly the knowledge producer becomes the supplier of individual counselling to the research project developed by each innovator. Thanks to new information and communication technologies, firms can access the competence, that is the technology to produce knowledge, of specialised firms in order to solve their own specific problems, and combine the competence stored in knowledge firms with their own tacit knowledge, so as to generate the localised knowledge necessary to feed the innovation process.

In this context, the diffusion of new information and communication technologies favours the demise of the tight vertical integration of research and search activities within industrial firms, and the increasing outsourcing of knowledge-generating activities. By means of computer communication firms can rely more and more on knowledge-intensive business service providers, who, acting as 'competent interfaces', implement the generation of new localised knowledge. The production of knowledge becomes the core activity of specialised firms, whose product consists of new technological and scientific information which can be sold in the market place, not only when appropriability can be enforced by means of property rights, but also when absorption costs are too high for potential competitors to imitate without the direction and advice, and hence agreement, of such producers of knowledge. Specialisation in the production of knowledge is dependent on the effectiveness of the legal protection of intellectual property, the tacit potential of new knowledge, and the ease with which knowledge producers can appropriate the economic rent generated by the application of new knowledge (Geroski, 1995).

Knowledge-intensive business service firms play a major role in offering each agent access to the technological and scientific information dispersed in the system. Such firms perform two important functions in the economic system: they are containers of proprietary 'quasi-generic' knowledge, extracted by means of repeated interactions between both customers and the scientific community; and they act as an interface between that knowledge and the tacit and implicit knowledge buried in the daily routines of firms. Specifically, knowledge-intensive service firms represent vital factors of connectivity and receptivity. The supply of knowledge-intensive business services to the rest of the economic system has important effects in terms of connectivity because the interface-activity of service firms increases the exchanges of tacit knowledge and localised competence between agents. With regard to receptivity, each firm purchasing such services has an opportunity to learn from the experience of other firms via the services of consultants and advisers (Miles *et al.* 1995).

An array of new knowledge-intensive business service industries has been growing in recent years in European economies, covering a wide range of products and activities such as: computer and related information technologies services; hardware consultancy services; software consultancy and supply services; data processing services; database activities; advanced communication services; R&D services; technical testing and quality control; logistic services; patent bureaus; economic and management services; labour recruitment and provision of personnel; and training activities. Outsourcing of knowledge-intensive business services to firms specialising in the production and dissemination of localised knowledge is increasingly practised, especially in metropolitan regions. In turn, the remote access to knowledge-intensive business service, made possible by new information and communication technologies, gives these firms a global scope of action with significant and growing flows of exports and foreign direct investments so that multinational knowledge-intensive business service firms can gradually emerge combining the advantages of proximity and variety (Antonelli, 1989a; Miles *et al.*, 1995; Den Hertog *et al.*, 1995).

The diffusion of new information technology and the related specialisation of the knowledge-intensive service industry can also be considered a powerful connectivity-enhancing factor within the architecture of innovation systems. The spatial stochastic interactions probability and the speed of communication, of both technological information and technological knowledge within economic systems, is likely to increase, along with the division of labour in the production of knowledge.

The emerging specialised mode of production, based upon on-line access to the competence of knowledge producers rather than the supply of technological information, greatly enhances both the communication capability and private efficiency of knowledge production. The cumulative dynamics of positive feedback means that the more 'questions' the knowledge-producer receives, the more answers it is able to generate, and the larger the revenue and size of activity, the greater the opportunity to generate new knowledge which applies to a variety of conditions and uses. On-line provision of competence and long-term research contracts positively influence efficiency because any potential knowledge customer can purchase accordingly and every interaction potentially increases the general amount of knowledge available in the system. Furthermore, and perhaps more importantly, this mode of production can also reduce the social waste apparent in the duplication of production and absorption costs which occurs as a result of the separation of the production of knowledge from its subsequent communication and absorption (See Table 8.1).

In this way, the knowledge trade off is partially appeased: on-line interaction in problem-solving activities leads to a new institutional market where customers have little opportunity to 'steal' the competence itself; the assessment of competence is possible in terms of reputation; and the incentive for specialised firms to build competence is clear because of the positive market-signalling it provides.

In some ways, evolving out of the problems associated with the previous modes, the specialised mode of production ranks very high with respect to all the assessment criteria, provided a number of relevant conditions are observed. It is well known that the specialisation of knowledge production represents the best form of organisation from the viewpoint of the amount of incentives to enter into business. As Arrow (1962b) has shown, the independent inventor who is able to sell its knowledge in the market place will retain a larger post-innovation revenue than both a vertically-integrated innovator, who was already in business, and a competitive industry where the innovation is introduced by any firm and immediately imitated by all the others. Provided a market for knowledge can be institutionalised and the basic conditions to buy and sell knowledge enforced, the availability of resources to innovate would be readily secured by the market dynamics (Kitch, 1977).

If there is an appropriate interaction between tacit learning processes and codified knowledge, the private efficiency of this mode of production should be very high, as a result of the effects of division of labour and specialisation of productivity, known in economics ever since Adam Smith. However, the dissemination capability of the specialised production of knowledge, when associated with a strong intellectual property rights system, increasingly comes under question when the monopolistic effects of patents are properly considered. Long-lasting patents prevent imitation and this increases the incentives for innovators to duplicate research activities. This is particularly culpable when patents impede the dissemination of radical technological knowledge that may have significant applications in a wide range of products and industries unrelated to the ones in which the original innovator is active. The cumulative character of technological change and the important role of convergence among seemingly un-related technologies add on here to stress the social limitations of the present intellectual property rights system (Scotchmer, 1991).

Mandated licensing of key technological information already generated in previous 'telematic market' interactions might help in reducing the negative effects of proprietary information with respect to other potential users, further increasing the social utility of the new specialised mode of knowledge production. The evolution of intellectual property rights away from the excludability conditions of patents, instead designed to increase appropriability, and thus the incentives to codification of the copyright model, as a reward for the right to use a codified knowledge, could increase the pace of technological change. Such evolution would increase the benefits of cumulativeness in the generation of knowledge, reduce the wastes of duplication, and increase the speed of circulation of scientific and technological knowledge within innovation systems.

The emergence of a specialised industry for the production of knowledge has significant effects on institutional variety and the academic system in particular. The funding of universities is likely to come under close scrutiny because of direct competition from firms performing a similar role in the economic system and the risk of crowding out. However, the assessment of the quality of research conducted in universities and its effects on the economic system becomes increasingly possible and reliable due to the ability to compare the efficiency and organisation of labour in university departments with that of knowledge firms. The very boundaries between the knowledge industry and the academic community are shifted as more and more universities are induced, by restrictions in publicly-funded budgets, to finance their research programmes by offering their own competence and technological knowledge for sale in the market place.[1] Risks of cross-subsidisation between profit-oriented and non-profit academic activities becomes pertinent: knowledge firms may be prey to unfair competition from low-priced services supplied at variable costs while fixed ones are tax-paid. Provided proper terms of co-operation are established, though, the close interaction of knowledge firms and universities might well increase the overall efficiency of both institutions. In this regard knowledge firms could act as connecting agents, specialising in the transfer of technological information from universities to industrial firms; a link which is to some extent missing in the institutional relationship between universities and entrepreneurship, as articulated in the continental European system.[2]

Conclusions

The enforcement of appropriability conditions of new localised knowledge and the consequent increase in the incentives to generate new knowledge, coupled with the restrictions on the conditions of use, and the social and private advantages which stem from the enhanced dissemination of new knowledge (associated with the decline in the amount of resources available to innovate), that is to say the conflicting elements of the knowledge trade off, emerges as the key problematic issue in the organisation of the production of knowledge. Appropriability conditions, such as intellectual property rights and market power, represent the basic incentive for agents to produce knowledge and subsequently extract economic wealth in order to produce further knowledge and so on. However, the current direction of technological change, characterised by cumulativeness and convergence of seemingly unrelated technologies, means that the exclusive assignment of patents and similar rights to inventors, have significant negative effects on social welfare. The resolution of the dilemma appears to lie in the progressive un-bundling of technological knowledge, which involves the creation of a specific market for such knowledge and the separation, from vertically-integrated corporations, of knowledge-producers, operating instead as specialised firms within the new knowledge economy (Dasgupta, 1987; Dasgupta and David, 1987).

As we have seen, this process and solution are the burgeoning result of the introduction of new information and communication technologies and its effects on the organisation of the production of knowledge. The evolution towards a specialised mode of organisation – a specialised industry for the production and distribution of knowledge and a specialised market for its supply and demand – still includes revised elements of entrepreneurship, institutional variety, vertical integration and technological co-operation. The growing globalisation of vertical integration means that the monopolistic tendencies of this mode are kept in check, while their invention and innovation, in the sense of research and learning, are continually encouraged. Institutional variety and technological co-operation come to define one another, as knowledge-intensive business service firms become the productive interface on which such relationships, between agents and universities and agents themselves, are established and developed. The continued specialisation in the organisation of knowledge production, and its positive effects on innovation capability generally, relies upon the proper distribution of knowledge services throughout economic systems, the introduction of network-wide knowledge-production processes, new forms of contractual interactions and appropriate mandatory licensing.

In conclusion, the diffusion of new information technology increases the connectivity and receptivity of information networks, fuelling the growth of a market for knowledge-intensive business services, and the firms involved in such services, and enhancing the innovative capability of the system as a whole. This process is clearly recursive, generating in turn more such technology and an ever-increasing array of product and process innovations. What emerges is a radical structural change, re-shaping completely the position of service industries and emphasising the function of knowledge-based service sectors as the pillars of this new system in terms of innovative capacity and the all-important competitive edge.

9 The dynamics of technological externalities and the evolution of technological co-operation

Technological co-operation, an important organisational innovation, is increasingly becoming an integral part of industrial systems, and many firms are involved in systematic co-operation activities aimed at generating new scientific and technological knowledge with a view to eventual technological innovation. Recently, lots of economic literature has been dedicated to this organisational innovation; but attention has been focused mainly on the static analysis of the firm rather than investigating the properties of the system in which the co-operation takes place or its evolution over time.[1] Recent advances in the economics of science and technology and the distinction between generic and localised knowledge, can offer new ways of analysing the economic rationale behind the dynamics of technological co-operation.

In the traditional analysis, the production of knowledge and innovation as a public good is deemed to be suboptimal because there is little incentive for potential innovators and it is difficult to correctly assess and assign property rights to the results of the innovation process. Fiscal allowances and public subsidies have become the standard recommended way to sustain levels of innovation. When the tacit component of technological knowledge is identified, the characteristics of information networks, as a key attribute of industrial systems, in which technological information is shared and percolates from one firm to another, become relevant and new tools of industrial and innovation policies warrant greater attention.

Here the first section briefly outlines the need and potential of technological co-operation via clubs and other collective associations. The second section considers some implications of the application of the methodology of spatial stochastic interactions to the rationale behind co-operation, in particular the active role of firms in facilitating 'percolation'. The benefits and drawbacks of co-operation are then considered within an identifiable endogenous and historical dimension in the third section, which identifies the various forms of technological co-operation and recalls their dynamic relation with new information technology. The core of the chapter, section four, is dedicated to the evolution of technological co-operation over the technology life cycle: following some general considerations, co-operation is analysed through the stages of innovation, diffusion and maturity. In conclusion, co-operation is seen as an effective innovation policy tool within the context of calculated public subsidy, as evidenced by the European Union.

Technological co-operation

In our approach, the amount of technological knowledge a firm is able to generate is determined by the relationship between the amount of internal resources devoted to R&D and learning activities, and the levels of internalisation of external technological information, both tacit and codified; which, in turn, depend on the extent to which technological externalities and effective communication among innovators percolate through the system, influencing both the research process and its outcome (Antonelli, 1996a and b). This approach has important implications for assessing new technology strategy. Every effort a firm makes to increase the local interaction probability of its own innovation environment will have strong positive effects on its innovative efficiency for any given amount of resources invested in learning and research activities; and a new pattern of technology strategy may be built on these premises (Antonelli, 1994a).

The creation of technology clubs for firms which are involved in complementary innovation activities, where local technological externalities exist, becomes a potential strategy for firms and public intervention; such activities lead to an increase in the productivity of resources invested in innovation activities (Metcalfe, 1995). Specifically, technology clubs, formed with the help of public subsidies, can offer firms the opportunity to internalise the spillover of localised technological knowledge within the club. As a result, the levels of appropriability of the codified component of technological knowledge are increased and consequently a fair return is possible for the investment of resources in R&D activities. More importantly, the actual productivity of resources invested in research and learning is enhanced. The sponsoring of technological clubs can thus be viewed as an institution-setting intervention favouring the re-allocation of intellectual property rights. Proper definition of the static and dynamic characteristics of technological co-operation and the evolution of specific forms of technology clubs seem to be essential if the real potential of such an innovation policy tool is to be exploited.

Spatial stochastic interactions and technological co-operation

The use of the methodology of spatial stochastic interactions in the analysis of the incentives and dynamics of technological co-operation, in the form of technology clubs, has a number of important implications. Codified, scientific and technological knowledge with low levels of natural excludability, which can be assessed by all firms with minor communication effort, can be assumed to exert an external pressure. It is probable that all the firms in a system will be able to receive a new piece of technological information consisting of highly codified knowledge, even in situations of low levels of connectivity and receptivity and where the density of agents may be low. In fact, the source of information can be considered great enough to reach all the agents in the system directly: a new radical scientific discovery exerts a strong effect on the whole system.

The properties of spatial stochastic interactions systems become much more relevant when technological knowledge is strictly localised. Its successful communication implies also the transfer of both tacit knowledge, acquired by means of learning processes and bottom-up processes of technological induction, together with the exchange of explicit science-based generic and codified knowledge. The generation of new localised knowledge offers 'spontaneous' externalities only to those agents operating in close technological, industrial, regional and institutional proximity, as well as it can rely only on local externalities. Connectivity and receptivity probabilities become relevant when the communication and assimilation of new technological knowledge requires important additional and dedicated efforts, beyond reading blue-prints in scientific magazines.

Individualistic efforts of each firm to build up receptivity and connectivity probabilities often have no influence and/or are too expensive. The actual effect of local technological externalities is closely related to the levels and quality of communication among contiguous partners as well as the general communication characteristics of the innovation system. The creation of additional levels of connectivity probabilities engendered by such events as the investments in new communication channels, or the implementation of receptivity probabilities by each firm by means of organisational changes, generates important externalities and hence a divide between private and social returns. In this situation, a collective undertaking for communication systems to be properly assessed and funded seems necessary.

A new communication channel between agents A and B, or stronger receptivity in either, also benefits all the other agents already linked to A or B. Connectivity and receptivity probabilities may thus be thought of as non-pure private goods. Proper levels of co-operation in communication among partners can only be achieved through a collective undertaking. All efforts to build up connectivity probabilities between partners are to the mutual advantage of all parties. Connectivity and receptivity building is clearly a positive sum game: the larger the number of firms, the greater the local interaction probability and hence the innovative efficiency of each firm in the innovation system. If these parameters of interaction probability, which govern the technological communication in an innovation system, are recognised as endogenous and dynamic rather than exogenous and static, then the significance of such an equation becomes crucial. Connectivity and receptivity probabilities can be built up and implemented through positive action, such as the creation of new institutions, e.g. technology clubs (See Chapter 5).

The trade off of technological co-operation

In our earlier assessment of spatial stochastic interactions models as an interpretative example of the generation of technological knowledge, it became apparent that in the real world the distribution of interaction probability in an innovation system varies across technologies and regions and over time. The endogenous characteristic of spatial stochastic interactions probability was also demonstrated: effective connections in terms of succesful communication is the result of deliberate action and not given circumstance. Spatial stochastic interactions probability at time t affects the behaviour of agents, not only in terms of the levels of research and learning activities, but also in the extent of active measures to build up connectivity and receptivity, which enhance the efficiency of the very funds invested in research and learning activities. Subsequently, the spatial stochastic interactions probability at time $t + 1$ is influenced but, due to its stochastic nature, not entirely determined by the conduct of firms at time t.

Within this context, technology clubs can be defined as institutionalised systems of relationships among firms aimed at internalising technological externalities and increasing communication in terms of interaction probability. So far, they represent the result of explicit strategic action taken by their members to increase communication in terms of connectivity and receptivity levels.

Clearly a firm's decision whether or not to join a technology club can be analysed in terms of the trade off between the benefits and losses derived from actual co-operation. Benefits arise from the internalisation of technological externalities that spill over from the R&D and learning activities carried out by other firms. Losses are generated by the risks of uncontrolled imitation and the increased difficulty in appropriating the results of the research and learning activities because of the opportunistic behaviour of fellow members. Association requires some dedicated resources which in turn generate governance costs, highly specific to the management of the technology club. Firms are likely to join a technology club only when, for a given desired level of innovative output, the sum of governance costs and expected losses, in the form of increased technological rivalry, is lower than the expected advantages, in terms of lower research and learning costs (Buchanan, 1965; Antonelli and Foray, 1992).

Diverse forms of technology clubs can be identified in the wide range of empirical and theoretical literature on technical co-operation now available. Important distinctions are made between R&D cartels (Kamien, Muller and Zang, 1992), where firms collectively decide what levels of R&D activity they will undertake in their own research laboratories, and knowledge-sharing agreements (d'Aspremont and Jacquemin, 1988), or technology clubs proper, where instead firms share their knowledge completely. Technological co-operation can be: horizontal – that is within one industry; lateral – among firms that operate in lateral industries; or vertical – i.e. among firms that produce goods which are the input of the other firms (Chesnais, 1988). It can also be purely industrial or extended to include universities. While industrial consortia require the co-operation of all the firms in an industry, most technology clubs have a limited number of partners. Patent-swopping agreements are based on symmetrical access to the use of technological knowledge already patented. Technological co-operation is either symmetrical, involving partners on an equal basis, or asymmetrical, between partners who differ in terms of sale, market power and technological advantage (Ordover and Willig, 1985).

New information technologies and technological co-operation

As we have seen in the previous chapter, technological co-operation is heavily influenced by the diffusion of new information technologies. On-line co-operation between firms increases the extent to which partners can actually exchange tacit knowledge and competence and share the complexities of the research process by establishing common research standards and evaluation protocols. Electronic communication also provides partners with access to internal data banks and software. Partners can participate in co-design processes in cases of complex innovation requiring a variety of new components. Opportunistic behaviour can be effectively sanctioned by excluding members from the data communication systems. New communication technology enables partnership between remote members, with the added effect of reducing the time lag in the international diffusion of technological change. Technical assistance is also easier using on-line systems. The performance of those new capital goods which embody innovations can be controlled remotely, thus increasing the appropriability of returns, benefiting the vendors of patents and technological know-how (Antonelli, 1988). The incentive for technological co-operation is evident: the diffusion of new information technology enables the levels of governance costs for technology clubs to be reduced and for the spectrum of effective co-operation in real time to be extended.

Technological co-operation in the technology life cycle

The dynamics of technological co-operation are influenced by the evolution of the parameters which characterise the particular technology and industry. The specific structure of technological co-operation and the incentive to join clubs both evolve with the parameters of the innovation system (Cainarca, Colombo and Mariotti, 1992). The different forms of technological co-operation that prevail at various stages of the technology life cycle can be explained by the methodology of spatial stochastic interactions models, when the time stratification of percolation structures is properly accounted for.

The wide ranging literature on the technology life cycle provides some basic considerations:

1   The number of firms follows a clear evolutionary path. After the initial innovation is introduced by a limited number of firms, waves of imitators enter the market; entries are much more frequent than exits so the number of firms in the market grows. Eventually however, there has to be some selection and the rates of exit become much higher than those of entry. Ultimately, the number of firms progressively drops and stabilises at lower levels (Klepper and Graddy, 1990). As a result, the density of the innovation system and related information links in place among firms – ultimately affecting the communication probability – is likely to increase during a large part of the technology life cycle.

2   Localised technological knowledge eventually becomes industry and region specific. Local externalities spill over among firms that are part of the same innovation system. The net result is that the 'spontaneous' communication probability, as given by the extent to which all agents have access to global technological externalities, is likely to increase along the technology life cycle.

3   Technological rivalry, based on the introduction of new competing products among firms, slows down as a dominant design emerges (Abernathy, 1978). The competition process is now characterised by monopolistic competition. When other imitators enter, the market evolves towards a mature stage where price differentiation is based upon reputation, brand names and advertising (Klepper and Grady, 1990).

4   The demand for products follows the well-known logistic pattern of diffusion processes. In the early stages, consumers are slow to learn about the new product. Only when imitation, due to the inter-dependence of the utility function, and emerging demand externalities provide the basic push, does demand reach a sustainable level. The introduction of process innovations and the increase in competition cause the market price for the innovated goods to fall; equilibrium demand grows further, though at a lower rate. In the final stages demand approaches an asymptotic level where saturation is reached.

The dynamics of technological co-operation is also influenced by the evolution of governance parameters. Learning processes are fundamental in shaping the evolution of dedicated governance activities. Here, learning to co-operate is a function of time and the total number of technology clubs of which a firm is a member. Consequently, the incentive to join a technology club increases over time. Since receptivity probability is more effective than connectivity probability in influencing the local communication probability – and hence the productivity of R&D activities – firms are likely to make more effort to increase their own receptivity levels towards external technological and scientific knowledge (David and Foray, 1994; Cohen and Levinthal, 1989). Subsequently, highly receptive firms, that is to say firms which have done everything possible to increase their own receptivity probability, command an internal capacity which may be used in a variety of different clubs.

Overall, what we see is that firms with experience of technology club membership tend to replicate that strategy more systematically than firms that have never joined a club; and such persistence in membership occurs across the board, involving a wide variety of alliances and clubs. Because the value of incentives and constraints changes over time we observe the systematic evolution of the forms and intensity of technological co-operation along the standard phases of the technology life cycle (Mueller, 1972; Abernathy, 1978; Utterback, 1994). This can be analysed in detail with respect to the three basic stages of innovation, diffusion and maturity (See Table 9.1).

Innovation

When there is a technological breakthrough, the incentives to establish a technology club are important but not very high; the likelihood that technological co-operation actually takes place is uneven. The number of firms in the market and hence the 'natural' levels of connectivity between them is still very low. The character of technological knowledge is essentially tacit and the natural excludability of new scientific knowledge relevant enough so that co-operation is influential in enhancing the productivity level of R&D activity. The positive effects of joint research on costs are also significant, at this stage demand is still latent and fragmented, and full market competition is still too far away to be certain of having any substantial effect. Governance costs for the formation and implementation of a technology club are, however, very high: it is difficult to locate the complementary competences and the communication links that are most likely to encourage internal research and learning activities. The technological field is still largely unexplored and it is difficult to focus and direct receptivity properly. Indeed the risks of 'dating the wrong partner' are very high, also in terms of opportunistic behaviour because of firms' limited experience in a common environment. Finally, investment in building up receptivity and connectivity probabilities is long term and hence leads to significant increasing returns; but it also involves high levels of upfront costs with important thresholds (Arrow, 1974, 1996).

At this stage, the incentives for technological co-operation are very high because the expected profitability is high; but the high levels of risk and uncertainty, and the high levels of investment required to initiate active co-operation, may discourage most firms. This stage is characterised by

Table 9.1 The evolution of technological clubs and the technology life cycle

	Innovation		Diffusion			Maturity	
	Break-through	Localised technology	Adoption and imitation	Selection and dominant design	International diffusion	Process innovation	Saturation
Density	*	**	***	***	****	**	*
Firm tacit knowledge	***	****	***	**	**	****	*
Industry tacit knowledge	**	**	**	***	**	****	*
Codified knowledge	*	*	**	****	*****	*****	*******
Demand levels	*	*	**	*****	******	****	***
Price elasticity	*	*	**	***	***	*****	*****
Technological rivalry	*	**	***	**	**	****	**
Price competition	*	*	*	***	****	****	******
Governance costs	**	*	***	***	***	****	**
Frequency	*	***	**	*	**	***	*
Forms of technological clubs	Inter-industrial clubs	Horizontal and regional clubs	Vertical clubs	Standard clubs	International clubs	Industry consortia	Project specific JV

* measures the relative weight.

inter-industrial technology clubs open to universities and other scientific institutions, based on symmetrical knowledge-sharing agreements, set up by firms which are active in a variety of industries and technologies, and also by the joint introduction of research standards and research technologies. Technological co-operation is aimed at increasing the levels of receptivity probability of each agent. Public subsidies to pre-competitive research may be necessary to help reluctant firms join technology clubs (Mody, 1993; Clarysse, Debackere and Van Dierdonk, 1995; Quintas and Guy, 1995).

When technological knowledge is still mainly based upon tacit knowledge, co-localisation within industrial districts is an effective tool to implement informal technological co-operation. Co-localisation can even be a substitute for formalised co-operation. Technological districts develop because of the intentional entry and concentration of new technology-intensive firms in that area and the localisation of research laboratories there by firms based elsewhere (Antonelli, 1986 and 1994a).

In the stage of development of localised product technologies, the effects of technological co-operation on total costs are still substantial and the negative effects on the demand curve are low. In fact, firms can extract important benefits from technological co-operation in terms of reducing duplication, and signalling dead-ends and promising avenues. Effects on revenues, as determined by the downward shift of the more elastic demand curves, due to technological leakages and imitative entry, are not very strong as a result of the sustained rates of growth of demand found in the take-off phase of the logistic curve. The number of firms increases because of the continued entry of new competitors and imitators: the variety of products and market niches in potential markets for fellow members of the technology club is very high. Moreover, governance costs to locate potential partners decline substantially since the technology field is now much more clearly defined. The increasing density of agents means that spontaneous interaction probability rises and with it the opportunity for informal communication. At this stage, the incentives to create technology clubs are very high. Such clubs are, however, mainly horizontal, that is to say, members are active in the same industry and technology, because of the strong specific and industrial characteristics of the information exchanges between firms involved in similar learning processes. Technological co-operation is based on R&D cartels, where firms agree on the separate, individual levels of R&D activity, and now aimed at increasing the connectivity levels of each agent (Arora and Gambardella, 1990; Arora, 1995).

Diffusion

During the stage of diffusion of product innovations, the balance of the effects of technological co-operation is reversed. Negative effects on the demand curve of each firm and therefore on its revenue become stronger: the rates of growth of demand slow down.

The risks of opportunistic behaviour are greater, but so too are the dangers of imitation and anticipated entry. Conversely, technological co-operation is likely to have less effect on the costs of carrying out R&D activities. At this stage, firms that have been able to implement their own receptivity probabilities are likely to show a high propensity to move across technology clubs. Overall levels of membership tend to decline, especially in horizontal clubs; vertical and lateral clubs now become increasingly prominent. Technological co-operation is stronger in user-producer and subcontracting relations, across industries that are vertically complementary (i.e. *filières*), between firms which are active in different industries – but use the new products introduced upstream, or provide complementary inputs. There is less risk of opportunistic behaviour in vertical clubs because the scope of the activity of the firms is different; important lines of communication about technological knowledge acquired through the interaction of learning to use and learning to do are kept open. Here co-operation is aimed at increasing the receptivity probabilities of each agent and firms that have already been able to build up high levels of receptivity competence are likely to play a leading role in the management of clubs (Von Hippel, 1988; Lundvall, 1985; Hagedoorn, 1995).

When the diffusion of innovated products is enhanced by network externalities, co-operation among firms clearly offers incentives to shift towards forms of product standardisation. This is true for both consumer goods and capital goods. Product standardisation for consumer goods increases network externalities in terms of collective learning and compatibility. Similarly, standardisation for capital goods enhances network externalities based upon reductions in skill requirements; consequently benefits consist mainly of reductions in training and other adoption costs, such as maintenance and repairs, which also affect consumer goods. Co-operative innovation is likely to be consolidated when it can lead to the introduction of industry-wide standards and hence generate network externalities with the familiar positive 'excess momentum' effects on the level and slope of overall demand (Katz and Shapiro, 1985; David and Greenstein, 1990; Antonelli, 1994b).

The international diffusion of product innovations offers new opportunities for technological co-operation. Late comers have a strong incentive to join technology clubs, managed by firms already established in the field, for they have the opportunity to speed up the learning process for new technologies at a lower cost. Established firms have an incentive to join, in order to maintain better control over both unintended leakage or imitation of new radical technological knowledge, and the introduction of incremental innovations generated by new applications of the new radical technological knowledge. In this context, technology clubs show strong asymmetrical relations between innovators and imitators since they are mainly used to implement unidirectional licensing and technical assistance (Arora, 1995). In some circumstances, innovators may join technology clubs to impede aggressive imitation (Ordover and Willig, 1985). In any case, the international character of technology clubs becomes pre-eminent: late comers are often localised in peripheral countries, while established firms are based in core regions. Technology clubs become an alternative governance institution that complements, and possibly even substitutes, multinational growth for established firms (Mowery, 1989).

Maturity

The shift from product innovation to process innovation coincides with the substantial decline in the number of firms and the progressive codification of technological knowledge. The natural levels of the interaction probability decline because of the reduced density, but this is more than compensated for by the substantial increase in the external pressure of scientific knowledge. Effects on R&D costs decline because firms now have access to more explicit and codified knowledge which can be absorbed with lower levels of structured interaction. The costs of club membership are increased and the incentive to join is negatively affected if there is a risk of anticipated imitative entry at stagnant demand levels. However, technological co-operation can take on more institutionalised forms. With regard to the innovation process, collective research by industrial consortia, carrying out long-term R&D with a strong scientific bias, is likely to be the most frequent form of technological co-operation (Link and Bauer, 1989; Aldrich and Sasaki, 1995).

When the stage of maturity is reached, the focus of the innovation process shifts even more towards the introduction of new processes aimed at reducing production costs. During this stage co-operation is again active because it offers important opportunities to reduce total costs. However, due to the large minimum break-even size of plants and firms and product differentiation – based on reputation, brand name, distribution facilities and post-sales assistance – barriers to entry are lowered by the cross-entry of new cost-effective competitors who are already active in related industries and technologies: this means that the risk of opportunistic behaviour is high. Demand reaches saturation point, price elasticity is very high and revenue elasticity is now very low. Cross-licensing and cross-patenting become important tools as exchange hostages in order to control the risk of opportunistic behaviour (Williamson, 1985). Project-specific joint ventures, often aimed at introducing new components into the final product, constitute an important form of co-operation.

Finally, in the stage of decline, the role of price-competition increases. The effects of technological co-operation on total costs are not expected to be very important except for late comers who have not yet adopted the new processes. However, the consequences of having to face more cost-effective competitors and more elastic demand curves are likely to drastically reduce firms' revenues. Vertical technological co-operation is reduced to the minimum of providing *ex post* technical assistance and *ex ante* technical analysis via company-funded independent research institutes within the context of strong contractual agreements (Kogut, Walker and Kim, 1995).

Conclusions

Technological co-operation, parallel in some ways to the specialisation we saw above, is emerging as one of the most important organisational innovations in the production of knowledge since the move away from the rigid vertical integration that characterised the US and most OECD countries at the end of the Second World War (Mowery, 1995). New information technology is highly influential in this context, increasing communication control and interaction – the very means of co-operation – between firms with regard to research and learning processes and their outputs. Indeed, the diffusion of technological and organisational innovations, such as new information technologies and technological co-operation, reinforce each other, with the result that the circulation of localised technological knowledge in the economic system is increased. Spatial stochastic interactions methodology provides a useful tool with which to understand the dynamics of knowledge flows within innovation systems. Technological knowledge is generated by the continuous process of recombination and socialisation of both tacit and codified knowledge. Localised technological knowledge spills over into a limited, local area where firms are in close industrial, regional and technological proximity. Local technological externalities can be internalised by means of technology clubs. The dynamics of technology clubs and the changing rationale of technological co-operation over the product life cycle offer innovation policy a major possibility to enhance the levels of innovative activities.

The application of the methodology of repeated spatial stochastic interactions based upon the time stratification of a sequence of Random Markov Fields has produced a comprehensive framework which explains the physiological evolution of technological co-operation over a number of phases involving:

1   symmetrical, receptivity-building and knowledge-sharing agreements;
2   horizontal, connectivity-building R&D cartels;
3   technological districts;
4   vertical and lateral receptivity-building clubs;
5   standard clubs;
6   asymmetrical and international diffusion clubs;
7   industrial consortia;
8   project specific joint ventures;
9   independent research institutes.

Within such a dynamic framework pathological relations among firms, aimed more at enforcing collusive agreements than developing new technologies, can be more easily detected by anti-trust authorities.

Incentives for firms to form technology clubs alter the rationale for co-operation during the introduction of new localised technologies. In this phase, the risks of inappropriable leakage are very high and compensation, in the form of the advantages offered by technological externalities in undertaking R&D, are still uncertain. Encouraged by innovation policy, our analysis shows that the creation of technology clubs reduces the governance costs of co-operation substantially, because the learning processes are specific to the government of those clubs. The social notion of trust becomes relevant in this context. The value of membership in a technology club is reduced by the threat of opportunistic behaviour. However, the risks are lower the larger the number of technology clubs in the industry and the larger the number of partners. The first wave of technology clubs, sponsored by public subsidies, is likely to set off a self-reinforcing mechanism, lowering the reluctance of firms to join technology clubs because of the perceived risks of opportunistic behaviour. The likelihood that co-operation, once started among firms because of an external push – e.g. subsidies – may be consolidated throughout the technology life cycle, appears high.

Timing in the creation of technology clubs, and in granting subsidies accordingly is thus absolutely central. Combining R&D subsidies with technology clubs is likely to generate higher returns than straightforward subsidies. Sponsoring a technology club means encouraging co-operation among firms and should increase the effectiveness of given amounts of R&D subsidies. Sponsored membership of technology clubs can become a very effective tool of technology policy and used to sustain the innovative efforts of small firms. Most research programmes are characterised by very high threshold levels in terms of sunk costs which small firms cannot afford. R&D subsidies to technological clubs could be tied to the membership of small firms.

In considering the necessity and efficacy of subsidising technological co-operation, as part of a general effort to enhance the operational, 'percolating' framework for the generation of technological innovations, it is appropriate to recall that the general efficiency of an innovation system can be severely impaired if the receptivity and connectivity probabilities fall below some minimum thresholds. If no deliberate effort is made to implement the connectivity and receptivity probabilities of each agent within the economic system, some parts, in certain periods of the technology life cycle, may experience connectivity and receptivity levels below minimum thresholds, creating 'spotty' innovation networks with empty areas where innovation falls to very low levels. In fact, the earlier the system falls below such levels in the technology life cycle, the lower the overall technological capability of the whole innovation system; and all subsequent phases are harmed by the earlier failure.

Within such an analytical framework, the provision of incentives to R&D activities only via technology clubs, as practised by the European Union, appears to be an ingenious tool of industrial policy which could help to overcome the reluctance of many firms to co-operate. The innovation policy drawn up by the European Union and initiated by the ESPRIT Programme radically affects just such decision-making. Such programmes, drawn up to favour European integration, have led to a significant increase in industrial and technological co-operation among European companies. The subsidies granted under the auspices of the EU Innovation Programmes (after ESPRIT, RACE and BRITE, many others have been implemented) significantly lowered the costs associated with the monitoring of co-operation activities, consequently lowering the overall constraint on firms to co-operate (Folster, 1995).

To conclude, there are a number of reasons why sponsored technology clubs appear to be an effective innovation policy tool to implement the innovation system. Technology clubs make it possible to:

1   share localised and tacit knowledge;
2   reach minimum threshold levels in setting up R&D programmes, which are often beyond the reach of medium-sized firms;
3   reap the advantages of economies of scale and scope in carrying out R&D activities;
4   reduce the duplication of R&D efforts and consequently better focus each firm's R&D programme;
5   increase the number of spillovers across industries and technologies;
6   reduce adoption costs and increase user-producer interaction, thus fostering diffusion.

10 The evolution of standards as economic institutions

The generation of technological knowledge rests on the competence of firms able to manage the complex mix of learning, socialisation, recombination, and R&D. A key interface between internal and external knowledge is provided by standardisation processes. Standards are vital for technological change, especially in network technologies where the complementarity between the innovative efforts of a variety of firms contributes to the pace of technological advance.

Economic analysis has made a lot of progress recently in understanding and appreciating the key role of standards as institutions that shape both markets and organisations. The large and still growing literature on the subject has concentrated on the emergence of standards as a process driven mainly by demand-side forces: firms adhere to standards because of the incentives generated by network externalities and the subsequent larger demand for their products. Less attention has been paid to the analysis of the role of standards on the supply side of firms, both with respect to the relationship between standards, technological knowledge and technological change, and to the supply conditions of standards themselves.

This chapter attempts to provide an integrated approach to the study of standards, one which considers the many advances made on the demand side analysis about the role of network externalities and user inertia, and also elaborates on the supply-side conditions of standards. In particular, it focuses on standards as specifications of new technologies and on the role of the producer switching costs necessary for firms to adhere to a standard. The costs of switching from own product specifications to a common standard are relevant and become all the more important, the more localised the process of technological change in the specific, idiosyncratic features of a firm's environment.

Standardisation costs are then compared with the benefits, so as to provide a general rationale for understanding the features of the emergence of standards in an economic environment characterised by localised technological change, technological variety, asymmetries among firms and selection processes.

The first section briefly outlines the variety of standards identified in the literature and summarises the role of standards in economic systems. The second section concentrates on the implication of standards as vectors of technological and organisational communication and on their role in the generation of localised technological knowledge. The third section comprehensively analyses a model of a standardisation club, from a simplistic hypothesis to a complex series of recursive interactions, enumerating the factors affecting its formulation and the extent of its own effects on the industrial and economic environment. The conclusion identifies the supply-side influences on the standardisation process and locates that process within the wider circumstances of technological and organisational change.

Standards as institutions: an overview

The exploration of the variety of standards has produced a rich taxonomy. An initial distinction stresses the difference between product standards, document standards and compatibility standards: the former concerns actual products, the second refers to information codes, and the latter to processes (Farrell and Saloner, 1987; Besen, 1990). In turn such processes can refer to both production and consumption. With regard to the process that leads to standardisation and the related role of agents, more specific categories of standards have been elaborated. A basic classification distinguishes between mandatory and voluntary standards: mandatory standards are mandated by public authorities, whereas voluntary standards emerge in the market process. *De facto* standards emerge *ex post* in the market process as the result of interaction between agents and may be either unsponsored or sponsored standards according to the role of sponsoring entities. *De jure* standards are elaborated *ex ante* either by committees and agreements or standard-setting authority mandates (David, 1987; David and Greenstein, 1990). In functional terms, a further distinction has been drawn between standards that perform a reference function, and consequently reduce transaction costs, and standards that perform a compatibility function and consequently enhance or enable technical co-ordination between different components of a technological system.

From the large literature available, standards may be defined as institutions, which are vectors of technical, commercial and procedural communication. They emerge within the process of selection and diffusion of technological and organisational changes as a result of both selection processes and the interactive co-operative behaviour of learning agents within clubs. In substance, standards change the extent and context of the market and shape the competition process, radically, affecting the division of labour and the organisational set-up of firms. Standards thus represent institutions that 'provide the structure for exchange, that (together with the technology employed) determines the costs of transacting and the costs of transformation' (North, 1991: 34).

Institutions generally provide the structure for exchange and enable specialisation. Standards, as institutions that are carriers of technical and commercial information, reduce transaction costs in a variety of ways: they reduce the variety of asset specifications by increasing the range of possible users and consumers for a given set of standardised products, so as to reduce bilateral dependence; they increase the frequency of transactions and limit market uncertainty; and they make it possible to increase the number of parties operating in the market place. Consequently, they help reduce the extent to which market exchanges are personalised and the scope for moral hazard, shirking and opportunistic behaviour (Williamson, 1985 and 1993).

Standards enable the reduction of transaction costs with given levels of governance costs and, as a result, the shrinking of the optimum size of firms. Similarly, they increase the division of labour among firms. Indeed, in some ways, standards can be thought of as substitutes for organisations (Demsetz, 1993). With low levels of standardisation firms find it more profitable to internalise exchanges and diversify in a variety of related activities so as to economise on transaction costs. Without standards and with constant average production costs, the costs of the internal bureaucratic co-ordination of exchanges between complementary production processes are lower than the costs of arm's length transacting in the market place.

Historically, the effects of the diffusion of procedural standards, such as bar codes on the vertical separation of retailing, can be traced from many mass manufacturing industries where the dynamics of scale and scope have pushed firms to integrate downstream into distribution (Chandler, 1990). However, the relationship between communication and organisation is actually much more complex: Brousseau (1994) explores the interactions between the standardisation of communications procedures and the changes in the organisation of firms.[1]

The demand for standardised products may be higher because of relevant network externalities. Due to lower inertia, as determined by producer switching costs, demand may be more elastic for consumers and users of previous units of durable products. Demand for standardised products may also be higher because of the important revenue effects generated by the lower transaction costs of acquiring information about the characteristics of the products and their performances (Farrell and Saloner, 1987; Saloner, 1990).

When analysis focuses on new products, standards play an even greater role in enhancing demand. They reduce the risks for users to be locked into previous vintages of durable products. Consequently, they help reduce the adoption lags associated with new products. Empirical analysis confirms that standards enhance diffusion rates among both competitors and consumers (Link and Tassey, 1987).

Standards affect both the demand and supply conditions of firms, shaping market structure in many ways. With larger and more elastic demand curves, and increasing returns in production, for both economies of scale and learning, equilibrium unit costs for standardised products are likely to be lower. Independent of production costs, mandatory standards lower market prices: such standards provide the basic function of spreading information, reducing the monopoly power of innovators and, consequently, the barriers to entry and extra profits. Mandatory standards reduce the amount of tacit knowledge necessary to actually command in order to manufacture a new product and make it easier to enter new markets. Standards help to reduce information asymmetries between members of the same standardisation club. Hence they can help in fitting a small monopolistic niche into a larger oligopolistic market.

Voluntary standards can be fundamental in building multiple barriers to entry. As the outcome of standardisation clubs, they can make entry more difficult on both demand and supply sides for potential competitors and rival suppliers in differentiated markets. Within a given aggregate demand for a family of new products, performing similar functions but fragmented into a variety of niches, the demand for standardised products is likely to grow faster and attract consumers from the adjacent market niches because of the powerful effects of network externalities. At the same time producer switching costs on the supply side make entry more difficult for potential competitors.

Innovating firms that operate in the durable goods markets – with repeated purchases – may be reluctant to adhere to industry standards because of the potential loss of the advantages offered to first-comers down to the inertia among users of durable products. Lack of standards provides first-comers with a protection of their market shares that is equal to the consumer switching costs for buyers of incompatible products supplied by rivals. In this context, public standard-setting institutions can have a significant influence. The analysis of Swann and Shurmer (1994) shows that the pre-announcement of institutional standards by a standard-setting authority has important and positive effects on the dynamics of the competitive process.

Standards can substitute for regulatory interventions directed towards price-output combinations, when their introduction is likely to lower market prices and the overall costs of manufacturing firms. From this viewpoint, standards may be a substitute for regulation. Mandatory standards can be designed so that firms are obliged to leave their small market niches and enter into competition in larger markets. They can be especially effective when the markets themselves have been unable to provide the appropriate amount of voluntary standards due to lack of active participation in standardisation clubs, which may be determined by locking-in effects of the monopolistic rents made available to individual innovators by their small, fragmented, demand niches.[2]

Standards and technological knowledge

The innovation capability of firms rests upon various combinations of tacit and codified knowledge. The former consists of knowledge acquired via learning processes embedded in the specific production process and the market for products and for inputs, in which each firm operates, while the latter consists of more explicit and codified technological and scientific information that is elaborated and communicated by means of common procedures. Technological changes, based upon localised knowledge, consequently lead to a variety of product and process specifications. Building upon its own learning process and the innovative stimuli provided by the particular economic environment, the firm attempts to introduce innovations. Therefore, at any point in time a variety of rival product innovations are generated and introduced into the market place. Each product innovation is partially in competition with the others in that it performs similar functions and addresses similar needs of potential users and consumers.

Standardisation is relevant in the economics of innovation from two different and yet complementary dynamic approaches. The first approach stresses the role of standardisation processes as an important aspect of the process of diffusion, selection and adoption of technological changes. According to Utterback (1994), product standardisation takes place when a dominant design is selected out of the variety of product innovations. In fact, when product standards are defined as that specification 'which is accepted for current use through authority, custom, or general consent' (Utterback, 1994: 29), the concepts of standards and dominant design overlap. This overlapping offers important insights into the relationship between product standards, compatibility standards and procedure standards (Abernathy and Clark, 1985; Clark, 1985). Following the emergence of a dominant design, the flow of rival product innovations shrinks and competition between firms shifts to the new battleground of process innovations. Compatibility standards emerge as a result of the selection process leading to the exclusion of the rival alternative production technologies in the market place.

In this literature standards are viewed as the outcome of a process of technical and economic selection that reduces variety to a common, dominant design (Metcalfe and Gibbons, 1988; Metcalfe, 1992, 1997). The original variety of rival technological innovations consists of a plurality of alternative new product specifications that are introduced by each firm according to its own localised innovation processes. Market selection and incremental innovations induce each firm to converge towards the dominant standard, and less adaptive firms are pushed out of the market. As Metcalfe and Miles (1994) show, standardisation can be thought of as one aspect of a possible, yet not deterministic, process of technological convergence and selection that follows the generation of innovations and parallels their adoption. The adoption of innovations is enhanced by standardisation and its related inducement, such as the reduction in costs from increasing returns, the reduction in market prices from the fall of barriers to entry, and the new competition brought in by imitators. Standards favour diffusion, especially when they help turn small monopolies into larger oligo-polies, and increase the value for users by means of network externalities.

The outcome of standardisation processes is consequently deeply inter-twined with the dynamics of market selection. It is influenced by the amount of initial variety and diversity among the original designs, the extent to which the positive feedbacks of network externalities affect con-vergence, and the extent to which producer switching costs – in terms of localised learning – and sunk costs on the supply side and inertia induced by consumer switching costs on the demand side, slow the process. The timing of standardisation reflects the balance that exists between the incentives to converge and give way to standards and to resist and stand up to them.

A complementary approach has been recently developed: it focuses atten-tion on the role of standards in the generation of new localised knowledge (David and Greenstein, 1990; David and Steinmueller, 1994; David and Foray, 1995). A standard is defined as a set of technical, commercial and procedural specifications that define the functions and the composition of an economic artefact: hence standards perform the basic role of carriers of technical information about the way to use and to manufacture an economic good.[3] If we accept the proposition that both the knowledge and computa-tional capability of the decision-maker are severely limited;[4] then commu-nication costs are significant in defining the economic environment into which firms and economic agents operate and behave.

Standards are influential in making more explicit the tacit knowledge on which new products and manufacturing processes are based. Standardisation processes can be considered a key component of the more general process of conversion of tacit into codified knowledge, which also favours the recom-bination of available codified knowledge. Standards perform a notable, though unintentional, activity as carriers and converters of tacit knowledge; they actually codify the characteristics of new products and new processes that command market recognition, and make explicit a number of technical specifications that become effective instructions for standards adopters (Winter, 1993).

The elaboration of voluntary standards within standardisation clubs involves the co-operation of firms in the definition of common technical specifications with each member of the club sharing the information and know-how specific to their own production processes and localised learning procedures. From this point of view, standards are not only carriers of tacit knowledge but also, and most importantly, converters of tacit knowledge into codified knowledge.

Hence, standardisation processes can be thought to be, both the result of high levels of co-operative interaction and interdependence among agents in innovation systems, as well as the basis for enhanced levels of technological communication within innovation systems – in terms of higher levels of connectivity and receptivity among agents. It is clear that standardisation enables the spreading of relevant technological externalities into the economic system. Moreover, because standardisation is associated with increasing returns in production, as determined by the economies of scale and learning, it generates important pecuniary externalities for downstream users, as well.[5]

The economics of clubs provides useful insights into an understanding of the dynamics of standardisation processes. Standardisation is the outcome of a co-operative process that takes place both *ex ante* and *ex-post* and responds to the basic trade off of club membership[6] as analysed by Buchanan (1965). In the analysis of standardisation, connectivity among agents and receptivity to external information are at stake and it is clear that they are endogenous variables which firms are able to influence and bear clear costs for the parties involved in the standardisation process.

Irrespective of the character of the standard – whether mandatory or voluntary, *de facto* or *de jure*, and the role of each firm in its elaboration – whether active or passive – the adoption of a given standard by each economic agent is by no means free: each producer has its own highly specific production features that affect the product (Berg, 1989). The adoption of a given standard, that is a set of product characteristics, which differ from the type of product that each agent would manufacture and deliver, entails a variety of costs that may be summarised as producer switching costs. In order to share a given standard, a firm has to change the topological character of its localised production process, the features of the intermediate inputs available in its environment, the know-how and experience accumulated in its own specific learning process. When a standard is voluntary and a firm participates in its elaboration, sponsoring costs add to and interact with adoption costs. Sponsoring costs consist of the resources necessary to participate in committees and other clubs involved in drawing a standard, out of the variety of technical specifications of a given class of products performing similar functions, offered by each producer and required by each user.

It should be clear that the more localised the technological knowledge, and the greater the topological variety of firms in the relevant technical and product spaces, the higher the producer switching costs for firms to adhere to a common standard. Conversely, the more firms rely upon codified knowledge based upon common and generic technological and scientific principles, the lower the costs to adhere to a common product specification.

In this context, the definition of standards as public goods seems no longer appropriate. Kindleberger (1983) argued that standards 'clearly fall within Samuelson's (1954) definition of public goods in that they are available for use by all and that use by any one economic actor does not reduce the amount available to others' (p. 377). Yet the standardisation of each agent's products entails two distinct classes of costs: adoption costs when standards are given, and elaboration costs for standards not yet established. The role of both adoption costs and sponsoring costs for firms adhering to a standard suggests that Romer's (1990) notion of non-pure private goods is applicable also to standards. Standards, like 'a design for a new good can be used as many times and in as many different production processes as desired'. As such goods, standards constitute a non-rival input, are productive and to some extent excludable.

In sum, as vectors of technical and commercial communication, standards are productive in that they make available the benefits of technological and network externalities. Moreover, the disclosure of technical and commercial information can be so articulated as to partially exclude certain firms. Standards, especially voluntary standards, can be thought of as non-pure private goods generated and distributed to the members of a club who have decided to share various technical and commercial information and, consequently, the market demand for their products, and the use of the same pool of intermediate and primary inputs. Within the club, technical information is shared and its use is non-rival; it is also productive because it provides access to more efficient production processes and higher levels of demand. Finally, and most important, membership in a club gives each firm the power to influence the final specification of the standard, minimising the technical distance between the standard itself and the technical specifications of each firm's current products and processes. Outsiders, moreover, may face considerable disadvantages when adhering to a standard; hence standards are partially excludable (Steedman, 1987; Parrinello, 1993).

A simple standardisation club model

We shall now try to model the emergence of *de facto* standards on the supply side as the result of co-operative co-ordination between rival innovators and as part of the process of introduction, diffusion and selection of new technologies. The economics of standards and the economics of technological change seem to be so intertwined that they cannot be separated.

De facto standards are the outcome of the emergence of standardisation clubs: membership in a standardisation club entails both gains and costs for firms and can be passive and active. Active membership involves dedicated efforts to specify new standards; passive membership consists of the efforts necessary to adopt the specific requirements of standards that have been designed by active members. In both cases, the standards and their specifications emerge out of each firm's balanced decision process of whether to adhere to the standardisation club or remain out of it. Such a decision, in turn, depends on a variety of factors that this simple model of club membership should help to clarify.

According to our approach to localised technological knowledge and change, we model the aggregate market for new similar products as a collection of niches, each with its own negatively sloped market demand where each innovator is a local monopolist (Greenstein, 1990). Let us assume that two identical firms have introduced, at the same time, rival product innovations that perform similar functions in two independent market niches. As innovators, the two firms enjoy the advantages of lead times and barriers to entry and are transient monopolists in their respective niche markets. Their identical costs and demand functions are respectively:

$$CT_1 = A + b\,(Q1) \tag{1}$$

$$CT_2 = A + b\,(Q2) \tag{2}$$

$$P_1 = B - d\,(Q1) \tag{3}$$

$$P_2 = B - d\,(Q2) \tag{4}$$

Their total profits will be determined, according to the usual maximisation procedures, by the price-output combination where marginal costs (dCT) equal the marginal revenue (dRT):

$$dCT_i = dRT_i \quad (i = 1,2) \tag{5}$$

The decision to standardise rests on n assessing the effects of four different sets of changes:

1   The effects on the total costs of each monopolist of the producer switching costs that are necessary to meet the changes, with respect to their 'natural' design, to manufacture and deliver a new product based upon a common standard;
2   The amount of sponsoring costs required to elaborate and establish the technical specifications of a standard;
3   The effects on the demand for the new standardised product for each firm with respect to the two independent demand curves;
4   Whether these changes are symmetric for the two firms or induce asymmetric costs and demand-share conditions.

In order to assess these issues we have to explore the product space into which the firms are localised. The simplest product space can be thought of as monodimensional, in which firms are distributed linearly along a segment. Their products reflect the specifications of their production processes, their primary and intermediate inputs, and the localised character of their learning processes. The distance of each firm from the others measures the extent to which each firm has to modify this set of production specifications in order to manufacture and deliver a product that respects the standards. Consequently, that distance also measures the amount of producer switching costs that each firm has to expend in order to assimilate the technical specifications of its products to those of the others (von Weizsäcker, 1984).

The adoption of a standard implies some producer switching costs: and the more localised the production process and innovation capabilities of each firm in a narrow area of the product space, the larger the producer switching costs. Such producer switching costs are both actual and perspective: a firm that adopts a standard not only changes the product specifications which were closer to its own localised knowledge, but also loses the opportunity to enhance its learning capability and hence its capacity to generate potentially higher productivity levels and new product innovations. The higher the producer switching costs, the more irreversible are the location decisions in the product space (Eaton and Lipsey, 1978).

Producer switching costs (SW) for each firm can be modelled as a function of the distance between the vector of the technological characteristics of the standard (a) and the vector of the characteristics of the localised technology (b):

$$SW_i = s(a - b) \tag{6}$$

The technological distance (a − b) between the standardised technology and the localised technology can in turn be identified as the geometric distance between the technical point representing the standard (a) and the technical point representing the localised technology (b) in a simple technique space with two technical characteristics (X, Y):

$$d(a - b) = ((X_a - X_b)^2 + (Y_a - Y_b)^2)^{1/2} \tag{7}$$

In such a context the relative localisation of the proposed standard, with respect to the boundaries of the original product space, is an important consideration: the closer the standard to the specifications of a particular firm the lower the producer switching costs for that firm.

Sponsoring costs matter when the firms are actively involved in the definition of the technical specifications of the standards: a firm that does not participate in the definition of a standard, but only adopts it, has no elaboration, and little opportunity to influence the standard. In this case the emerging standard is likely to be 'distant' from its 'natural' design. The first result of our analysis should make clear the alternatives between passive and active membership in a standardisation club. A trade off emerges: a firm that adopts a *de facto* standard has no sponsoring costs, but higher producer switching costs and *vice versa*.

On the demand side, we assume that the introduction of a voluntary standard makes it possible for potential users to take advantage of lower transaction costs, larger choice sets and network externalities. Users of a standardised product have lower transaction costs in assessing their quality and product characteristics, so they can devote their revenue exclusively to actually purchasing the products. Without product standards an important share of consumer revenue would be expended in assessing the characteristics of the products. A standardised product has lower search costs.

Compatibility standards are especially relevant for products that are part of broader technological systems. Compatibility increases the number of systems that can be operated with a given component and the number of components that can be used with a given system. Compatibility standards consequently increase both component variety and system variety (Matutes and Regibeau, 1987). The value for consumers of products that are compatible because of standards, is also enhanced by the effects of network externalities, for each user will have more opportunities to interface its products with other complementary products. In this case the stock and the aggregate demand for the compatible product enter the utility function of each consumer and consumers' demand becomes interdependent (Rohlfs, 1974; Allen, 1988).

The final demand of households and the derived demand of firms, for products that are standardised, with respects to both their quality, performance and compatibility with other complementary products, is likely to be much larger and more elastic, Such a demand is an important incentive for a firm when deciding to adhere to a standard. We are now in a position to consider the effects of standardisation for the two innovating monopolists on both cost curves and demand curves. Their cost curves will be higher, both because of sponsoring costs and producer switching costs. They will be symmetrical if the standard is equidistant from each firm and both share the sponsoring costs. Cost curves may be steeper because of competition in the same markets for intermediate inputs and skilled labour, which the two firms originally purchased in two distinct markets. The new demand curve is now larger than the sum of the two previous demand curves, but is also shared by the two firms.

The distribution of demand shares, purchasing costs, sponsoring costs and producer switching costs among the two firms is significant in determining the outcome of the standardisation process. Let us analyse the perfectly symmetric case with two identical firms who elaborate a standard that is perfectly equidistant from the two original product specifications, so that the two firms face the same levels of purchasing costs and producer switching costs in order to adhere to the standard, and the same amount of sponsoring costs in order to establish the technical specifications of the standard itself. We assume they are able to collude perfectly and symmetrically share the outcome of the standardisation process. The new cost curves will be:

$$CT_1 = SC_1 + SW_1 + A + b'(Q) \tag{8}$$

$$CT_2 = SC_2 + SW_2 + A + b'(Q) \tag{9}$$

where SC are the sponsoring costs, SW are the producer switching costs, and b' are augmented purchasing costs for intermediary inputs in markets where supply curves have a positive slope.

Because of network externalities and revenue effects, determined by lower information and transaction costs, the new demand for the two firms is now expressed by one higher curve with a larger price elasticity:[7]

$$P = W - w(Q) \tag{10}$$

with respect to the demand curves (3) and (4), we assume here that $W > (2B)$ and $w < (2d)$. If the two firms decide to share the new demand symmetrically they will collude and operate on the market place as a cartel. Hence, the standardisation club model opens the door to co-operation and co-ordination designed to regulate the production, pricing and marketing of goods. Now the profits will be defined as the outcome of the maximisation of revenues stemming from the combined cost curves of the two firms with the given common demand curve:

$$dCTT = dRT \tag{11}$$

where CTT are the total costs of the cartel. It is evident that the total profits of the cartel may be higher than the sum of the profits of the two independent monopolists, but they also may not be: the effects in the changes of price-output combinations within a monopolistic market structure are highly unpredictable. Cartel profits will be larger, not only if the new demand curve is sufficiently larger to offset the increase in costs but also, and, most importantly, if the new equilibrium point on average costs is further from the price.

Our analysis now indicates that standardisation will occur only when the profitability of the new market structure is larger than that of the two separate market niches. Sponsoring and producer switching costs must be lower than the incremental revenue from standardisation, in other words, the lower the technological variety of firms, the greater the chances of standardisation. Equally, the effects on the slope of marginal costs created by increased competition in intermediary markets should be smaller than the reduction in the slope of aggregate demand. Economies of scale and learning affect the manufacturing cost curves: standardisation is more likely when the positive slope of the new aggregate supply curve in the equilibrium quantity is smaller than each of the supply curves of the two firms. With regard to the demand curves and the likelihood of standardisation, the new aggregate demand curve should not only be higher but also more elastic than the previous ones; and the aggregation of the two demand curves should have no effect on the monopolistic control of the cartel on the market.

The transformation of the standardisation club into a cartel by the two participating firms enhances the standardisation process generally as well as maximising joint profits. If we also consider increasing returns in production as incentives to the formation of standardisation clubs, then timing becomes relevant. When returns are determined by learning economies in the form of an L-shaped, long-term cost curve, i.e. strongly affecting the slope of average costs only in the early stages of production, the window for standard setting is reduced to the time-span along which learning economies display their effects; after this period, the incentive to join a club declines.

The collusive and monopolistic behaviour of the standardisation club is an important condition that requires additional consideration: if the two firms are unable to transform the standardisation club into a cartel, the risks that standardisation does not take place are higher and the chances of this are increased when we relax the simplifying assumption that only two firms enter the club and the cartel first. It is clear that the larger the number of firms involved the lower the chances that such a cartel may be obstructed by regulatory interventions or impeded by the opportunistic behaviour of each member. Thus, the fewer members, the larger the chances that standardisation takes place. Larger differences in the cost and demand functions of firms reduces the chances; under such conditions, it is more likely that an explicit profit-sharing agreement will be required (Fellner, 1949; Phillips, 1962).

All of these considerations lead us to a more realistic hypothesis; that the firms are able to agree upon the definition of a standard but are unable or impeded in transforming the standardisation club into a cartel. The firms now operate in the new market place as oligopolists and their essential behaviour can be analysed by means of the traditional Cournot model.

In a Cournot model of duopoly the larger the number of firms, the lower the equilibrium price and accordingly the profits. Now the equilibrium conditions imply that:

$$dP_1/dQ_1 = dR_1/dQ_1 - dC_1/dQ_1 = 0$$
$$dP_2/dQ_2 = dR_2/dQ_2 - dC_2/dQ_2 = 0$$

(12)

The Cournot equilibrium conditions for firms in an oligopolistic market enable us to consider a variety of asymmetric effects: those of the original conditions of the firms, which may now differ in size and efficiency; those between the firms, in terms of economies of scale and learning; those associated with standardisation, i.e. differentiated purchasing costs, producer switching costs and sponsoring costs; and those related to different cross-demand elasticities.

The distribution of localised innovators in the product space exerts a significant influence here. While a homogeneous distribution has no effect on the creation of asymmetries, it is clear that any two players that happen to be co-localised in the same product space have lower producer switching costs in adhering to a common standard, and lower sponsoring costs because the two products are already very close. Co-localised players are likely to become core members of any standardisation club quickly. Our analysis further indicates that the larger the extent to which firms rely on tacit and localised knowledge in introducing innovations, the larger the producer switching costs; consequently, the chances of the rapid introduction of standards in an innovation system are enhanced as the role of codified knowledge increases.

Each firm will still join the standardisation club only if the expected profits in the new oligopolistic market are larger than those from its smaller monopolistic niche. Because of the asymmetries that are now allowed, though, some firms will be earning more profits than before, and others less: the extent of the larger profits, however, depends on the membership decisions of those firms with lower profits. The slope and position of the demand curve is determined by the membership of all the firms. This has two more implications for the emergence of standardisation clubs. As incentives to join clubs, side-payments, from core members to potential marginal members, appear in a variety of forms, such as reductions in sponsoring costs, the development of standards in order to reduce the amount of producer switching costs for marginal members, and privileged access conditions to input markets. Beneath this interaction lies another incentive structure, that which originally induces core members to allow either active marginal membership, involving interference with the definition of standards (to lower the producer switching costs of the new members), or passive membership, where marginal members can adopt but not influence standards.

Full appreciation of cost asymmetries between firms, as determined by switching costs, highlights the dynamics of *de facto* standards. *De facto* standards can emerge in the market place when imitators decide to enter adopting the standard introduced by innovators: here, however, innovators do not bear the costs of switching from their own original design. Under such conditions producer switching costs, as sunk costs, become a source of barriers to entry, and limit pricing for innovators. Former monopolistic innovators can react to this entry, by fixing the market price for their products where demand equals the long-term average costs for new competitors, who also bear producer switching costs. Formally, we see that:

$$P_L = P_C(1 + E)$$
$$CT_m = A + SW_m + b(Q)$$
$$CT_i = A' + b'(Q) \tag{13}$$
$$P_Q = Z - z(Q)$$
$$E = (CT_m - CT_i)/Q_e$$

where P_L is limit price, P_C is the competitive price, E is the premium for the established firm; CT_i is the cost curve of the innovator, CT_m is the cost curve of the imitator, SW_m are the producer switching costs for imitators, P_Q is the demand curve for the standardised product, and Q_e is the equilibrium demand with limit price.

From equation (13) it would appear that the higher the levels of producer switching costs for imitators and the greater the equilibrium demand (and the smaller the slope of the demand curve), the higher the profits for innovators. However, *de facto* standards are convenient for both innovators and early imitators when production exhibits increasing returns, demand increases over diffusion curves and is characterised by network externalities, and entry occurs sequentially. The shift of the demand curve towards the right, augmented by network externalities, encourages the innovator and the first imitators to take advantage of larger markets with an even larger price elasticity. Limit prices remain at a higher level, taking into account the larger production costs of *late* imitators. Clearly, there is a strong incentive for incumbents, as early innovators, to select highly idiosyncratic, dominant designs for their products which are eventually likely to become *de facto* standards, in order to maximise the producer switching costs, for their potential and actual competitors, and hence barriers to entry, limit prices and profits.

Standards that emerge in the market place are likely to be strongly influenced by a path-dependent market process, where they represent the idiosyncratic and irreversible dominant designs of early innovators, and are specified under the influence of product rivalry in conditions far away from competitive equilibria. With significant and non-recoverable relocation costs in the product space, Hotelling's principle of minimal differentiation does not apply, and a sub-optimal variety of standards is likely to persist (Hotelling, 1929; Eaton and Lipsey, 1978).

Within this oligopolistic arena the intervention of public authorities able to reduce sponsoring costs and to establish mandatory standards is likely to be beneficial only to the extent that standardisation was previously impeded by the effects of sponsoring costs. Mandatory standards, especially at the international level, which oblige firms to adhere to a common standard, can generate considerable switching costs and a reduction in welfare even if they lead to reductions in market prices. However, mandatory standards in intermediate markets are likely to generate a large net welfare gain if the effects of price reduction in upstream markets offer important, positive, technological externalities favouring the diffusion of innovations in that industry, and pecuniary externalities in downstream industries that use the standardised input in their own production processes.

Conclusions

Standards emerge under circumstances of rival co-operation, technological change and monopolistic competition, where behaviour is necessarily out-of-equilibrium. As a result, standardisation, even without increasing returns, is a highly path-dependent process. The eventual technical features of standards, and their final distribution across the original variety of products and production processes, depend upon a number of identifiable factors: the sequence of actual events; the characters of the original localised technological knowledge; the resources necessary to introduce new technological innovations and their irreversibility, and the nature of the market structures. In particular, the outcome of the standardisation process is determined by the specific and highly idiosyncratic effects of producer switching costs stemming from non-recoverable and irreversible resources invested in the accumulation of localised knowledge and localised technologies (David, 1992a and b; David, 1993a).

Consequently, each standard is by no means necessarily the best possible technical specification from a given set of technical and economic alternatives. Rather it reflects the complexity of the environment and the behaviour of agents in their ability to decipher and order both that environment and the balance of forces between themselves and other players (North, 1991).

In this approach, standards are viewed as part of a more general process of institutional and technological change where the behaviour of firms is influenced by their original location in the product space, the characteristics of the market structure and the economic environment, and it is not limited to price-output adjustments.

A much wider field of action exists consisting of the generation of technological knowledge and the introduction of technological innovations, organisational changes and the elaboration of new institutions. Hence, like other factors in the overall general process of technological change, standardisation can be viewed itself as a process of recursive structural change, where firms adjust to a given set of structural features with, on the one hand, traditional price-output changes and, on the other, the generation of new knowledge and the introduction of technological and organisational innovations (Phillips, 1970).

On the supply side, we have seen that the outcome of the standardisation process is strongly influenced by a specific set of productive and technological characteristics such as:

1   the technological diversity of firms;
2   the localised character of the innovation processes, and consequently the extent to which firms rely on tacit rather than codified knowledge, either internal or external;
3   the levels of irreversible and non-recoverable producer switching costs necessary to adopt a new standard;
4   the distribution of the firms in the product space in terms of relative density;
5   the role of increasing returns in production in terms of economies of scale and learning economies;

6   the ability of core members of potential standardisation clubs to fund side-payments in order to encourage or exclude marginal members;

7   the actual number of innovating firms that have introduced products likely to be standardised;

8   the timing of standardisation efforts;

9   the active role of public authorities to establish mandatory standards or help standardisation committees by lowering sponsoring costs;

10   the effects of externalities in terms of internal gains.

The long-term effects of standards, in terms of lower levels of transaction costs, higher levels of specialisation, more effective division of labour, higher levels of receptivity and connectivity among firms and higher rates of diffusion, appear to be distinctive features of national systems of innovation (Nelson, 1993). In addition, they go a long way towards explaining the differentiated capability of countries to generate technological knowledge and achieve higher levels of productivity.

The retreat of firms into small monopolistic niches, dictated by the prevailing role of localised knowledge and related irreversibilities in terms of producer switching costs, impedes adherence to standards but also prevents firms from taking advantage of the larger opportunities to generate further technological innovations offered by new scientific break-throughs. Conversely, the initial push exerted by the positive feedback of the standardisation processes may prevent firms from being locked into the specific limits of their localised knowledge. As another example of the Schumpeterian trade off between static and dynamic efficiency, positive feedback between standards and access to codified knowledge should make for a successful standardisation process.

11 New information technology and the knowledge-based economy

The European evidence

At this point in the study we are in a position to discuss the empirical effects of the interaction between new information and communication technology and the knowledge-intensive business service industry. The general outcome of such an interaction, that is the development of a veritable knowledge-based economy, has already been elaborated and illustrated in previous chapters (in particular Chapters 2 and 8). New information technology affects both the operational conditions of information – from access to process – and the characteristics of the information itself – its separability and tradeability. Taken together this means structural change, i.e. the creation of a knowledge economy based on the information-intensity of a good (or service) or its production: the flow of generation of new knowledge and introduction of new technologies regenerates itself via the continuous generation, introduction and diffusion of information.

Knowledge-intensive business services are the main medium of this recursive process; and in turn are also influenced and improved by it. As well as offering access to existing, codified scientific information, these service firms provide the interface between the tacit knowledge and competence of individual firms, thus enabling the continual and accumulated production of technological and organisational innovation, including new information technologies.

As we have seen, the overarching tendency is towards specialisation and co-operation in the production of knowledge. Receptivity and connectivity in the communication system are actively built up, creating a fully-operational, 'percolating' information network. The development of the economy, aided by appropriate public intervention and private activity, is characterised by new markets increasingly specific to the environment of the individual firm, an associated increase in the social division of labour, rising revenues from rising numbers of information exchanges, higher levels of information appropriability, and new systems of co-operation between private businesses and public institutions such as universities and research centres. Overall productivity growth is the expected net result.

The effective capability of a knowledge system – i.e. the ability of a firm or industry to generate cost-effective technological innovation – is dependent on the implementation of new information and communication technology via the operations of knowledge-intensive business services.

This chapter empirically assesses two fundamental hypotheses of the knowledge-based economy. The first section outlines the argument of these hypotheses, articulating the productivity-enhancing function of communication and business services. The main part of the chapter, the second section, presents the empirical data and illustrates the fairly convincing evidence in support of the assumptions, with regard to the European economy at the end of the 1980s. The conclusion confirms the positive results of this examination of the knowledge economy and the influence of new information technology via communication and business services, under a recognisable and explicable situation of disequilibrium.

The hypotheses

Having established the fundamental dynamics of the process, our basic argument can now be articulated. The aggregate effects of the diffusion of information and communication technology are likely to accelerate the parallel diffusion of knowledge-intensive business services; and together, in turn, these should enhance the innovative capability of agents and systems via increased interaction between the different knowledge components. Completing the dynamic circuit, enhanced innovative capacity means accelerating the rates of introduction and diffusion of new information technologies (Petit, 1988; Brousseau, Petit and Phan, 1996).

Consequently, we expect to see a systemic correlation between the rates of penetration of both new information and communication technologies, and business services, and the rates of introduction of new technological and organisational innovations, as measured by the rates of growth of total factor productivity. In accordance with the general analysis outlined so far, with respect to the European economy, we intend to provide some empirical evidence in support of two essential hypotheses:

1   The co-evolution of the usage of communication and business services, that is correlation between the levels and rates of growth of the use of communication and business services, respectively;
2   The productivity-enhancing effects of this co-evolution, that is correlation between the rates of growth of the use of communication and business services and the rates of growth of total factor productivity.

The empirical evidence

The data

Input/output tables offer a valuable set of data from which the amount of services provided by the communication service industry and the business service industry, can be extracted respectively, in relation to the rest of the economic system, articulated in terms of industries (See Appendix on Chapter 11).

Tables 11.1–4 show the distribution of the intensities of communication and business services with respect to value added in Italy, Germany, France and UK. The data shows that communication services account for a marginal share of value added (c/av) in all countries and sectors, ranging from low values in the region of 0.5% in most manufacturing industries, to high values of 3% in many service sectors, such as hotel and catering, credit and insurance, transport, trade and actual business services themselves. The

Table 11.1 The distribution of communications and business services intensity in the Italian economy in 1985 and 1988

Italy sectors	c/av % (1988)	c/av % (1985)	bs/av % 1988	bs/av % 1985
1 Agriculture	.030	.030	.750	.200
2 Energy	1.217	.777	1.352	1.084
3 Minerals	3.196	4.020	19.255	20.272
4 Clay & Glass	2.417	2.523	13.377	13.288
5 Chemicals	2.805	3.067	15.755	16.029
6 Metal products	2.504	2.214	18.121	15.677
7 Machinery	2.441	2.401	11.458	10.079
8 Precision & informatics	2.786	2.962	16.092	14.370
9 Electrical machinery	1.484	1.538	12.997	12.176
10 Motor vehicles	1.859	1.851	10.667	9.776
11 Ships & aeronautics	1.512	1.160	9.897	7.372
12 Meat & products	.773	.982	13.134	14.705
13 Milk & products	1.499	1.680	15.307	15.139
14 Other food industries	1.662	1.469	14.865	13.934
15 Drinks	1.232	1.287	17.036	14.567
16 Tobacco	.049	.145	3.816	6.934
17 Textiles & Apparel	2.405	.240	16.011	14.051
18 Leather & shoes	1.426	1.424	14.578	12.865
19 Wood & furniture	2.144	2.055	18.070	15.243
20 Pulp, paper & printing	2.840	2.898	15.175	12.912
21 Rubber & plastics	1.767	1.564	9.410	8.243
22 Other manufacturing	2.242	2.404	19.931	20.127
23 Building	.511	.490	9.960	9.520
24 Repair and maintenance	2.950	2.410	33.186	33.237
25 Wholesale & retail	1.587	1.478	44.075	37.503
26 Lodging & catering	1.422	1.371	25.957	19.840
27 Inland transportation	.839	.241	19.065	12.082
28 Sea & air transportation	3.948	3.091	20.413	16.731
29 Other transportation	4.076	3.619	3.980	3.762
30 Communications services	3.464	2.614	27.945	37.590
31 Credit & insurance services	2.700	1.840	44.320	39.980
32 Business services	2.040	1.970	39.870	38.760

Table 11.2 The distribution of communications and business services intensity in the German economy in 1986 and 1990

Germany sectors	c/av 1986	c/av 1990	bs/av 1986	bs/av 1990
1 01/Agricultural, forestry and fishing	.323	.339	4.035	3.919
2 06/Coal, petroleum and gas	.753	.801	7.983	10.413
3 13/Ferrous & non-ferrous products	.643	.719	15.021	20.511
4 15/Non-metallic and mineral products	.904	.874	17.405	21.970
5 17/Chemicals and pharmaceuticals	1.367	1.486	21.183	24.675
6 19/Metal products	1.485	1.536	12.285	16.740
7 21/Machinery	1.755	2.185	14.703	22.656
8 23/Office equipment	2.087	1.909	28.391	30.597
9 25/Electrical machinery	.670	.674	10.959	15.048
10 28/Transport equipment	.476	.610	16.344	23.358
11 36/Food beverages and tobacco	.977	1.242	16.779	27.042
12 42/Textiles, clothing, leather products	2.128	2.511	16.002	25.260
13 47/Paper and printing products	1.051	1.126	9.802	15.028
14 49/Rubber and plastic products	1.170	1.125	15.140	18.790
15 48/Other manufacturing industries	1.426	1.628	13.221	20.184
16 53/Building	1.363	1.566	13.226	18.780
17 56/Repair and wholesale & retail	2.278	1.992	10.829	11.839
18 59/Hotel and catering services	2.884	3.081	8.531	15.403
19 61/Domestic transportation	2.777	2.678	8.240	9.518
20 67/Communication	1.428	2.064	.171	.587
21 69a/Credit & insurance	1.983	1.709	17.538	19.422
22 74/Business services	.737	.746	9.806	14.087
23 86/Non-market services	1.474	1.402	5.551	8.136

share of business services to value added (bs/av) is much larger everywhere; on average accounting for a value of 15% in most sectors.

Specifically, we see that in Germany the ratio of communication services to value added was 1.23% in 1986 and 1.39% in 1990, while the ratio of business services to value added increased from 14.9% to 15.5%. In the United Kingdom, the ratio of telecommunication services to value added actually declined from 1.12% to 1.02% in 1990, while the cost share of business services in the same time interval rose from 16.6% to 19.3%. Finally, in France, the cost share of communication services over value added increased from 0.89% to 0.95% and the ratio of business services to value added increased from 14.1% to 16.3%. In assessing the evolution of the cost share of communication services, the sharp increase in the capability of transmission equipment in telecommunications due to the increasing share of data communication should be taken into consideration, resulting in an effective reduction of the hedonic prices for telecommunication services.

On such a basis the amounts of communication services and business services purchased by each industry may be converted into intensities in terms of the percentage ratio of input to value added (respectively c/av and

Table 11.3 The distribution of communications and business services intensity in the French economy in 1986 and 1990

France sectors	c/av 1990	c/av 1986	bs/av 1990	bs/av 1986
1 01/Agricultural, forestry and fishing	.040	.030	1.618	1.649
2 06/Coal, petroleum and gas	.657	.629	13.260	8.615
3 13/Ferrous & non-ferrous products	1.606	1.309	4.774	3.121
4 15/Non-metallic and mineral products	.271	.252	13.917	10.160
5 17/Chemicals and pharmaceuticals	2.400	1.952	20.764	18.964
6 19/Metal products	2.913	2.633	8.148	5.086
7 21/Machinery	1.618	1.394	47.382	38.350
8 23/Office equipment	2.981	2.743	19.705	15.618
9 25/Electrical machinery	1.441	1.281	21.048	17.778
10 28/Transport equipment	1.306	1.363	32.319	19.966
11 36/Food beverages and tobacco	1.056	.967	25.292	17.496
12 42/Textiles, clothing, leather products	1.273	1.184	21.589	14.985
13 47/Paper and printing products	2.755	2.630	20.835	14.139
14 49/Rubber and plastic products	1.163	1.070	30.859	19.964
15 48/Other manufacturing industries	2.101	1.916	17.848	14.290
16 53/Building	.966	.861	37.306	25.640
17 56/Repair and wholesale & retail	1.737	1.655	6.180	4.192
18 59/Hotel and catering services	1.118	1.034	8.509	5.457
19 61/Inland transport	.998	.944	5.525	3.940
20 67/Maritime and sea transport	1.920	1.926	26.653	20.730
21 65/Auxilliary activities	.457	.413	5.844	4.219
22 67/Communication	2.652	2.183	2.617	2.829
23 69a/Credit & insurance	3.153	4.640	31.882	18.916
24 74/Business services	2.732	2.767	12.976	9.151
25 86/Non-market services	1.459	1.430	4.687	4.169

bs/av in Tables 11.1–4). This will give an understanding of the cost share of these services and their effects on the productivity of the users. The levels and changes in the usage of these key services can be used as dummies for assessing the dynamics of receptivity and connectivity, which are enhanced by the very diffusion of communication and business services respectively; and in turn, such dynamics accelerate the rate of introduction of localised innovations in organisation and production processes, and hence the growth of total factor productivity. According to the evidence and the analysis so far, we maintain that the levels of usage of communication and business services by firms in the European economy are an indicator of the technological and organisational capability of the different industries. We now wish to test the hypothesis that the diffusion of communications and business services within the European economy is associated with an increase in total factor productivity.[1]

Table 11.4 The distribution of communications and business services intensity in the British economy in 1984 and 1990

UK sectors		c/av 1984	c/av 1990	bs/av 1984	bs/av 1990
1	Coal mining	1.649	.481	7.113	9.183
2	Petroleum and gas	•	•	•	•
3	Metal ore mining	0	•	16.667	•
4	Other mining	.227	.980	5.000	4.314
5	Food products	.622	.667	8.609	10.099
6	Beverages	.879	.643	11.905	11.340
7	Tobacco	.467	.301	12.336	6.541
8	Textiles	.957	.863	4.858	9.391
9	Clothes	.884	.916	3.979	6.947
10	Leather products	1.071	1.000	3.571	12.333
11	Footwear	.577	.845	4.038	6.901
12	Wood products	1.624	1.333	7.094	10.278
13	Furniture, fixtures	1.176	1.059	8.162	11.451
14	Paper and products	1.045	.933	7.351	9.733
15	Printing, publishing	2.876	2.909	7.819	18.555
16	Industrial chemicals	.869	1.071	6.802	9.887
17	Other chem. products	.629	.635	7.614	7.904
18	Petroleum refineries	.305	.484	8.244	5.565
19	Rubber products	.980	.651	6.667	6.095
20	Plastic products	1.126	.931	7.117	9.113
21	Pottery, china, etc	1.132	1.098	6.038	6.585
22	Glass and products	.845	.769	7.042	7.436
23	Non-metal products	.748	.791	4.829	6.759
24	Iron and steel	.421	.265	4.142	7.263
25	Non-ferrous metals	.769	.577	5.983	10.705
26	Metal products	1.439	1.082	7.888	11.320
27	Machinery	1.357	1.068	6.776	9.674
28	Electrical machinery	1.153	1.214	6.886	10.335
29	Transport equipment	.653	.512	5.814	9.303
30	Professional goods	1.463	1.561	7.073	8.341
31	Other industries	4.043	1.218	8.723	7.756
32	Electricity, gas	1.270	1.199	4.920	2.854
33	Water works	1.181	1.154	4.173	4.375

Evidence of the co-evolution of usage of business and communication services in Europe

The dynamic interaction of new information and communication technology and knowledge-intensive business services enables the generation and diffusion of a growing variety of goods and services to an equally increasing range of remote users. We foresee a strong association between both the levels and the rates of growth of communication and business services across the main sectors and industries of the European economy. Specifically, the larger the usage intensity of communication services, the larger the use of business services.

The first part of this hypothesis, regarding levels of usage, can easily be specified as follows:

$$BS/AV = a + b \ (C/AV) \tag{1}$$

where C/AV measures the intensity of communication services purchased by each industry with respect to value added, and BS/AV the intensity of business services, in 1988 for Italy and 1990 for the United Kingdom, Germany, and France.

The econometric test yields a strong positive result for all the countries:

$$BS/AV = 0.047 + 3.382 \ (COM/AV) \tag{2.1. ITALY}$$
$$(10.211)$$

R^2 0.781; F = 104.258; (Student t-values in parentheses)

$$BS/AV = 0.247 + 2.885 \ (C/AV) \tag{2.2. UK}$$
$$(8.211)$$

R^2 0.881; F = 124.212; (Student t-values in parentheses)

$$BS/AV = 0.168 + 3.312 \ (C/AV) \tag{2.3. DEU}$$
$$(9.901)$$

R^2 0.741; F = 104.867; (Student t-values in parentheses)

$$BS/AV = 0.297 + 2.966 \ (C/AV) \tag{2.4. FRA}$$
$$(12.311)$$

R^2 0.901; F = 96.578; (Student t-values in parentheses)

These results confirm that the levels of usage of communications and business services were strongly related in the European economy at the end of the 1980s.

The second part of the hypothesis asserts that the rates of growth in the intensity of communications services led to, or are significantly associated with, the growth of the intensity of business services. Actually, the causal link can easily work both ways: increased use of new technology, in the form of information and communication technologies, enables greater and more efficient market access for business services, which in turn propagates that new technology, facilitating and encouraging the generation of more. The hypothesis can be specified as follows:

$$\log \ (BS_t/BS_{t-1}) = a + b \log \ (C_t/C_{t-1}) \tag{3}$$

where C_t, C_{t-1}, BS_t and BS_{t-1} are the natural logarithms of the growth rates of the use of communications and business services in each of the industries, respectively, retained between the years 1985 and 1988 for Italy, 1984 and 1990 for the United Kingdom, and 1986 and 1990 for Germany and France. The logarithmic specification of equation (3) enables us to read the outcome of the econometric test directly in terms of elasticity, so that b measures the elasticity of the growth in the use of business services in relation to the growth in communications services. Once again, the results of the econometric test are very clear:

$$\log (BS_t/BS_{t-1}) = 6.227 + 0.607 \log (C_t/C_{t-1}) \qquad \text{(4.1. ITALY)}$$
$$(8.819)$$

R^2 0.733; F = 77.771; (Student t-values in parentheses)

$$\log (BS_t/BS_{t-1}) = -3.705 + 0.789 \log (C_t/C_{t-1}) \qquad \text{(4.2. UK)}$$
$$(9.819)$$

R^2 0.739; F = 57.987; (Student t-values in parentheses)

$$\log (BS_t/BS_{t-1}) = -9.905 + 0.753 \log (C_t/C_{t-1}) \qquad \text{(4.3. DEU)}$$
$$(7.908)$$

R^2 0.813; F = 71.951; (Student t-values in parentheses)

$$\log (BS_t/BS_{t-1}) = -6.535 + 0.831 \log (C_t/C_{t-1}) \qquad \text{(4.4. FRA)}$$
$$(8.115)$$

R^2 0.782; F = 77.549; (Student t-values in parentheses)

The results are important on two accounts: first, they show that the econometric link between the growth in the usage of communications services and the growth in the usage of business services is statistically very strong. The two variables exhibit a strong correlation value. Second, and most important, the large estimated value of b, the elasticity parameter, in equations (4.1.)–(4.4.) suggests that growth in the usage of business services is strongly stimulated by growth in the usage of communications services.

The productivity effects of the co-evolution of usage between communications and business services: the residual hypothesis. The Italian evidence.

According to our approach, firms' ability to implement new networking technology, via communications and business services, has a significant influence on the general efficiency of the production process.

In an initial attempt to assess empirically the use of communications and business services as an indicator of the introduction of new localised technologies we used the well-known residual methodology. This consists of estimating the residual of a standard growth accounting procedure, based on the standard evaluation of the direct effect on output growth of all increases in capital stock and labour force. The residual of output growth, that is the portion of output growth 'not explained' by the increase of the two fundamental factors, may be attributed to factors increasing general efficiency levels, as well as to errors in the measurement of the proper contribution of capital and labour (Griliches, 1979 and 1995). If we then assume that the spread of communications and business services is a reliable indicator of both the introduction of new technology and its positive effects on general efficiency, then the residual may be 'explained' in terms of that diffusion process. It is clear that there is no justification for considering that the residual of the empirical estimation of the production function is due solely to the diffusion of communications and business services. For our purposes, however, it is sufficient to assess the diffusion of such services as a sign of a more general process of modernisation and hence of innovative capability; and as one factor, among others, in the actual increase of total factor productivity.

Formally this argument leads to the following equation:

$$Y_i(t) = A_i(t) \ (K_i(t)^a \ L_i(t)^b) \tag{5}$$

where Y is the output of the *i*th firm in terms of value added at time *t*; K is the capital used by the *i*th firm; L is the labour used by the *i*th firm at time *t*; A is the general efficiency parameter; and a and b are the output elasticity of the capital and labour of the *i*th industry, respectively. With some calculation, total differentiation of equation (5) leads to:

$$(dY/dt) \ / \ Y = (dA/dt) \ / \ A + a(dK/dt) \ / \ K + b(dL/dt) \ / \ L \tag{6}$$

The residual generated by the empirical estimate of equation (6) may be considered a reliable proxy for the value of *dA/dt*, which is considered to be a dependent variable of BCS, that is the diffusion of communications and business services:

$$dA/dt = f(dBCS/dt) \tag{7}$$

Using this methodology, an initial econometric estimate of the productivity-enhancing effects of an increase in the usage of communications and business services can be made as follows. The econometric specification of equation (6) is:

$$Y(1985/1988) = a + b \ K(1985/1988) + c \ L(1985/1988) \tag{8}$$

where Y is the natural logarithm of the relative growth in real terms of value added in the years 1985–1988 for the thirty-two sectors available; K is the natural logarithm of the relative increase of capital (estimated from investments) in the years 1986–88; L is the natural logarithm of the relative increase in real terms of total labour costs in the years 1985 and 1988.

The OLS estimates of equation (8) provide satisfactory results:

$$Y(1985/1988) = 3.945 + 0.516\,K(1985/1988) + 0.473\,L(1985/1988) \qquad (9)$$
$$(3.389) \qquad\qquad (7.479)$$

$R^2 = 0.749$; F = 47.162;
(Student t-values in parentheses)

The residuals were calculated and their distribution across the sectors may be considered a proxy for that portion of output growth unaccounted for by the two established production factors. It therefore represents an indicator of the 'unexplained residual', also seen as the outcome of the increase in the general efficiency of the production process that occurred between 1985 and 1988. As stated already, the subsequent idea is that the diffusion of communications and business services is a reliable indication of the level of introduction of new technology and innovation.

Because of the strong correlation between the diffusion of both services, it is impossible to obtain reliable estimates of their joint effect on the residual. We thus specified the following two distinct regression equations, one for each group of services:

$$RE = a + b\,d\mathrm{COM}/dt\ (1985/1988) \tag{10}$$

$$RE = a + b\,d\mathrm{BS}/dt\ (1985/1988) \tag{11}$$

where RE are the residuals from the estimate of the production function of equation (9) and $d\mathrm{COM}/dt$ (1985–1988) and $d\mathrm{BS}/dt$ (1985–1988) are the natural logarithms of the increase in the levels of usage of communications and business services, respectively, in the years considered across the thirty two sectors. The results of the OLS estimates of equations (10) and (11) are as follows:

$$RE = -1.39 + 0.128\,d\mathrm{COM}/dt\ (1985/1988) \tag{12}$$
$$(2.196)$$

$R^2 = 0.116$; F = 4.823;
(Student t-values in parentheses)

$$RE = -1.717 + 0.135\,d\mathrm{BS}/dt\ (1985/1988) \tag{13}$$
$$(1.852)$$

$R^2 = 0.083$; F = 3.433;
(Student t-values in parentheses)

The independent variables perform quite well statistically. On the basis of these results we may assume that a significant portion of the residuals was strongly associated with the diffusion of communications and business services in the years considered.

A more direct assessment of the 'causal' relationship between the diffusion of communications and business services and the increase in the levels of output is provided by the econometric estimate of a 'technology production function' (Griliches, 1979). Here, communications and business services are considered a reliable indicator of the extent to which new and better technologies have been introduced in each sector. Substitute equation (7) into equation (6) we obtain:

$$(dY/dt)/Y = a(dK/dt)/K + b(dL/dt)/L + c(dBCS/dt)/BCS \qquad (14)$$

With this methodology, a value of the productive efficiency of communications and business services can be directly computed and estimated with the following econometric specification, where $dCOM(1985/1988)$ and $dBS(1985/1988)$, specified as the ratio of the logarithmic values, enter the equation separately:

$$dY(1985/1988) = a + b \; dK(1985/1988) + c \; dL(1985/1988) + \qquad (15)$$
$$d \; dCOM(1985/1988)$$

$$dY(1985-1988) = a + b \; dK(1985/1988) + c \; dL(1985/1988) + \qquad (16)$$
$$d \; dBS(1985/1988)$$

where all variables are specified as in the previous equations.

The OLS estimates of equations (15) and (16) perform very well statistically:

$$dY(1985/1988) = 3.153 + 0.461 \; dK(1985/1988) + 0.398 \; dL(1985/1988)$$
$$(6.805) \qquad\qquad\qquad (2.584)$$

$$+ \; 0.111 \; dCOM(1985/1988) \qquad (17)$$
$$(1.904)$$

$R^2 = 0.871; F = 61.77;$
(Student t-values in parentheses)

$$dY(1985-1988) = 0.204 + 0.487 \; dK(1985/1988) + 0.338 \; dL(1985/1988)$$
$$(4.445) \qquad\qquad\qquad (1.764)$$

$$+ \; 0.270 \; dBS(1985/1988) \qquad (18)$$
$$(2.449)$$

R^2 0.881; F = 67.765;
(Student t-values in parentheses)

In terms of adjusted R squared, total variance explained reaches the 0.8 levels. All the variables are significant in terms of the t statistics. The result seems particularly important when we consider the estimated value of the elasticities of output growth in relation to the increase in the usage levels of communications and business services. The value of the former parameter is 0.111, and it is significant at 0.968%; the value of the latter is 0.270, and is significant at 0.978%. It is equally important when we compare the estimated output elasticities of communications and business services with their cost shares; 1.48% in 1985 and 1.68% in 1988, and 14.45% in 1985 and 15.66% in 1988, respectively. Estimated output elasticities are therefore more than six times and almost two times as large as their cost shares, respectively.

These results confirm that the diffusion of communications and business services is strongly associated with the growth of output, under the control of the rate of increase of the two basic production factors. They also show that the effects of this diffusion, in terms of the output elasticity of communications and business services as strategic intermediary inputs, are very high. The results serve to indicate the extent to which the diffusion of communications and, to a lesser extent, business services can be considered a reliable proxy of the rates of adoption and effective implementation of the wide array of technological and organisational changes in the Italian economy in the second half of the 1980s.

The effects of the co-evolution of usage of communications and business services: a simple accounting approach. The European evidence.

With regard to the general analytical framework outlined in the work, we maintain two notions. The first is that the general efficiency of the production process is significantly affected by the extent to which firms are able to take advantage of opportunities to introduce new networking technologies by means of the systematic use of communications and business services. Communications and business services industries are the new strategic sector of the emerging knowledge-based economy. Their products are key intermediary inputs to the rest of the economy. A small increase in their use makes it possible to increase significantly the output levels. Hence we expect to measure their strong and positive effects on the rest of the economic system by the empirical estimates of their output elasticity.

Second, the adoption and implementation of the new technologies takes place in the context of a disequilibrium process. In equilibrium, cost shares of production factors should equal their output elasticity. In out-of-equilibrium conditions instead, cost shares and output elasticities may diverge. Such conditions emerge when factor markets are imperfect and/or major technological changes are being diffused, so that only a fraction of the total population of firms is able to properly adjust the use of the new production factors, embodying significant innovations, to product elasticity. Under such conditions product markets may also reflect out-of-equilibrium conditions, so that innovators and/or fast adopters are able to command quasi-rents associated with the timely introduction of the new technologies.

An attempt to assess empirically the effects of the use of communications and business services can be based on the standard production function where 'communication and business services' are specified as distinct production factors. The econometric specification of a standard Cobb-Douglas production function, which explicitly includes the use of communications and business services, gives us the following:

$$Y = a + bK + cL + dCBS \tag{19}$$

where Y is the natural logarithm of value added for the available sectors in each country; K is the natural logarithm of capital stock (estimated from investments); L is the natural logarithm of labour costs; and CBS is the natural logarithm of the flow of either the communications inputs (C) or business services (BS) purchased by each industry, in 1988 for Italy and in 1990 for the United Kingdom, Germany and France.

Again, due to the strong correlation between the services it is impossible to obtain reliable estimates of the joint effects of both services. Hence we have specified two distinct regression equations. The OLS cross-section estimates of equation (19) for communications services provides satisfactory results:

$$Y = 2.678 + 0.321\ K + 0.693\ L + 0.085\ C \qquad \text{(20.1. ITALY)}$$
$$ (3.576) \quad\ (7.679) \quad\ (3.211)$$

$R^2 = 0.713$; $F = 45.193$; (Student t-values in parentheses)

$$Y = -4.281 + 0.354\ K + 0.349\ L + 0.208\ C \qquad \text{(20.2. UK)}$$
$$ (5.483) \quad\ (3.956) \quad\ (2.34)$$

$R^2 = 0.\,953$; $F = 182.635$; (Student t-values in parentheses)

$$Y = 0.945 + 0.196\ K + 0.779\ L + 0.155\ C \qquad \text{(20.3. DEU)}$$
$$ (2.741) \quad\ (3.615) \quad\ (1.498)$$

$R^2 = 0.859$; $F = 24.162$; (Student t-values in parentheses)

$$Y = 2.185 + 0.662\ K + 0.161\ L + 0.088\ C \qquad \text{(20.4. FRA)}$$
$$ (9.389) \quad\ (1.879) \quad\ (2.211)$$

$R^2 = 0.913$; $F = 73.162$; (Student t-values in parentheses)

The OLS cross-section estimates of equation (19) for business services provide equally satisfactory results:

$$Y = 3.945 + 0.516 \text{ K} + 0.433 \text{ L} + 0.271 \text{ BS} \qquad \text{(21.1. ITALY)}$$
$$ (3.489) \quad\; (7.279) \quad\; (3.611)$$

R^2 0.749; F = 47.162; (Student t-values in parentheses)

$$Y = -4.389 + 0.332 \text{ K} + 0.473 \text{ L} + 0.424 \text{ BS} \qquad \text{(21.2. UK)}$$
$$ (6.415) \quad\; (5.479) \quad\; (4.567)$$

R^2 0.929; F = 154.342; (Student t-values in parentheses)

$$Y = 3.945 + 0.216 \text{ K} + 0.473 \text{ L} + 0.287 \text{ BS} \qquad \text{(21.3. DEU)}$$
$$ (7.989) \quad\; (6.429) \quad\; (2.211)$$

R^2 0.899; F = 231.162; (Student t-values in parentheses)

$$Y = 3.945 + 0.616 \text{ K} + 0.273 \text{ L} + 0.263 \text{ BS} \qquad \text{(21.4. FRA)}$$
$$ (4.89) \quad\; (3.422) \quad\; (3.811)$$

R^2 0.889; F = 76.890; (Student t-values in parentheses)

In order to appreciate the influence of time within the limited series available and the specific sectoral effects, pooling regressions were tested. The OLS estimates of equation (19) for communications services for the years 1985 and 1988 for Italy, 1984 and 1990 for the UK and 1986 and 1990 for Germany and France, provide the following positive results:

$$Y = 3.945 + 0.516 \text{K} + 0.473 \text{L} + 0.113 \text{C} + 0.231 \text{DUM4} \qquad \text{(22.1. ITALY)}$$
$$ (7.479) \quad\; (3.567) \quad\; (2.765) \qquad (3.389)$$

R^2 0.949; F = 137.192; (Student t-values in parentheses)

$$Y = -4.415 + 0.327 \text{K} + 0.444 \text{L} + 0.327 \text{C} + 0.680 \text{ DUM7} \qquad \text{(22.2. UK)}$$
$$ (6.411) \quad\; (5.479) \quad\; (2.11) \qquad (3.081)$$

R^2 0.931; F = 155.362; (Student t-values in parentheses)

$$Y = 3.945 + 0.151 \text{ K} + 0.78 \text{ L} + 0.152 \text{ C} + 0.596 \text{ DUM2} \qquad \text{(22.3. DEU)}$$
$$ (3.389) \quad\; (7.479) \quad\; (3.211) \qquad (3.786)$$
$$ - 0.314 \text{ DUM18}$$
$$ (4.732)$$

R^2 0.949; F = 147.162; (Student t-values in parentheses)

$$Y = 3.945 + 0.716\,K + 0.173\,L + 0.113\,C + 0.467\,DUM7 \qquad \text{(22.4. FRA)}$$
$$ (3.389)\ \ (7.479)\ \ (3.012)\qquad (2.553)$$

R^2 0.895; F = 87.042; (Student t-values in parentheses)

The pooled OLS estimates of equation (19) for business services, are as follows:

$$Y = 3.945 + 0.516\,K + 0.473\,L + 0.273\,BS + 0.231\,DUM4 \quad \text{(23.1. ITALY)}$$
$$ (7.479)\ \ (3.567)\ \ (2.765)\qquad (3.389)$$

R^2 0.945; F = 137.0192; (Student t-values in parentheses)

$$Y = -4.41 + 0.32\,K + 0.444\,L + 0.327\,BS + 0.68\,DUM7 \qquad \text{(23.2. UK)}$$
$$ (6.411)\ \ (5.479)\quad (2.11)\qquad (3.081)$$

R^2 0.931; F = 155.362; (Student t-values in parentheses)

$$Y = 3.945 + 0.151\,K + 0.78\,L + 0.280\,BS + 0.596\,DUM2$$
$$ (3.389)\ \ (7.479)\ \ (3.211)\qquad (3.786)$$

$$ - 0.314\ DUM18 \qquad\qquad\qquad\qquad \text{(23.3. DEU)}$$
$$ (4.732)$$

R^2 0.949; F = 147.162; (Student t-values in parentheses)

$$Y = 3.945 + 0.616\,K + 0.273\,L + 0.261\,BS + 0.467\,DUM7 \qquad \text{(23.4. FRA)}$$
$$ (3.89)\ \ (7.479)\ \ (2.011)\qquad (2.553)$$

R^2 0.895; F = 87.042; (Student t-values in parentheses)

Finally, to assess the twin effect of communications and business services together, an interactive variable was introduced to measure the output elasticity of the combined usage of the two key services. The following equation was specified:

$$(Y = a + bK + cL + d(C+BS) \qquad\qquad\qquad (24)$$

where all variables are as before and (C + BS) was set as the natural logarithm of the sum of C and BS.

Pooled OLS tests were conducted on the same data as in equations 23.1. to 23.4, with the following results:

$$Y = 3.945 + 0.516\,K + 0.473\,L + 0.273\,(C+BS) + 0.231\,DUM4 \quad \text{(25.1. ITALY)}$$
$$ (7.479)\ \ (3.567)\qquad (2.765)\qquad\quad (3.389)$$

R^2 0.899; F = 187.82; (Student t-values in parentheses)

$$Y = -4.41 + 0.32\,K + 0.444\,L + 0.327\,(C+BS) + 0.68\,DUM7 \qquad (25.2.\ UK)$$
$$ (6.411) \quad (5.479) \qquad (2.11) \qquad\quad (3.123)$$

R^2 0.941; F = 173.390; (Student t-values in parentheses)

$$Y = 3.945 + 0.151\,K + 0.78\,L + 0.292\,(C+BS) + 0.596\,DUM2 \qquad (25.3.\ DEU)$$
$$ (3.389) \quad (7.479) \quad (3.211) \qquad\quad (3.789)$$

$$ - 0.314\,DUM18$$
$$ (4.732)$$

R^2 0.969; F = 149.621; (Student t-values in parentheses)

$$Y = 3.945 + 0.616\,K + 0.273\,L + 0.273\,(C+BS) + 0.467\,DUM7 \qquad (25.4.\ FRA)$$
$$ (4.763) \quad (3.876) \quad (2.987) \qquad\quad (2.257)$$

R^2 0.895; F = 87.042; (Student t-values in parentheses)

Total explained variance reaches, in terms of adjusted R squared, the 0.9 levels. Again, this appears an important result particularly when we concentrate on the relation between output growth elasticities and the use of communications and business services. The estimated value of the former is above a mean of 0.10 in most countries, and is significant at 0.9%. The value of the estimated parameter for business services is much larger, around a mean value of 0.270, and is significant at no less than 0.95% for all countries.

These results warrant attention for three reasons. First the output elasticities so far estimated are very high and are close to the values of the two basic inputs: labour and capital. This result is all the more interesting when returns to scale are considered: in no case does the sum of output elasticities of three factors considered significantly exceed unity. In Italy and Germany the estimated output elasticity of communications services (0.085 and 0.155, respectively) is close to output elasticity of capital. In France the output elasticity of communications services is 0.088 against an output elasticity of labour of 0.161. In the United Kingdom the estimated output elasticity reaches the highest value among the countries considered at 0.208 against an output elasticity of capital and labour between 0.354 and 0.349 respectively. Where business services are concerned the results are even stronger. In Germany, Italy and France the estimated output elasticity of business services in 1990 was 0.28, 0.27 and 0.26 respectively. In the United Kingdom the output elasticity of business services fetched the 0.42 level. Although a direct comparison of the results across the four countries considered is impeded by heterogeneity in the data, it seems useful to note that the output elasticities of communications and business services reach the highest values in the UK, a country well ahead in the transition towards a knowledge-based economy; Germany ranks second, France third and Italy fourth. This ranking is consistent with OECD international statistics based upon other indicators about the role of intangible assets and knowledge-intensive inputs (Foray and Lundvall, 1996 and OECD, 1996; Mansell and Wehn, 1998).

Second, the estimates show that the inclusion of communications services in the econometric equation has some negative, non-negligible effects, on the output elasticity of capital in all countries. On the contrary, the estimated output elasticity of labour declines when business services are accounted for in the econometric estimates. These two results deserve some attention in that they might supply some indirect and very preliminary evidence that communications services capture some of the output elasticity of capital and business services capture some of the output elasticity of labour. This might in turn suggest that the inclusion of communications and business services capture the efficiency of the portion of capital and labour more directly involved in the use of data communications and knowledge-intensive business activities respectively.

Finally, considerable differences may be noted between the output elasticity of communications services and their cost share. In Italy, estimated output elasticity of communications services is 0.085 against a cost share of 1.78%, i.e. almost five times larger. It is a similar situation in Germany, where output elasticity is 0.155 compared to a cost share of 1.39%. The output elasticity of such services in France is 0.088, at a cost share of 0.95%; while the United Kingdom has the highest value of output elasticities of the four countries considered, at 0.208, but against a cost share ratio of 1.02%. Such striking discrepancies across the board confirm that in Europe the use of communications services takes place far away from equilibrium.

The out-of-equilibrium conditions in the use of business services are instead much weaker. In fact, the cost share of business services was 16.9% in Italy, 16.9% in France, 15% in Germany, and 19.3% in the UK; this compares to output elasticities values of 0.27, 0.26, 0.28 and 0.42, respectively. Finally, the estimated parameter for the interactive variable (C+BS) reaches an average value of 0.25, while the combined cost share of the two services, in the four countries considered, has an average of 17%.

These results, just like those for Italy alone, illustrate the strong association between the diffusion of communications and business services, and output growth, and the notable extent of the output elasticity of the services with respect to their actual cost share. In the mid-1980s, usage of communications and business services was clearly at the basis of a strong disequilibrium, and yielded a marginal product far larger than their share of total costs. In particular, the discrepancy between output elasticity and cost share is greater in the use of communications services than business services.

Conclusions

Innovation relies on new technological knowledge, which, beyond the learning processes of internal R&D, is increasingly created through the daily interaction, communication and exchange of information between private companies, business service firms and public institutions. As the main factors of connectivity and receptivity, the use of communications and business services by industries in a system enhances the innovative capability of that system. In this context, communications services clearly aid the receptivity of these interactions, subsequently influencing business services. And as active interfaces between learning agents, knowledge-intensive business services become 'converters' of external codified, scientific knowledge into localised competence and *vice versa*: they benefit the system in terms of connectivity. More information exchanges, that is to say increased interaction between tacit and codified knowledge components, based on improved receptivity and connectivity, generates more technological and organisational innovations. Thus, we may say that the spread of communications and business services would explain much of the innovative capability of the European economy.

We may conclude in general that the systematic use of communications and business services, and the associated creation of an operative information network, which enhances the communication intensity of a system, enable firms to capitalise on new technologies, improving general production efficiency. The implementation of this efficiency-enhancing network takes place under conditions of disequilibrium. Such conditions most likely involve several parallel processes, reflecting the fact that the spread of new information and communication technology affects not only a firm's competence but also product and factor markets. Thus, seemingly high output elasticity levels are explained by early technology adopters increasing their market share and profitability.

Based on empirical evidence, the results support our original hypotheses, with respect to the European economy, that the expected co-evolution in the usage of communications and business services has a positive influence on productivity. Our analysis confirms a correlation between the diffusion of communications and business services and the growth of total factor productivity, and partially explains the increase in the latter as experienced by the European economy in the late 1980s.

Appendix

Matching input/output data with national accounts statistics

Data from the input/output statistics can be cross-checked with data from standard industrial statistics (ISTAT, 1988) so that the amount of communications and business services purchased by each industry as intermediary inputs may be compared with figures on value added, labour costs and capital (estimated from investments series) obtained from industrial value added statistics. The matching of these two statistical sources is necessary in order to obtain data on investments, and hence capital, so as to estimate a produc-

Table 11.5 Conversion from the Italian input/output classification into the NACE

No	NACE	I/O compatible
1	011−030	01
2	111+120−17	07
3	211−224	09
4	231−248	13
5	25−26	15
6	311+312+313+314+315+316	17
7	321+322+323+324+325+326+327+328	21
8	33+371+372+373+374	23
9	341+342+343+344+345+346+347	25
10	351+352+353	27
11	361+362+363+364+365	29
12	412	31
13	413	33
14	411+414+415+416+417+418+419+420+421+422+423	35
15	424+425+427+428	37
16	429	39
17	431+432+434+435+436+437+438+439+453+454+455+456	41
18	441+442+451+452	43
19	46	45
20	47	47
21	48	49
22	491+492+493+494+495+496	51
23	505−509	53
24	620+671+672+673+675	55
25	61+63+64	57
26	661+662+664+665+667	59
27	710+72+730	61
28	741+742+750	63
29	761+762+763+764+771+772+773	65
30	790	67
31	811+812+813+820	69
32	83+84+84+85+93+94+95	74

tion function. Neither capital nor investment data are made available by input/output statistics, and the procedure involves some statistical problems due to the heterogeneity of the sources. Industrial statistics do not include very small firms, below ten employees, while input/output statistics do. Moreover, factory data is aggregated in the input/output statistics while firm data is aggregated in the industrial ones. However, a check on the intensities of communications and business services carried out with value added provided by input/output statistics and industrial statistics respectively, suggests that these discrepancies are negligible in most cases. Whenever the discrepancy between input/output value added and industrial value added was significant, corrections were made using the ratio between the two value added statistics as a factor to adjust investments and wage figures.

Table 11.6 Conversion from the German input/output classification into the NACE

	Germany NACE – I/O sectors	Germany: input/output
1	01/Agricultural, forestry	C1+C2
2	06/Coal, petroleum and gas	C3−C10
3	13/Ferrous & non-ferrous	C16+C17
4	15/Non-metallic and minerals	C13+C14+C15
5	17/Chemicals and pharmaceuticals	C9
6	19/Metal products	C18+C19+C20+C28
7	21/Machinery	C21
8	23/Office equipment	C22+C27
9	25/Electrical machinery	C26
10	28/Transport equipment	C23+C24+C25
11	36/Food beverages and tobacco	C38+C39+C40
12	42/Textiles, clothing, leather products	C35−C37
13	47/Paper and printing products	C32+C34
14	49/Rubber and plastic products	C11+C12
15	48/Other manufacturing industries	C29−C31
16	53/Building	C41+C42
17	56/Repair and wholesale and retail	C43+C44
18	59/Hotel and catering services	C52
19	61/Domestic transportation	C45+C46+C48+(B24−B26)
20	67/Communication	C47
21	69a/Credit & insurance	C49+C50
22	74/Business services	C55
23	86/Non-commercial services	C56+C57+C58

This is the case for repair and maintenance, building, wholesale trade, transportation and primary industries. Table 11.5 shows the criteria used to convert input/output aggregation of the forty-four industries into the NACE classification. In Italy data was available for thirty-two sectors in the primary,[2] manufacturing and service industries in 1985 and 1988. Input/output and national accounts data was also collected for the years 1984 and 1990 in the United Kingdom, and 1986 and 1990 in France and Germany. The classification of economic activities across these countries differs all the more when we try to maximise the number of observations, that is the number of industries. Therefore the four countries do not provide a homogeneous group of industries. Tables 11.6–8 indicate the conversion criteria for the UK (Table 11.6), France (Table 11.7) and Germany (Table 11.8).

Data from national accounts was used to match the input/output statistics, complementing the information on the usage of communications and business services with that on value added, wages and investments[3] for each industry considered. Matched data[4] was available in the United Kingdom for thirty-two sectors of the primary and manufacturing industries

Table 11.7 Conversion from the French input/output classification into the NACE

	France NACE – I/O sectors	France: NACE
1	01/Agricultural, forestry	S01+S02+S03
2	06/Coal, petroleum and gas	S41+S42+S51+S52+S53+S06+S07+S08
3	13/Ferrous & non-ferrous	S09+S10+S11+S12+S13
4	15/Non-metallic and minerals	S14+S15+S16
5	17/Chemicals and pharmaceuticals	S171+S172+S18+S19
6	19/Metal products	S20+S21
7	21/Machinery	S22+S23+S24+S25
8	23/Office equipment	S27+S34
9	25/Electrical machinery	S28+S291+S292+S30
10	28/Transport equipment	S311+S312+S33
11	36/Food, beverages and tobacco	S35+S36+S37+S38+S39+S401+S402+S403+S41+S42
12	42/Textiles, clothing, leather products	S43+S441+S442+S443+S451+S452+S46+S47
13	47/Paper and printing products	S50+S51
14	49/Rubber and plastic products	S52+S53
15	48/Other manufacturing industries	S54+S48+S49
16	53/Building	S55
17	56/Repair and wholesale and retail	S65+S66+S57+S64+S56
18	59/Hotel and catering services	S67
19	61/Inland transport	S68+S691+S692+S70
20	67/Maritime and sea transport	S71+S72
21	65/Auxilliary activities	S73+S74
22	67/Communication	S75
23	69a/Credit & insurance	S88+S89
24	74/Business services	S76+S77+S78+S79+S80+S811+S812+S82+S83+S85+S86
25	86/Non-market services	S90−S98

Table 11.8 Conversion from the British input/output classification into the NACE

UK Sectors		Input/output classification	NACE/CLIO classification
1	Coal mining	03	210
2	Petroleum and gas	04	220
3	Metal ore mining	09	230
4	Other mining	13	290
5	Food products	57+58+59+60+61+62+63+64+ 65+66	311+312
6	Beverages	67+68	313
7	Tobacco	69	314
8	Textiles	70+71+72+73+74+75+79+	321
9	Clothing	78	322
10	Leather and products	76	323
11	Footwear	77	324
12	Wood products	80	331
13	Furniture, fixtures	81	332
14	Paper and products	82+83	341
15	Printing, publishing	84	342
16	Industrial chemicals	19+20+21+22+23+24	351
17	Other chem. products	25+26+27+28	352
18	Petroleum refineries	05	353
19	Rubber products	85	355
20	Plastic products	86	356
21	Pottery, china, etc	18	361
22	Glass and products	17	362
23	Non-metal products	14+15+16	369
24	Iron and steel	10	371
25	Non-ferrous metals	11+12	372
26	Metal products	29+30+31+32+33	381
27	Machinery	34+35+36+37+38+39+40+41+ 42+43	382
28	Electrical machinery	44+45+46+47+48+49+50+51	383
29	Transport equipment	52+53+54+55	384
30	Professional goods	56	385
31	Other industries	87	390
32	Electricity, gas	06+07	410
33	Water works	08	420

only. German and French statistics provided data for twenty-three and twenty-five sectors, respectively, across the economy.

Aggregation among the four countries also differs, in terms of the content of the service sector[5] and the communication one. For example, communications services in the United Kingdom only consist of the telecommunication services, while in the other three countries they include mail and postal services as well. Consequently, the four sets of data cannot be compared and should be regarded as four different case studies.

12 Conclusion

The laws governing the creation of new knowledge and the introduction of technological and organisational innovations are central to understanding the dynamics of economic systems. A comprehensive economics of knowledge can be built bringing together the Marshallian and the Schumpeterian traditions. Specifically the Marshallian tradition of analysis which focuses on increasing returns and partial equilibrium has been combined with the Schumpeterian tradition of analysis about structural change, that is the endogenous creation of new knowledge and introduction of new technologies, organisations and institutions.

In the neoclassical theory, firms and, more generally economic agents, can adjust either prices or quantities to market signals within a given set of structural or environmental features, such as technology, consumer preference and primary resources. Within the received theory, firms cannot intentionally change the characteristics of the economic environment: such changes take place exogenously (Arrow, 1996). Technological knowledge and more generally the features of production and utility functions, and institutions such as property rights and standards belong to the same class of environmental features, so firms are not expected to play a role in their emergence (North, 1991). In our approach, instead, the scope of agents' interactive behaviour is not limited to traditional price-output combinations, but embraces search and action intentionally directed towards the introduction of structural changes which make the economic environment less restrictive for each agent (Phillips, 1970). Importantly, we do not assume that firms and agents are in equilibrium when the search process and the related decision-making takes place. The notion of behaviour itself implies that our agents are situated in a dynamic environment where they receive some feedback and have some objectives, which are far from optimal solutions (David, 1987; North, 1991).

In this book the generation of new knowledge and the introduction of technological, organisational and institutional change has been analysed specifically as the result of the dynamics of exchanges out-of-equilibrium. Out-of-equilibrium exchanges do take place in Marshallian markets and, because of irreversibilities, indivisibilities and structural change, i.e. the endogenous creation of knowledge and the introduction of innovations by Schumpeterian agents in out-of-equilibrium conditions, the convergence towards equilibrium is continuously deferred by the changing structural elements of the system: the attractors keep moving.

Out-of-equilibrium agents do make long-term choices which affect in historic time their conduct as well as the performances and the strategies of competitors, suppliers and customers, because of irreversibilities, indivisibilities and especially the endogenous capability to create new knowledge and introduce technological, organisational and institutional change. As a result, new potential equilibria would arise which are clearly different from the previous ones. In such a dynamics, a historic sequence of virtual equilibria can be traced, but no actual equilibrium point can be found. The process and the path are the single, relevant units of analysis: the corridors along which such sequences take place define the range of possible outcomes.

The localised constraints imposed by irreversibilities, indivisibilities and previous structural changes – and their effects in terms of producer switching costs, learning capabilities, product and factor markets disequilibria and the topological characteristics of the economic spaces into which firms are embedded – define the rate and the direction of the accumulation of new knowledge and the introduction of new technologies (as well as the rate of change), hence the shape of the flexible corridors or trajectories into which the system keeps moving.

The analysis of differences between systems in terms of generation of technological knowledge, the rate of introduction and diffusion of innovations, and productivity growth provides an outstanding opportunity to test the relevance of the approach so far elaborated. The hypotheses developed have been applied to understand the emergence of the knowledge-based economy, characterised by the increasing economic role of the rate, direction, production, transfer and use of knowledge in the most advanced countries and the parallel introduction of new information and communication technologies. Based on the growth of the new information technology system within the structure of the European economy, we are witnessing a new global division of labour, between OECD countries specialising in knowledge-intensive products on the one hand, and newly-industrialised countries concentrating on manufactured goods on the other. In such a situation, the competitivity and innovative capacity of the European economy is increasingly seen to depend on the generation of new information and communication technology and, consequently, the function of the knowledge-intensive business service sector.

In analysing this process of structural change, we have emphasised the utility of three notions, namely the dynamics of localised technological knowledge and change, path-dependence and technological communication based upon the spatial stochastic interactions methodology.

The dynamics of technological knowledge and industrial change

The examination of the generation of knowledge has undergone a thorough revision in recent time, and the traditional 'Arrovian' microeconomic conception of knowledge and information as a single, indivisible public good is now being challenged by a Schumpeterian approach, stressing the distinction between information and knowledge. According to the standard idea, knowledge is generated via a deductive chain involving the application of scientific discoveries and methodological procedures from pure 'scientific' research to the specific 'technological' activities of a firm. The actual flow of information is regarded as a spontaneous characteristic of economic systems. Technological knowledge is thus considered non-excludable and non-rival in its use, transferred and learnt at little cost; and though it cannot be appropriated by innovators, it has a wide variety of applications. Intellectual property rights can increase appropriability but would reduce the scope for the socialisation of innovation benefits (Arrow, 1962b, 1969 and 1996).

The new approach to the generation of knowledge emphasises the active necessity of the individual competence and skills of firms: information represents only one input in knowledge production. Technological knowledge is created and assimilated in tacit learning processes related to the specific background and experience of the innovator. It becomes 'localised' in well-defined technical, institutional, regional and industrial situations, as such it is partly appropriable and its use is, instead, largely excludable and partly rivalrous. Next, the new approach stresses the key role of technological communication in the generation of new knowledge.

Now the generation of new localised technological knowledge is viewed as the result of the complementary interaction between four, indispensable knowledge components: external and internal knowledge; tacit and codified knowledge. Individual learning processes enable the accumulation of tacit knowledge, whilst collective processes, built on industry- and region-wide technological communication processes (consisting of exchanges of information and experience), generate and share a common knowledge infrastructure. R&D activities gather codified knowledge via the different forms of communication and via the exchange of technological information and implement the tacit knowledge accumulated.

There is now a growing consensus that the production and assimilation of technological knowledge offers important positive feedbacks and increasing returns associated with internal learning-to-learn processes and communication of technological externalities. Cumulative learning processes and formal research are oriented towards the specific problems surrounding production bottlenecks, fast-rising prices of particular inputs, and market constraints. Localised technological knowledge is seen to emerge from daily routines and tacit experience, that is from using, producing and manufacturing goods, and interacting with customers and other manufacturers. In this respect, it is the result of a systemic, bottom-up process of induction from actual experience, and contrasts sharply with the individualistic, top-down, deduction from-scientific-principle model on which the previous theory of knowledge was based.

Potential innovators, in out-of-equilibrium conditions are exposed to relevant producer switching costs arising from changes in the economic environment. In order to cope with the new economic conditions, they try to innovate, drawing on their own particular history and experience. Out-of-equilibrium leads to the generation and implementation of new knowledge and the introduction and adoption of new technologies within processes which are highly sensitive, both to situations prevailing in the system at each point in time and to the interaction of agents – in other words to high levels of path-dependent irreversibility.

In summarising localised technological knowledge and localised technological change, in the overall assessment of the factors shaping the dynamics of structural change, our approach identifies the topological determinants of the innovation capability of an economic system. The general levels of technological opportunities via scientific breakthroughs are still a key external issue, as are the communication properties of the system in terms of channels in place, connectivity and the distribution of receptive agents. Internally, so to speak, the amount of resources devoted to generating innovation by each agent, the agent's receptivity to technological knowledge generated by third parties, and the level and characteristics of its accumulated competence, together with the actual levels of producer switching costs, are all important considerations. Finally, innovation capability rests on the dynamics of internal increasing returns as shaped by learning processes and technological externalities.

The interplay between excess momentum and inertia plays a major role here. Excess momentum is given by endowment factors; excess inertia by producer switching costs. Endowment factors represent the learning opportunities, both internal and external to each firm, associated with the range of familiar techniques and location in a multidimensional space providing fast and efficient access to new knowledge. Producer switching costs are the resources needed to adjust the present input composition to the new desired levels determined by changes in either production prices or demand. For a given environmental change and level of producer switching costs, a firm innovates, that is generates technological knowledge and introduces technological and organisational change, according to both the interaction between R&D and learning processes and its access to and absorption of knowledge spilling in from other firms and research institutions in the same innovation system.

It is in this context that a first attempt to build an economic topology has been made applying network analysis and the methodology of spatial stochastic interactions to the analysis of innovation systems.[1] As information networks, innovation systems may be thought of as spatial stochastic interactions structures through which technological communication takes place. Network analysis provides important tools to understand the static characteristics of communication networks. Spatial stochastic interactions methodology can help to understand the aggregate dynamics of technological externalities. Specifically, for given levels of external pressure and density, percolation probability is measured by the combined result of the probabilities of receptivity and connectivity. This relation can be used to study the probability within innovation systems that the flows of effective communication and the exchanges of information take place, actually implementing the productivity of the research and learning efforts of each firm in the system. The interaction between the rate and direction of technological change and the topological characteristics of the system, which shape the mixed percolation probability at each point in time, provides the basic understanding of the path-dependent dynamics of structural change.

Path-dependence is concerned with the different yet complementary analyses of the evolution in historical time of the system itself and the performance of each agent within it. The outcome of the latter analysis provides the information to understand the former. According to the values of the topological parameters of the economic system, such as the distribution of agents in the relevant multidimensional spaces, their density and distances, the network structure of their relations and the quality and quantity of their connectivity and receptivity, we can describe the dynamics of the system and the performance of its agents (David, 1997).

At any point in time, however, these parameters may be affected and ultimately changed by the conduct of each agent, via entry and exit, connectivity and receptivity investment, membership in technological alliances, standardisation clubs and new localisations in the relevant economic spaces. Hence the topological parameters of the system cannot be viewed as exogenous or given-once-and-for-ever, but are the outcome of the past conduct of agents as well as of the dynamic properties of the system itself. Because of the stochastic character of Random Markov Fields, small events may sometimes activate chain reactions that drastically change the parameters of the entire system, while in other periods of time and different contexts of co-action the outcome of the same efforts is much smaller. Hence the character of path-dependence, where hysteresis and determinism are mitigated by the localised context of action and their multiple effects on the transition probabilities from one state to another.

The analysis of path-dependence provides a general framework to explain the evolution of industrial economics, from the structuralist approach of the 1960s (Scherer, 1980), through Schumpeterian developments, up to the ultimate evolutionary steps of the 1980s (Dosi, 1988) in terms of a fully elaborated dynamic structuralism (Antonelli, 1995c). Such a broad framework, drawing upon both the Marshallian and the Schumpeterian traditions, offers a context which takes into account the topological interaction between agents and structures. This fundamental aspect is not taken into account by the neoclassical model which is based upon co-ordination processes achieved by means of equilibrium market transactions fully cleared by market prices.

Instead, this approach instead can accommodate both the effects on the topological structure of the past behaviour of agents and the Lamarckian process of agent survival via learning and adaptation to that environment. Dynamic structuralism uses path-dependence to model the effects of historical time on the behaviour of agents who are, nevertheless, able to modify their development at any point in time. This seems especially appropriate in understanding the dynamics of the generation of localised technological knowledge and the introduction of localised technological and organisational change when the interplay between internal and external sources of technological knowledge are properly appreciated.

This view is further enhanced when we realise that the topological characteristics of spatial stochastic interactions structures cannot be considered as irreversible or equally distributed through the structures.[2] Instead of global symmetric interacting systems, in which all agents have the same probability of networking and the same number of connections, innovation systems appear characterised by distributions of interactions which are highly asymmetric and regionally and industrially localised, where agents have access to differentiated connections and act intentionally to build and implement them. In an innovation system characterised by localised interactions, the innovative capability of each agent depends on the number of communication channels in place and the related connectivity and receptivity probabilities, and a hierarchy of agents is likely to emerge. Each connection requires a certain effort to be established; so connections become the outcome of intentional action and may be considered endogenous. The productivity as well as the levels of funds invested in R&D activities can also be thought to be influenced by the number of connections. As a matter of fact, firms, with given amounts of financial resources available to generate new knowledge, might be induced to substitute internal R&D activities for connections in order to increase innovative output. In a dynamic process however, where innovation is the main competitive tool, the larger and more effective the number of connections, the larger the innovative output, and thus profits; and consequently, the larger the amount of resources devoted to R&D activities, building and implemented connections.

Here the path-dependent nature of the topology of communication channels becomes fully clear. A given structure of communication channels and related connectivity and receptivity probabilities in place at time t, affects the rates and direction of introduction of localised technological changes. These in turn exert feedbacks on the distribution and use conditions of communication channels within the system. The states at time t have effects on the states at time $t + 1$, both directly and indirectly, via the changes they make on the probability of transition from one state to the next. The effects on the process of the stochastic character of the spatial interaction systems call for the application of inhomogeneous Markov chains.

The topological properties of innovation systems, conceived as communication networks that emerge in our general model enable us to understand the clustering of innovations in time, technologies and defined regional spaces, the introduction of complementary innovations and the micro-economics of discontinuous growth. In particular, it offers explanations of the growing effect of new information and communication technology on the introduction of technological innovation, the importance of knowledge-intensive business services, and standards on the innovative capability of the system, and the scope for technological co-operation as part of both firm strategy and innovation policy. The interaction between the dynamics of localised technological changes and spatial stochastic interactions paves the way towards a new innovation policy based upon measures designed to strengthen the technological communication and co-operation between firms and between firms and universities.

New information and communication technology

At the centre of the new and evolving knowledge-based economy, increasingly based on localised knowledge, new information and communication technologies determine the current state of technological innovation. The creation, adoption and diffusion of new technologies is a long and complex process involving several basic requirements. Internally, a well-trained and experienced workforce and increased integration between the different functions of a firm through network-organisation are essential for the evaluation and control of new information and the creation of competitive advantage. Equally, there is a need for intensive capital investment in an infrastructure accessible to the largest possible number of users; and in tandem, high levels of complementarity and interrelatedness between the production processes of different firms in different industries to accommodate successful developments in the division of labour and speed of production. The overall aim is for increased interaction between unharnessed tacit knowledge and available codified technology; this involves the internal workforce, external sources of knowledge and the activities of business services, in the creation, evaluation and implementation of new information systematically based on a firm's particular context.

New information and communication technologies can be considered as a complex cluster of radical innovations. They consist of a variety of applications of computer-based information processing procedures. Telecommunications constitute an essential component of this emerging information and communication technological system. New uses of telecommunication services are strongly associated with the introduction and diffusion of new information and communication technologies. Interdependence between the introduction of new technologies and the strategies of innovating companies is important here. The analysis of the direction of technological change in telecommunications confirms the vital influence of the multiple interaction between the introduction of alternative and competing innovations, their selection, adoption and implementation according to their complementarity with existing technologies (Arthur, 1989, 1994). In this framework, technological convergence represents the outcome of collective efforts to build a new technological system from complementary and compatible innovations deliberately introduced by innovators who draw on their localised competencies. Specifically, two strategies of collective innovation seem to be at work. On the one hand, centripetal forces push technological change towards higher levels of integration within the centralised network structure, building new complementary uses out of the existing infrastructure. On the other, new complementarities, based mainly on large user needs are implemented, creating an alternative technological system. A battle of technological systems thus seems to be emerging within the convergence of telecommunications and information technology; a battle of systems, whose outcome is likely to be shaped by the dynamics of lock-in and path-dependence. Innovative uses of information technologies are associated more and more with systematic networking of computers by means of telecommunication services.

The conceivable impact of new information and communication technology on the whole industrial matrix, from its original inception to its refinement and imitation by downstream users, makes of it a radical innovation. The wide-ranging effect of a great many localised innovations in products, processes and organisation, change the very nature of existing industries and their technologies. Obviously, this potential differs greatly according to the role of information within the products or processes of a particular nucleus of the industrial matrix. All service products, for example, usually have high levels of information, indeed the product is actually specified by its information. The information content of raw or manufactured goods is lower, but is still a factor in the production process in terms of output and delivery times. The effect of new information and communication technology on the very conditions of information, and ultimately its tradeability or commercial potential, will influence all products and processes according to their information content.

The actual generation and organisation of knowledge, both industrially and institutionally, is heavily influenced by the new information and communication technologies. The full vertical integration of knowledge-generation activities, characteristic since the Second World War, is being progressively and systematically replaced by selective outsourcing based upon the institutional creation of an information exchange market, based on real-time, on-line interaction between customers and knowledge producers. Customer accessibility and supplier competence are the major evolution here. Firms requiring specific solutions or advice, beyond recognised R&D measures, are able to interface their own internal knowledge with the scientific and technological competencies available in their external environment, thereby enhancing their own technological capacity. The classic exchange of good and coin is in this context represented by a process of market co-operation involving *ex-ante* contractual agreements, which enable the appropriation and distribution of knowledge and the supply of specific problem-solving competencies on demand.

The new organisation of knowledge production: knowledge-intensive business service industry

Knowledge-intensive business service firms are the protagonists in this emerging market, a dynamic source of 'quasi-generic' knowledge and an interface between a firm's own tacit and implicit knowledge and the codified knowledge available within the economy as a whole. Such a situation, as has been said, improves and increases connectivity and receptivity, as exchanges of tacit knowledge and localised competencies mean increased learning opportunities from the share of experience between the various customers of knowledge firms. The beneficial effects are clearly circular: the greater the diffusion of computerised networks, the greater the volume of electronic communication, thus the greater the blending of tacit and codified knowledge, and *vice versa*; all in turn increasing and being increased by the generation of new information and communication technology and the attendant opportunities of knowledge-intensive business services. Business and communications services will be the primary engineers and beneficiaries of knowledge markets and economies, which may well affect the social division of labour on a global scale.

The net result of such activity is increased specialisation in the production of knowledge and the creation of a veritable knowledge economy. A comparison with the software market is telling, where on-line interaction exists with independent software houses (i.e. knowledge producers) and their packages (i.e. knowledge competencies). What emerges is a highly-individual interaction between the customer, in search of specific solutions or generic information to turn its own tacit know-how into localised knowledge and innovation, and the supplier. The penetration of new information and communication technology encourages just such a trend, affecting the actual conditions of information, in terms of its exchangeable parts, separating new information from the technical expertise and competence used to generate and assimilate it. New technology provides an opportunity for business services to store and market knowledge, and for firms to access and purchase it.

Again the effects are reciprocal. The growth of direct, on-line, question–answer interactions in turn creates more and more opportunities to generate new codified knowledge with increasingly wider applications. The dynamics of positive feedback could have a positive influence in terms of both private and social efficiency in this system. Increased activity is obviously economically beneficial to knowledge-intensive business firms, with regard to size and revenue, but at the same time improves the overall distribution of the knowledge exchanged through the accumulation experience and increasing interactions. Customers are able to acquire the specific amount of information they require, while at the same time the total amount of knowledge increases. The interdependent nature of this exchange system means that new information technologies and the feedback they generate should contribute to the reduction of the wasteful duplication of costs which can occur due to the separation between the production and the (subsequent) absorption of knowledge. Knowledge not only becomes on-line, but also tailor-made.

The knowledge trade off is thus to some extent appeased: the incentive for specialised firms to build competencies is apparent in the positive market signalling it provides; the assessment of competencies is possible in terms of reputation; and in such an institutional market there is little opportunity for customers to 'steal' actual competencies. Moreover, the negative effects of intellectual property rights, with respect to other potential users, may be countered by mandated licensing of key technological information, generated in previous 'telematic market' interactions, in turn increasing the socialisation of this new specialised generation of knowledge.

Such a specialised industry for the production of knowledge, conceived and generated by new information and communication technologies, will ultimately affect the institutional generation of knowledge. Universities, and scientific centres in general, will face questions about the funding, efficiency and quality of research, as private business service firms doing the same work come to compete directly. The increasing compatibility and comparability between universities and knowledge firms may equally have positive effects. The evaluation of such things as the quality of research and the efficiency of the workforce in a publicly-funded institution becomes more and more viable as that institution more and more resembles a private knowledge firm. In fact, this similarity may even affect the traditional distinctions between university and (knowledge) industry, whose regulated interaction and co-operation could well increase overall efficiency in the knowledge system. Pressures of budget cuts on academic institutions on the one hand, and the threat of unfair competition between low-priced publicly-funded services and tax-paying ones on the other, are forces which will certainly bring about discussion and change. In Europe, the historical antagonism, or at least lack of established communication and co-operation, between industry and scientific centres may well be bridged by knowledge firms, acting as connectors and mediators in the exchange of technological information.

New information and communication technology is likely to exert most important influences on the new organisation of production of knowledge and especially on the role of knowledge-intensive business services within innovation systems. It affects the state of information itself, changing its divisibility and storage, its processing, transportation and communication, and consequently its accessibility and tradeability. This in turn increases the market opportunities and concentration of knowledge-intensive business service firms. By means of new information technologies, these firms gain greater command of the knowledge economy, building up connectivity and receptivity by establishing an interface between each member of the information network and the information itself. The impact of this should be visible in terms of increased innovative capabilities. More and more customers make increasingly specific demands on more and more knowledge suppliers, which implies enhanced interactions between tacit and codified knowledge – between the particular experience and ability implicit in each individual firm and the structured, technological and scientific information generally available. New information technology enables and enriches this situation, itself in turn benefiting from the acceleration in the generation and diffusion of new knowledge and technological innovations. The systematic support given to the introduction of complementary innovations, which fit into the idiosyncratic fabric of vintages of tangible and intangible capital of each firm, and the adoption of new information and communication technologies should be considered a major area for policy intervention.

Given this comprehensive analysis, we tested the systemic correlation, measured in terms of total productivity growth, between three interdependent factors: the penetration of new information and communication technologies; the diffusion of knowledge-intensive business services; and the generation and adoption of new technological and organisational innovations. Empirical analyses, based on the input/output statistics of the four main European economies demonstrated two hypotheses: the co-evolution in the use of business and communications services in respect of level and rate of increase, and the positive effect of this co-evolution on total productivity. In fact our analyses show high output elasticity levels for business and communications services, far above actual cost shares. Such a discrepancy may be explained within an out-of-equilibrium process – characterised by significant time delays and heterogeneity among both firms and industries – by temporary quasi-rents, linked to technological and organisational innovations made available by new information and communication systems, and the initial movement towards the said co-evolution of business and communications services in the European economy. It is this diffusion of new information and communication technologies that will promote knowledge-intensive business service firms, increase access to knowledge and, ultimately, determine productivity growth rates.

At this point it seems credible to propose that the European economy's technological and organisational capacity is a factor of its employment of communications and business services; and therefore, the diffusion of these services is proportional to the diffusion of new networking technologies, and such a demonstrable process should result in increased productivity levels. The use of communications and business services as strategic intermediary inputs by the rest of the economic system should be supported with policy schemes specifically designed to favour their development and diffusion both from the demand and the supply side.

Implications for innovation policy

Within the current situation as we have illustrated it, a framework of important policy implications becomes evident in conclusion. Until now, the economic importance of generic scientific knowledge as the unique result of formal R&D conducted intramuros by firms and scientific activities conducted by universities, has been exaggerated. R&D expenditure as an adequate indicator of a firm's productivity performance is equally misguided. As a consequence too much emphasis has been put upon R&D policies, and more generally science policies, as the basic tools to sustain the rates of accumulation of new knowledge. Tacit knowledge, acquired by localised personal experience and individual learning processes, is also a major source of technological knowledge. In fact, many small firms generate significant innovations based mainly on tacit localised knowledge; and many larger firms actually fail in the diffusion of innovative initiatives in unrelated activities because of a lack of tacit-learning appropriation opportunities. There is thus a basic need for an economic environment which encourages the accumulation of such tacit knowledge and enables its interaction with the codified counterparts.

In the generation of new technological innovations, firms rely on external knowledge acquired by means of informal interactions between themselves, sharing learning opportunities and experience, and with other, established sources of knowledge and information and more formal processes of technological co-operation. Outsourcing of research activities and the procurement of knowledge-intensive business services also plays an increasing role in assessing the innovative capabilities of each firm. The levels of outsourcing of knowledge-intensive business services should be accounted for when assessing the amount of inputs invested in the process of research and learning. The outsourcing of knowledge-intensive services could become an important recipient for policy interventions.

The innovative characteristics of the firm and the topology of the economic spaces into which it is embedded dictate the terms of communication and information exchange between firms, ultimately determining their innovative capabilities. We can identify three such 'architectural' factors in particular: the individual resources designated to the internal accumulation and implementation of tacit and codified knowledge; the receptivity to outside technological knowledge; and the connectivity and distribution network, in terms of knowledge, between firms. The quality of and accessibility to the information and communication technology infrastructure is also a significant indicator of an economy's innovative potential.

Finally, a strong competitive environment, characterised by diversity among firms, seems most conducive to foster the rate of accumulation of localised knowledge and its implementation in the actual introduction of innovations, both technological and organisational. Despite how it may appear, disorder and entropy at the microeconomic levels can actually direct economic systems towards high levels of virtuous performances at the macroeconomic level, provided that effective spatial stochastic interactions systems are in place.

Fast changes in industrial equilibria, consisting of shifts in aggregate demand levels, rivalrous conduct by competitors at the industry level and perturbations in relative factor costs can push firms to create new knowledge, introduce localised technological changes and eventually improve total factor productivity, for given levels of producer switching costs. However, high levels of perturbation in the economic environment and hence high producer switching costs can in turn hinder the general rate of growth. When the general conditions of the technological environment, and, specifically, the spatial stochastic interaction 'fabric' of communication of technological externalities, are appropriate, the introduction of localised technological changes is more likely to become the current strategy towards coping with economic fluctuations. Consequently, entropy can be an engine of economic growth only when important technological opportunities and the spillover of technological externalities help firms react by means of the introduction of productivity-improving localised technological changes. A competition policy that preserves the basic condition for a full display of the powerful effects of rivalry in the product and factor market place among different firms, and appreciates the key contribution of technological diversity, is a basic ingredient of an active innovation policy.

The topology of innovation systems and the quality of their communication networks can be greatly enhanced by the new key sectors such as the knowledge-intensive business services industries. The conditions of communication, dissemination, distribution, access and the quality of knowledge-intensive business services have important effects on the economic system in terms of innovative capacity. Countries with an advanced supply of knowledge-intensive business services are likely to have stronger communication capability in terms of connectivity and receptivity levels and hence higher innovation capabilities. The services of consultants and advisers improve connectivity between agents, sharing learning experiences and creating learning opportunities, thus also enhancing receptivity. Similarly, advanced business services, in terms of distribution, capillarity, competence and access, improve the interaction between tacit and codified knowledge, helping to introduce increasingly individual technological and organisational innovations. Such a dynamic situation can be of particular benefit to small and medium-sized firms, compensating for the high costs of in-house R&D and the technological knowledge it helps generate.

The useful distinction between innovation policies and diffusion policies, introduced by Ergas (1987) may be extended to articulate a further distinction between network-technology policies aimed at increasing the efficiency of innovation efforts by means of interventions on the degree of coherence of innovation systems and innovation policies designed to increase the amount of innovative efforts of firms. Granted this, we expect that countries with more systemic network approaches to industrial policy will experience higher rates of technological advance than countries with a more individualistic approach, for given levels of investment in research and learning activities. The strengthening of the complementarity of research and learning activities of firms in an innovation system is also likely to increase the generation of technology by each firm and by that system as a whole. *Ex ante* co-operation schemes in long-term technology projects offer useful guidance to firms in planning their efforts in a complementary way and co-operation among innovating firms is likely to have positive effects on connectivity. The creation and implementation of effective communication networks between firms, in turn influences all interventions that favour actual complementarity of research and learning activities among firms.

More generally, traditional innovation policies based upon incentive schemes mainly designed to increase the levels of R&D could be reoriented in order to take into account the communication properties of innovation systems, such as connectivity and receptivity. Policies enhancing technological co-operation between firms and between firms and universities are important in this context. Such co-operation may be defined as an institutionalised system of technological relationships aimed at internalising technological externalities and increasing spatial stochastic interactions probability. In fact, it is the result of explicit strategic action by members to increase communication via connectivity and receptivity levels.

The complementarity and compatibility of research agendas and thus network connectivity of innovation systems can also be increased by the introduction of meta-standards. Indeed standardisation policy can become an important complementary tool of technology policy (David and Greenstein, 1990; Antonelli, 1994a). In relation to the rationale behind the imposition of standards and policies of technological co-operation, property rights should also be re-assessed. The application of tight 'innovation oriented' intellectual property rights increases appropriation but is attended by a related reduction in the flow of communication between firms. An issue of under-utilisation arises with reference to the innovative capability of the network, with the existence of a clear trade off between static and dynamic efficiency. Systems with 'diffusion oriented' property rights regimes have higher chances of stimulating the flow of technological communication between firms, and consequently obtaining higher rates of return from resources invested in R&D activities (Ordover, 1991).

New information and communication technologies offer considerable opportunities to increase both the connectivity of innovation networks and the receptivity of firms in those networks. This in turn enhances the productivity of resources invested in research and learning activities, provided that open network architectures, maximising inclusion, are implemented. The diffusion and implementation of the new information and communication technology system, itself a product of the clustering of localised and complementary technological changes, are likely to interact with the general rate of introduction of localised technological changes enhancing the innovation capability of firms coping with changes in their economic environment. The modernisation of telecommunications infrastructure and organisation becomes central in this context.

The network of networks, as it is emerging in the daily experience of the European Union in the integration of different national telecommunications networks into a single European network, seems an organisational architecture especially conducive to foster the rate of introduction of innovation and accommodate the different directions, whether introduced by users or network operators. The notion of the network of networks promises the advantages of high rates of introduction of innovations and yet retains the coherence of the network and its established advantages in terms of interoperability and interconnectivity externalities. From a dynamic point of view, in the European Union, the network of networks is likely to emerge as a key policy tool both to induce and guide the evolution of European telecommunications and increase the rates of introduction of localised technological change in the European innovation systems.

Advanced countries with well designed innovation systems are likely, over time, to experience a continual increase in innovative capability levels provided that positive feedbacks, between the quality of connectivity and receptivity, and the levels of innovative capability, take place either 'spontaneously' or as a result of technology policies and strategies. Successful agents rooted within innovation systems can learn to communicate, in terms of both connectivity and receptivity, as soon as they realise that their innovation capability is positively influenced by the communication network and subsequently, they take advantage of increasing returns and positive feedbacks in learning both internal and external to each firm. When we take into account the possibility of interactions between productivity levels and the properties of innovation systems, the methodology of recursive spatial stochastic interactions models offers a conceivable explanation for cumulative self-sustained growth as led by learning to interact within the network. On the other hand, new industrialising countries and peripheral regions, where communications channels and complementarity are not yet established and organised, are likely to experience much higher innovation unit costs than industrialised countries where a long lasting practice of co-operation and complementarity is fully embedded in articulated innovation systems. For the same levels of perturbation in the economic environment, such countries are more likely to experience the drawbacks of producer switching costs rather then the positive inducement mechanisms associated with the introduction of localised technological changes.

Countries with high levels of technological capability in a given technological area, such as engineering industries in Italy, are likely to experience a continual advance in these areas accompanied by slight changes over time in related areas, such as the newly emerging mechatronics industry, generated by the merging of electronics and engineering. We can thus expect strong path-dependent features in the evolution of the technological specialisation of countries and firms. For given levels of perturbation in the economic environment, countries will react differently according to the characteristics of their topological structure i.e. the network relations in place among agents and the spatial stochastic interactions structure of their innovation systems. Countries are most likely to implement their own technological specialisation and to experience continual increases in productivity levels around the initial given composition of their industrial structure with an increasing specialisation in well defined technological fields and the complementary growth of the international trade in disembodied technology.

Notes

Foreword

1 This book brings together in an unitary framework, based upon systematic rewriting and reorganisation, after many exclusions and inclusions, preliminary materials and extracts from papers which were previously published in several journals. For a preliminary version of the text now in Chapter 1 see International Journal of Industrial Organization 15 (1997); for Chapter 3 see Economics of Innovation and New Technology 6 (1998); for Chapter 4 see Manchester School of Economic and Social Studies 44 (1996); for Chapter 6 see Industrial and Corporate Change 4 (1995), Information Economics and Policy 8 (1996) and Telecommunications Policy 21 (1997); for Chapter 7 see International Review of Applied Economics 10 (1996); for Chapter 8 see Cambridge Journal of Economics 22 (1998); for Chapter 9 see Empirica 24 (1997); for Chapter 10 see Information Economics and Policy 6(1994); for Chapter 11 see Review of Industrial Organization 12 (1997) and Journal of Evolutionary Economics 8 (1998).

Introduction

1 Arrow (1996) makes clear this point: 'The literature, especially the formal literature, in this field has largely traced the effects of a given information structure. An agent, for example, is assumed to observe a random variable, while the principal knows only the distribution of that variable. Not enough weight has been given to the possibility that information can be and is daily altered by economic decisions. A firm can buy information in one way or another or it can expend resources in research and development to wrest the information from nature. It is the treatment of information as a variable and its implications for economic behavior that needs further analysis'. (p. 646)

2 A distinction is made here between 'industrial economics' as it has been elaborated in the structure-conduct-performance tradition and the more game-theoretic 'industrial organisation' specialising in the analysis of oligopolistic markets (See Scherer, 1984; Scherer and Ross, 1990; Antonelli, 1995c).

1 Path-dependence in industrial economics and the economics of innovation

1 See the extensive literature reviewed by Paul Stoneman (1983).
2 See the extensive literature reviewed by Stephen Martin (1993: 136–163 and 261–296).
3 See Chapter 3 for the analysis of the endogeneity of localised technological change.

4 The specific steps are as follows:

$$\int_{t} \frac{dQ(t)}{[\alpha - Q(t)] \cdot Q(t)} = -\frac{1}{\alpha} \log \left| \frac{\alpha - Q(t)}{Q(t)} \right| = -\lambda \cdot Z \cdot t + C_1 \Rightarrow \frac{\alpha - Q(t)}{Q(t)} = C_2 \cdot e^{\alpha \cdot \lambda \cdot Z \cdot t}$$

$$\text{for } \left| \frac{\alpha - Q(t)}{Q(t)} \right| > 0 \quad Q(t) = \frac{\alpha}{1 + C_2 e^{\alpha \cdot \lambda \cdot Z \cdot t}} \quad \text{for } \left| \frac{\alpha - Q(t)}{Q(t)} \right| < 0 \quad Q(t) = \frac{\alpha}{1 + C_2 e^{\alpha \cdot \lambda \cdot Z \cdot t}}$$

5 Standard economics is (also) bound to assume a myopic behaviour: entrants and potential entrants are not aware of the congestion effects brought about by their own entry decision.

6 I owe these remarks to many discussions with Stan Metcalfe.

7 I owe to many discussions with Paul David many arguments elaborated in this paragraph as well as in Chapter 5.

8 See David (1988: 21) for the identification of this distinction and related discussion. David (1997) further elaborates this point and introduces the distinction between homogeneous Markov chains and inhomogeneous Markov chains: 'Transition probabilities that are not invariant functions of the current state also are characteristic features of so-called inhomogeneous Markov chains.' (David, 1997: 10).

2 The new economics of knowledge

1 To be fair to the rich, and ever increasing, contributions of Kenneth Arrow to the economics of innovation and technological change, this 'Arrovian' reference is made to his early and path-breaking papers (Arrow 1962a and b; 1969) and do not include the important advances made in more recent years (Arrow, 1974, 1994a, 1994b, and 1996), systematically quoted elsewhere in this book.

2 See Allen, 1983; Antonelli, 1992 and 1994a; Cohen and Levinthal, 1989; Malerba, 1992.

3 Arrow (1996) puts this very clearly: ' Increasing returns can occur for other reasons than information. But with information, constant returns are impossible. Two tons of steel can be used as an input to produce more than one ton of steel in a given productive activity. But repeating a given piece of information adds nothing. On the other hand, the same piece of information can be used over and over again, by the same or a different producer. This means both that the way information enters the production function is different than the way other goods do and that property rights to information take on a different form.' (p.648).

4 See Griliches, 1979, 1984 and 1988; Jaffe, 1986 and 1989; Katz and Shapiro, 1985; Arora and Gambardella, 1990; Carlsson and Stankiewicz, 1991.

5 See the path-breaking analysis of Francois Perroux on the role of economic spaces in assessing the full systems of interdependence among agents in economic systems. Only the analysis of economic spaces makes it possible to understand the co-ordination process within systems beyond the set of interactions cleared by market prices (Perroux, 1935 and 1964).

6 Within 'perfect' markets, without any form of externality, interdependence takes place all the time, but is *fully* mediated by prices.

7 See Allen, 1983; Von Hippel, 1988; Lundvall, 1985; Antonelli, 1994b.

8 See Teece, 1986; Klein, 1992; Nelson, 1993.

9 On-line engineering co-operation procedures among independent firms in the design of new automobiles are today common practice in the industry and provide a variety of examples of forms of exchange and trade of both tacit and

codified knowledge among teams of experts each specialising in the design of a complementary component.

10 See Arrow (1996): 'I would forecast an increasing tension between legal relations and fundamental economic determinants. Information is the basis of production, production is carried on in discrete legal entities, and yet information is a fugitive resource, with limited property rights. Small symptoms of these tensions are already appearing the legal and economic spheres. There is continually difficulty in defining intellectual property: the US Courts and Congress have come up with strange definitions. Copyright law has been applied to software, although the analogy with books is hardly compelling . . . These are still minor matters, but I would surmise that we are just beginning to face the contradictions between the systems of private property and of information acquisition and dissemination'. (p.652)

11 For similar conclusions see Porter, 1990; Saxenian, 1991 and Von Hippel, 1988.

3 The dynamics of localised technological changes: the interaction between factor costs inducement, demand-pull and Schumpeterian rivalry

1 See David (1975), von Weiszacker (1984), Beggs (1989) and Antonelli (1994c and 1995) for the evolution of the notion of producer switching costs, as distinct from consumer switching costs (Klemperer, 1995).

2 The new localised technology enables one to find a solution B which coincides with A in terms of factor requirements, but allows larger or identical output levels, but higher general efficiency and hence lower unit costs.

3 The technical distance between A and B can be measured with the Euclidean distance Δ:

$$\Delta AB = ((L_A - L_B)^2 + (K_A - K_B)^2)^{1/2} \tag{2}$$

4 In the case of the maximisation of possible adjustments the map of the FPA is clearly bordered by a maximum level of switching distances, corresponding to the distance AB, so that no larger switching distance can be selected. The map of isorevenues will exhibit diminishing slopes beyond the distance AC, taking into account the increasing incentive to introduce technological innovations that increase productivity in monetary terms as well.

5 Hence localised technological change is neutral: the factor intensity of the previous technical choice remains the same. In such a case, factor shares will change in the same direction as factor costs: for a given increase in wages, an entirely localised technological change will be introduced which mirrors the increase of the amount of revenue paid to workers.

6 In fact the dynamics of such a market, based on the combination of both Marshallian and Schumpeterian characters, reproduces the basic elements of classical competition as repeatedly analysed by Josef Steindl (See Steindl, 1947 and 1952).

7 On the basis of well-established empirical literature it is assumed here that the rates of introduction of innovations in industries specialising in the production of capital goods are higher than those in the industries producing consumer goods (See Pavitt, 1984).

8 Especially when the demand for capital goods exhibits more than unitary price elasticities in the relevant portion of the curve.

4 Localised technological change and Schumpeterian growth regimes

1 In Chapter 3.

5 Economic topology: the role of technological communication in the dynamics of localised technological change

1 When numbers are *sufficiently small* direct strategic interactions can be taken into account by means of game-theoretic approaches.

2 See Cohen and Levinthal (1989 and 1990) on the distinction between 'receptivity' and 'connectivity'.

3 See also Kirman, Oddou and Weber (1986) on the role of stochastic communication in coalition formation.

4 A variety of models, functional forms and specifications of spatial stochastic interactions is available in the literature: percolation is a class of models among many others (See for an excellent review Cefis and Espa, 1997).

5 The standard approach to obtain a dynamic system of spatial interactions consists in the assumption that at random points in time, firms can reassess their choices without any qualification about the effects of the previous points in time on each new situation (See David and Foray, 1994: 154). Our approach instead consists in making explicit the time stratification of different spatial interactions where the structural characterisitics of each interaction are influenced by the results of the previous. This approach to model the dynamics leads to the notion of historic time processes: hence with respect to percolation, we can introduce the notion of percolation processes which instead would seem unwarranted in the specification elaborated by David and Foray (1994: 159). This hypothesis is consistent with the use of 'Ising' spatial interactions models where 'energy' is endogenous. See David, Foray and Dalle, 1998.

6 Actually some firms might even consider substituting better communication links to internal R&D activities, but such substitution can take place only to a limited extent (See Chapter 2).

7 See Arrow (1974).

8 The consideration of the idiosyncratic characteristics of the technology life cycle makes it possible to better specify the time path along which the total number of information channels changes either via the entry and exit of firms and/or the explicit strategic conduct of firms such as the creation of technology clubs and generally the membership into technological co-operation schemes (See Chapter 9).

6 Localised technological changes in telecommunications and the network of networks

1 See Brock(1994): 'MCI was a new company founded by radio servicemen and entrepreneur Jack Goeken. Goeken proposed a limited microwave system costing about one-half million dollars that would have less capacity than many private systems. Goeken estimated he needed to obtain 35 users to break even and presented a research report that concluded he was likely to obtain between 58 and 204 customers.'

7 Localised technological change and unemployment in the global economy: a Schumpeterian approach

1 See Pavitt and Soete, 1982; Dosi, Pavitt and Soete, 1990; Archibugi and Pianta, 1992; Amendola, Dosi and Papagni, 1993 with regard to empirical evidence.

2 In imitating countries, other things being equal, there will be fewer job opportunities than in an innovating country, since the fixed coefficients on which the new superior technology is based, are not designed for consistent use with the factors available in the non-innovating countries. The localised character of technology will therefore also tend to cause relative unemployment in the imitating countries.

3 All the data is from OECD sources (IMF for investment) and includes all the member countries except Luxembourg and Iceland for obvious reasons and Mexico because it has only just joined.

4 High employment levels in the primary sector in these countries are likely to hide consistent shares of 'real' unemployment.

5 The results of the linear specification for R&D read as follows:

$$UE = 21.714 - 3.882\,(R\&D) - 0.297\,(INV) + 0.062\,(W) - 6.42\,(G) - 6.566\,(P) \quad (7)$$
$$\qquad\quad (3.267) \qquad\quad (3.539) \qquad\ (0.99) \qquad (3.186) \quad (4.789)$$

$R^2 = 0.608$; $F(1\text{-}63) = 20.24$
(Student t-values in parentheses)

8 New information technology and the evolution of the organisation of knowledge production

1 The long standing tradition of the Italian universities to allow for a distinction between part-time and full-time tenured professors can be considered in this context an interesting institutional device to favour the interaction between the business community and the academic one by means of the creation of professional markets for advanced research individual competences. Tenured professors can operate professionally as consultants and earn additional revenue in the market place but only after switching to the part-time condition. This implies a reduction in salary and academic duties. The ratio of part-time to full-time tenured positions is very high in scientific faculties, as well as in law, business, medical and engineering schools, for chair professors.

2 The personal relationship instead has been traditionally flourishing in Italy, due to the part-time professorial positions. The transition from a personal relationship to an institutional one, however, would enable the direct access of firms to universities as a whole, that is also to the entire academic organisation, including intangible and fixed capital infrastructure. Such an institutionalised relationship would seem more appropriate for sophisticated research tasks which require advanced laboratories with dedicated equipment, as well as team production, based on a variety of skills and large numbers of researchers. The traditional 'personal relationship' instead seems most efficient in securing the fast circulation of information, helping the diffusion of new technologies and increasing the connectivity and receptivity of agents in the system. The transition to an institutionalised relationship would also favour the full outsourcing of research activities by firms: the personal relationship often resorts to the inclusion of academic part-time personnel in research teams and intra-muros laboratories operated by firms (See Geuna, 1998 for a first attempt in the economics of university).

9 The dynamics of technological externalities and the evolution of technological co-operation

1 See Katz, 1986; Katz and Ordover, 1990; Grossman and Shapiro, 1986; D'Aspremont and Jacquemin, 1988.

10 The evolution of standards as economic institutions

1 Empirical evidence shows that the introduction of document standards, such as EDIFACT, enables the division of labour within large technological systems like the automobile components industries.

2 The introduction of GSM standards in the European mobile telephone industry, for example, has favoured competition in telecommunications services because of the international roaming that the pan-European standard engendered. In addition, the GSM standard has almost swept away the typical bilateral monopoly market structure in the telecommunications equipment industry, where one or a few large buyers usually confront one or a few suppliers. Now instead all European mobile service providers can procure standardised equipment from a variety of competitive suppliers (Hawkins, 1993).

3 As David and Steinmueller (1994) make clear: 'the economics of standards . . . belongs to the domain of information economics. The establishment of standards has the greatest significance when economic agents cannot assimilate without substantial costs all the relevant information about the commodities that may be exchanged with other agents; and about the processes by means of which those goods and services can be produced. In a very broad sense, then, to ask about the effects of standards upon economic competition simply is to inquire into the ways in which competitive processes may be affected by the creation and distribution of information' (p. 3).

4 See Simon, 1986 p. S210–211, quoted by North, 1991, p. 23; Lamberton, 1971 and Langlois, 1986.

5 Consequently standardisation appears to be an essential part of the process of virtuous, cumulative growth to which Young (1928) refers: 'Every important advance in the organisation of production regardless of whether it is based upon anything which in a narrow or technical sense, would be called a new 'invention' or involves a fresh application of the fruits of scientific progress to industry, alters the conditions of industrial activity and initiates responses elsewhere in the industrial structure which in turn have a further unsettling effect. Thus change becomes progressive and propagates itself in a cumulative way' (Young, 1928: 533).

6 Besen's (1990) careful analysis of the organisation and working procedures of ETSI (European Telecommunications Standards Institute) provides clear evidence on the structure and the functions of a typical standardisation institute as a club where membership, roles and powers of members are subject to severe scrutiny.

7 When the utility function is affected by network externalities and it is specified as follows:

$$U = x^{aZ} y^b \qquad (10)$$

where Z is the level of aggregate demand for compatible products, x is a standardised product, y a vector of other products; a and b are other conventional parameters; it is easily shown that both the intercept and the price elasticities of the demand for standardised products are larger (See equation (9) in Chapter 1).

11 New information technology and the knowledge-based economy: the European evidence

1 Because of differences in the quality and usage conditions of input/output statistics for Italy and the other three main European economies, i.e. France, Germany and the United Kingdom respectively, the empirical analysis was

carried out with two methodologies. The Italian data offered a longer time spell for investments and hence for capital figures, which enabled us to test empirically the 'residual' hypothesis. We thus present first the full set of results for the Italian evidence, then the other countries. The cross-industry estimates of the production function used for France, Germany and the United Kingdom, however was subsequently replicated for Italy, in order to present a full continental framework of analysis.

2 Data from national accounts has been used for the primary industries.
3 Capital figures were obtained using investments series.
4 Data for Germany and France was made available by the MERIT Data Bank whose support is gratefully acknowledged. Data for Italy was found in ISTAT (1992a and b). Data for the United Kingdom was found in the Central Statistical Office (1995) and UN (1995). The help of Andrea Panetta and Aldo Geuna in data collection and aggregation is acknowledged.
5 Business services in the United Kingdom include activities such as legal services, accountancy services, other professional services, advertising, computing services, other business services, renting of movables, in rows 107–108–109–110–111–112–113 respectively. The definition of the business service sector for the other countries is provided by the respective country tables.

12 Conclusion

1 See David (1996).
2 See Perroux, 1935 and 1964.

Bibliography

Abernathy, W. J. and Clark, K. B. (1985) 'Innovation: mapping the winds of creative destruction', *Research Policy*, 14, 3–22.

Abernathy, W. J. (1978) *The Productivity Dilemma*, Baltimore: Johns Hopkins University Press.

Abramovitz, M. (1938) 'Monopolistic selling in a changing economy', *Quarterly Journal of Economics*, 52, 191–214.

Abramovitz, M. (1986) 'Catching up, forging ahead, and falling behind', *Journal of Economic History*, 46, 385–406.

Abramovitz, M. (1989) *Thinking about Growth*, Stanford: Stanford University Press.

Acs, Z. J., Audretsch, D. B. and Feldman, M. P. (1994) 'R&D spillovers and the recipient firm size', *Review of Economics and Statistics*, 76, 336–40.

Aghion, P. and Howitt, P. (1998) *Endogenous Growth Theories*, Cambridge, MA: MIT Press.

Akerloff, G. and Yellen, J. (1985) 'A near rational model of the business cycle, with price and wage inertia', *Quarterly Journal of Economics*, 100, 823–838.

Aldrich, H. E. and Sasaki, T. (1995) 'R&D consortia in the United States and Japan', *Research Policy*, 24, 301–316.

Allen, D. (1988) 'New telecommunications services: network externalities and critical mass', *Telecommunications Policy*, 12, 257–271.

Allen, T. J. and Scott Morton, M. S. (eds) (1994) *Information Technology and the Corporation of the 90s*, Oxford: Oxford University Press.

Allen, R. C. (1983) 'Collective invention', *Journal of Economic Behavior and Organization*, 4, 1–24.

Amendola, G. (1988) 'The diffusion of synthetic materials in the automobile industry: towards a major breakthrough?' DRC Discussion Paper No.63, SPRU.

Amendola, G., Dosi, G., and Papagni, E. (1993) 'The dynamics of international competitiveness', *Weltwirtschaftliches Archiv*, 129, 451–471.

Amendola, M. and Bruno, S. (1990) 'The behaviour of the innovative firm: relations to the environment', *Research Policy*, 19, 419–433.

Amendola, M. and Gaffard, J. (1988) *The Innovative Choice. An Economic Analysis of the Dynamics of Technology*, Oxford: Blackwell.

Antonelli, C. (1982) *Cambiamento Tecnologico e Teoria dell'Impresa*, Torino: Loescher.

Antonelli, C. (1986) *L'Attività Innovativa in un Distretto Tecnologico*, Torino: Edizioni della Fondazione Agnelli.

Antonelli, C. (ed.) (1988) *New Information Technology and Industrial Change. The Italian Evidence*, Boston: Kluwer Academic Publishers.

Antonelli, C. (1989a) *L'Industria della Ricerca*, Torino: IRES.

Antonelli, C. (1989b) 'A failure-inducement model of research and development expenditures: Italian evidence from the early 1980s', *Journal of Economic Behavior and Organization*, 12, 159–180.

Antonelli, C. (1991) *The Diffusion of Advanced Telecommunications in Developing Countries*, Paris: OECD.

Antonelli, C. (ed.) (1992) *The Economics of Information Networks*, Amsterdam: Elsevier.

Antonelli, C. (1993a) 'Externalities and complementarities in telecommunications dynamics', *International Journal of Industrial Organization*, 11, 437–448.

Antonelli, C. (1993b) 'The dynamics of technological interrelatedness. The case of information and communication technologies, in Foray, D. and Freeman, C. (eds), *Technology and the Wealth of Nations*, London: Francis Pinter.

Antonelli, C. (1993c) 'Investment productivity growth and key-technologies: the case of advanced telecommunications', *Manchester School of Economic and Social Studies*, 41, 386–397.

Antonelli, C. (1994a) 'Technological districts localized spillovers and productivity growth. The Italian evidence on technological externalities in the core regions', *International Review of Applied Economics*, 8, 31–45.

Antonelli, C. (1994b) 'Localized technological change and the emergence of standards as economic institutions', *Information Economics and Policy*, 6, 195–216.

Antonelli, C. (1994c) 'Localized technological changes: a model incorporating switching costs and R&D expenses with endowment advantages', in Shionoya, Y. and Perlman, M. (eds) *Innovation in Technology, Industries and Institutions. Studies in Schumpeterian Perspectives*, Ann Arbor: University of Michigan Press.

Antonelli, C. (1995a) *The Economics of Localized Technological Change and Industrial Dynamics*, Boston: Kluwer Academic Publishers.

Antonelli, C. (1995b) 'Localized technological change in the network of networks. The interaction between regulation and the evolution of technology in tele-communications', *Industrial and Corporate Change*, 4, 737–755.

Antonelli, C. (1995c) 'Dynamic structuralism and path-dependence: industrial economics in Italy', *Revue d'économie industrielle*, 73, 65–90.

Antonelli, C. (1996a) 'Localized knowledge, percolation processes and information networks', *Journal of Evolutionary Economics*, 6, 281–296.

Antonelli, C. (1996b) 'Localized technological change and Schumpeterian growth regimes', *Manchester School of Economic and Social Studies*, 44, 351–370.

Antonelli, C. (1996c) 'The network of networks: localized technological change in telecommunications and productivity growth', *Information Economics and Policy*, 8, 289–316.

Antonelli, C. (1996d) 'Localized technological change and unemployment in the global economy: a Schumpeterian approach', *International Review of Applied Economics*, 10, 333–344.

Antonelli, C. (1997a) 'New information technology and the knowledge-based economy. The Italian evidence', *Review of Industrial Organization*, 12, 593–606.

Antonelli, C. (1997b) 'The economics of path-depencence in industrial organiza-tion', *International Journal of Industrial Organization*, 15, 643–676.

Antonelli, C. (1997c) 'A regulatory regime for innovation in the communication industries', *Telecommunications Policy*, 21, 35–46.

Antonelli, C. (1997d) 'Percolation processes technological externalities and the evolution of technological clubs', *Empirica*, 24, 137–156.

Antonelli, C. (1998a) 'The dynamics of localized technological changes. The interaction between factor costs-inducement, demand pull and Schumpeterian rivalry', *Economics of Innovation and New Technology*, 6, 97–120.

Antonelli, C. (1998b) 'The evolution of the industrial organization of the production of knowledge', *Cambridge Journal of Economics*, 22, forthcoming.

Antonelli, C. (1998c) 'Localized technological change, new information technology and the knowledge-based economy: the European evidence', *Journal of Evolutionary Economics*, 8, 177–98.

Antonelli, C. (1998d) 'Localized technological change and the dynamics of path-dependent growth: The case of FIAT 1900–1971', Paper prepared for the VII Schumpeter Society Conference, Vienna, 1998.

Antonelli, C. (1998e) 'Localized technological change and the dynamics of technological systems. The case of advanced telecommunications', Paper prepared for the IV Annual Conference of the Consortium for Research on Telecommunications Policy, University of Michigan, Ann Arbor.

Antonelli, C. (1998f) 'Locally Progressive and regressive technological change: reswitching out-of-equilibrium and unemployment', Paper prepared for the IV Franco-American Conference organized by CREST and NBER, Université de Nice.

Antonelli, C. (1999) 'The organization of production', *Metroeconomica*, 51, forthcoming.

Antonelli, C. and Foray, D. (1992) 'Technological clubs: cooperation and competition', *Economics of Innovation and New Technology*, 1, 37–48.

Antonelli, C., Petit, P. and Tahar, G. (1992) *The Economics of Industrial Modernization*, Cambridge: Academic Press.

Antonelli, C. and Marchionatti, R. (1998) 'Technological and organisational change in a process of industrial rejuvenation. The case of the Italian cotton textile industry', *Cambridge Journal of Economics*, 22, 1–18.

Archibugi, D. and Pianta, M. (1992) *The Technological Specialization of Advanced Countries*, Boston: Kluwer Academic Publishers.

Archibugi, D. and Michie, J. (eds) (1997) *Technology Globalisation and Economic Performance*, Cambridge: Cambridge University Press.

Archibugi, D. and Michie, J. (eds) (1998) *Trade Growth and Technical Change*, Cambridge: Cambridge University Press.

Arora, A. (1995) 'Licencing tacit knowledge: intellectual property rights and the market for know-how', *Economics of Innovation and New Technology*, 4, 41–60.

Arora, A. (1997) 'Patents licencing and market structure in the chemical industry', *Research Policy*, 26, 391–403.

Arora, A. and Gambardella, A. (1990) 'Internal knowledge and external linkages: theoretical issues and an application to biotechnology', *Journal of Industrial Economics*, 38, 361–379.

Arora, A. and Gambardella, A. (1994) 'The changing technology of technological change. General and abstract knowledge and the division of innovative labour', *Research Policy*, 23, 523–532.

Arrow, K. J. (1959) 'Towards a theory of price adjustment', in Abramovitz, M. *et al.*, *The Allocation of Economic Resources*, Stanford: Stanford University Press.

Arrow, K. J. (1962a) 'The economic implications of learning by doing', *Review of Economic Studies*, 29, 155–173.

Arrow, K. J. (1962b) 'Economic welfare and the allocation of resources for invention', in Nelson R. R. (ed.) *The Rate and Direction of Inventive Activity: Economic and Social Factors*, Princeton: Princeton University Press for N.B.E.R.

Arrow, K. J. (1969) 'Classificatory notes on the production and transmission of technical knowledge', *American Economic Review*, P&P 59, 29–35.

Arrow, K. J. (1974) *The Limits of Organization*, New York: W.W. Norton.

Arrow, K. J. (1994a) 'Information and the organization of industry', *Rivista Internazionale di Scienze Sociali*, 102, 111–124.

Arrow, K. J. (1994b) 'Methodological individualism and social knowledge', *American Economic Review*, P&P 84, 1–9.

Arrow, K.J. (1996) 'Technical information and industrial structure', *Industrial and Corporate Change*, 5, 645–652.

Arthur, B. (1989) 'Competing technologies increasing returns and lock-in by small historical events', *Economic Journal*, 99, 116–131.

Arthur, B. (1994) *Increasing Returns and Path-dependence in the Economy*, Ann Arbor: University of Michigan Press.

Atkinson, A. B. and Stiglitz, J. E. (1969) 'A new view of technological change', *Economic Journal*, 79, 573–578.

Audretsch, D. B. (1995) *Innovation and Industry Evolution*, Cambridge, MA: MIT Press.

Audretsch, D. B. and Stephan, P. E. (1996) 'Company-scientist locational links: the case of biotechnology', *American Economic Review*, 86, 641–652.

Baldwin, J. R. (1995) *The Dynamics of Industrial Competition*, Cambridge: Cambridge University Press.

Banerjee, A.V. (1993) 'The economics of rumors', *Review of Economic Studies*, 60, 309–327.

Bean, C. R. (1994) 'European unemployment: a survey', *Journal of Economic Literature*, 32, 573–619.

Becattini, G. (ed.) (1987) *Il Mercato e le Forze Locali*, Bologna: Il Mulino.

Beggs, A. (1989) 'A note on switching costs and technology choice', *Journal of Industrial Economics*, 37, 437–440.

Beniger, J. R. (1986) *The Control Revolution: Technological and Economic Origins of the Information Society*, Cambridge, MA: Harvard University Press.

Berg, S. V. (1989) 'The production of compatibility: technical standards as collective goods', *Kyklos*, 42, 361–383.

Berndt, E. and Fuss, M. (1986) 'Productivity measurements with adjustments for variations in capacity utilization and other forms of temporary equilibrium', *Journal of Econometrics*, 33, 7–29.

Besen, S. M. (1990) 'The European telecommunications standards institute', *Telecommunications Policy*, 14, 521–530.

Besen, S. M. and Raskind, L. (1991) 'An introduction to the law and economics of intellectual property', *Journal of Economic Perspectives*, 5, 3–27.

Binswanger, H. P. *et al.* (1978) *Induced Innovation*, Baltimore: Johns Hopkins University Press.

Boyer, R., Chavance, B. and Godard, O. (eds) (1991) *Les Figures de l'irréversibilité en économie*, Paris: Editions de l'Ecole de Hautes Etudes en Sciences Sociales.

Bresnahan, T. F. (1986) 'Measuring the spillover from technical advance: mainframe computers in financial services', *American Economic Review*, 76, 742–755.

Bresnahan, T. F. (1989) 'Empirical studies of industries with market power', in Schmalensee, R. and Willig, R. D. (eds) *Handbook of Industrial Organization*, Amsterdam: Elsevier.

Brock, G. W. (1994) *The U.S. Telecommunication Policy Process*, Cambridge, MA: Harvard University Press.

Brousseau, E. (1994) 'EDI and inter-firm relationships: toward a standardization of coordination process?', *Information Economics and Policy*, 6, 319–340.

Brousseau, E., Petit, P. and Phan, D. (1996) *Mutations des telecommunications des industries et des marchés*, Paris: Economica.

Brynjolfsson, E. and Hitt, L. (1995) 'Information technology as a factor of production: the role of differences among firms', *Economics of Innovation and New Technology*, 3, 183–200.

Buchanan, J. M. (1965) 'An economic theory of clubs', *Economica*, 34, 1–14.

Burns, A. (1934) *Production Trends in the United States since 1870*, New York: National Bureau of Economic Research.

Burt, R. S. (1992) *Structural Holes. The Social Structure of Competition*, Cambridge, MA: Harvard University Press.

Cainarca, G., Colombo, M. G. and Mariotti, S. (1992) 'Agreements between firms and the technological life cycle model: evidence from information technology', *Research Policy*, 21, 45–62.

Callon, M. (1991) 'Réseaux technico-économiques et irreversibilité', in Boyer, R., Chavance, B. and Godard, O. (eds) *Les Figures de l'irreversibilité en économie*, Paris: Editions de l'Ecole de Hautes Etudes en Sciences Sociales.

Cantner, U. and Westermann, G. (1997) 'Localized technological progress and industry structure. An empirical approach', *Economics of Innovation and New Technology*, 6, forthcoming.

Cantwell, J. A. (1989) *Technological Innovation and Multinational Corporations*, Oxford: Basil Blackwell.

Cantwell, J. and Barrera, P. (1998) 'The localisation of corporate technological trajectories in the interwar cartels: cooperative learning versus an exchange of knowledge', *Economics of Innovation and New Technology*, 6, forthcoming.

Carlsson, B. (1987) 'Reflections on "industrial dynamics". The challenges ahead', *International Journal of Industrial Organization*, 5, 135–148.

Carlsson, B. (ed.) (1989) *Industrial Dynamics. Technological Organizational and Structural Changes in Industries and Firms*, Boston: Kluwer Academic Publishers.

Carlsson, B. (ed.) (1995) *Technological Systems and Economic Performance: The Case of Factory Automation*, Boston: Kluwer Academic Publishers.

Carlsson, B. (1998) 'On and off the beaten path: the evolution of four technological systems in Sweden', *International Journal of Industrial Organization*, 15, 775–800.

Carlsson, B. and Eliasson, G. (1994) 'The nature and importance of economic competence', *Industrial and Corporate Change*, 3, 687–712.

Carlsson, B. and Stankiewitz, R. (1991) 'On the nature function and composition of technological systems', *Journal of Evolutionary Economics*, 1, 93–118.

Carter, A. (1989) 'Know-how trading as economic exchange', *Research Policy*, 18, 155–163.

Casson, M. (1997) *Information and Organization. A New Perspective on the Theory of the Firm*, Oxford: Clarendon Press.

Caves, R. E. and Porter, M. E. (1977) 'From entry barriers to mobility barriers:

conjectural decisions and contrived deterrence to new competition', *Quarterly Journal of Economics*, 91, 241–261.

Caves, R. E. (1982) *Multinational Enterprise and Economic Analysis*, Cambridge: Cambridge University Press.

Cefis, E. and Espa, G. (1997) 'Modelli di interazione spaziale: presupposti teorici e aspetti applicativi', Computable and Experimental Economics Laboratory WP 1997–05, University of Trento.

Chandler, A. D. (1990) *Scale and Scope: the Dynamics of Industrial Capitalism*, Cambridge, MA: Harvard University Press.

Chandler, A. D. (1992) 'Organizational capabilities and the economic history of industrial enterprise', *Journal of Economic Perspectives*, 6, 79–100.

Ciborra, C. (1993) *Teams Markets and Systems. Business Innovation and Information Technology*, Cambridge: Cambridge University Press.

Clark, K. M. (1985) 'The interaction of design hierarchies and market concepts in technological evolution', *Research Policy*, 14, 235–251.

Clarysse, B., Debackere, K. and Van Dierdonck, R. (1995) Research networks and organizational mobility in an emerging technological field: the case of bio-technology', *Economics of Innovation and New Technology*, 4, 77–96.

Coe, D. E. and Helpman, E. (1995) 'International R&D Spillover', *European Economic Review*, 39, 859–887.

Cohen, W. M. and Levinthal, D. A. (1989) 'Innovation and learning: the two faces of R&D', *Economic Journal*, 99, 569–596.

Cohen, W. M. and Levinthal, D. A. (1990) 'Absorptive capacity: a new perspective on learning and innovation', *Administrative Science Quarterly*, 35, 128–152.

Cowan, R. (1991) 'Tortoises and hares: choice among technologies of unknown merit', *Economic Journal*, 101, 801–814.

Cowan, R., Cowan, W. and Swann, P. (1997) 'A model of demand with inter-actions between consumers', *International Journal of Industrial Organization*, 15, 711–732.

Cowan, R. and Cowan, W. (1998) 'On clustering in the location of R&D: statistics and dynamics', *Economics of Innovation and New Technology*, 6, 201–230.

D'Aspremont, C. and Jaquemin, A. (1988) 'Cooperative and non-cooperative R&D in duopoly with spillovers', *American Economic Review*, 78, 1133–1137.

Dalle, J. M. (1995) 'Dynamiques d'adoption coordination et diversité', *Revue Economique*, 46, 1081–1098.

Dalle, J. M. (1997) 'Heterogeneity vs. externalities in technological competition: a tale of possible technological landscapes', *Journal of Evolutionary Economics*, 7, 395–414.

Dasgupta, P. (1987) 'The economic theory of technology policy: an introduction', in Dasgupta, P. and Stoneman, P. (eds) *Economic Policy and Technological Performance*, Cambridge: Cambridge University Press.

Dasgupta, P. and David, P. A. (1987) 'Information disclosure and the economics of science and technology', in Feiwel, J. (ed.) *Arrow and the Ascent of Modern Economic Theory*, New York: New York University Press.

Dasgupta, P. and David, P. A. (1994) 'Toward a new economics of science', *Research Policy*, 23, 487–521.

David, P. A. (1975) *Technical Choice Innovation and Economic Growth*, Cambridge: Cambridge University Press.

David, P. A. (1985) 'Clio and the economics of QWERTY', *American Economic Review*, 75, 332–337.

David, P. A. (1987) 'Some new standards for the economics of standardization in the information age', in Dasgupta, P. and Stoneman, P. (eds) *Economic Policy and Technological Performance*, Cambridge: Cambridge University Press.

David, P. A. (1988) 'Path-dependence: putting the past into the future of economics', Technical Report No. 533. The economics series. Stanford: Institute for Mathematical Studies in the Social Sciences, Stanford University,

David, P. A. (1992a) 'Why are institutions the "carriers of history"? Notes on path-dependence and the evolution of conventions organizations and institutions', Paper prepared for presentation in the Stanford Institute for Theoretical Economics Summer Program on 'Irreversibilities'.

David, P. A. (1992b) 'Intellectual property institutions and the panda's thumb. Patents copyrights and trade secrets in economic theory and history', Stanford: Center for Economic Policy Research, Stanford University.

David, P. A. (1992c) 'Path-dependence in economic processes: implications for policy analysis in dynamical system contexts', Stanford: Center for Economic Policy Research, Stanford University.

David, P. A. (1992d) 'Heroes herds and hysteresis in technological history', *Industrial and Corporate Change*, 1, 129–179.

David, P. A. (1993a) 'Knowledge property and the system dynamics of technological change', *Proceedings of the World Bank Annual Conference on Development Economics*, Washington, DC: The World Bank.

David, P. A. (1993b) 'Path-dependence and predictability in dynamic systems with local network externalities: a paradigm for historic economics', in Foray, D. and Freeman C. (eds), *Technology and the Wealth of Nations*, London: Pinter.

David, P. A. (1994) 'Positive feed-backs and research productivity in science: reopening another black box', in Granstrand, O. (ed.) *Economics and Technology*, Amsterdam: Elsevier.

David, P.A. (1996) 'Communication norms and the collective cognitive performance of invisible colleges', forthcoming in Navaretti, G.B. *et al. Creation and Transfer of Knowledge: Institutions and Incentives*, Berlin: Physica-Verlag Series Contribution to Economics.

David, P.A. (1997) 'Path dependence and the quest for historical economics: one more chorus of the ballad of QWERTY', working document, All Souls College, Oxford and Stanford University.

David, P. A. and Greenstein, S. (1990) 'The economics of compatibility standards: an introduction to recent research', *Economics of Innovation and New Technology*, 1, 3–42.

David, P. A. and Rosenbloom, J. (1990) 'Marshallian factor market externalities and the dynamics of industrial localization', *Journal of Urban Economics*, 28, 349–370.

David, P. A. and Foray, D. (1994) 'Percolation structures, Markov random fields and the economics of EDI standards diffusion', in Pogorel G. (ed.) *Global Telecommunications Strategies and Technological Changes*, Amsterdam: Elsevier.

David, P. A. and Foray, D. (1995) 'Accessing and expanding the science and technology knowledge base', *Science Technology Industry Review*, 16, 14–68.

David, P. A. and Steinmueller, E. (1994) 'Economics of compatibility standards and competition in telecommunication networks', *Information Economics and Policy*, 6, 217–242.

David, P. A., Foray, D. and Dalle, J. M. (1998) 'Marshallian externalities and the emergence and spatial stability of technological enclaves', *Economics of Innovation and New Technology*, 6, 147–182.

David, P. A., Foray, D. and Steinmueller, W. E. (1998) 'The research network and the new economics of science: from metaphors to organizational behaviours', in Gambardella A. and Malerba, F. (eds) *The Organization of Innovative Activity in Europe*, Cambridge: Cambridge University Press.

Day, R. H. (1986) 'Endogenous preferences and adaptive economizing', in Day, R. H. and Eliasson, G. (eds) *The Dynamics of Market Economies*, Amsterdam: Elsevier.

Day, R. H. and Eliasson, G. (1986) *The Dynamics of Market Economies*, Amsterdam: Elsevier.

Day, R. H. and Nelson, J. P. (1973) 'A class of dynamic models for describing and projecting industrial development', *Journal of Econometrics*, 1, 155–190.

De Bandt, J. (1996) 'Business services: markets and transactions', *Review of Industrial Organization*, 11, 19–33.

Demsetz, H. (1993) 'The theory of the firm revisited', in Williamson, O. E. and Winter, S. G. (eds) *The Nature of the Firm*, Oxford: Oxford University Press.

Den Hertog, P. *et al.* (1995) *Assessing the distribution power of national innovation systems. Pilot study: the Netherlands*, Apeldoorn: TNO.

Dixit, A. (1992) 'Investment and hysteresis', *Journal of Economic Perspectives*, 6, 107–132.

Dosi, G. (1988) 'Sources procedures and microeconomic effects of innovation', *Journal of Economic Literature*, 26, 1120–1171.

Dosi, G., Pavitt, K. and Soete, L. (1990) *The Economics of Technical Change and International Trade*, New York: Harvester.

Dosi, G. *et al.* (1988) *Technical Change and Economic Theory*, London: Pinter.

Ducatel, K. (ed.) (1994) *Employment and Technical Change in Europe*, Aldershot: Edward Elgar.

Dunning, J. H. (1981) *International Production and the Multinational Enterprise*, London: Allen and Unwin.

Dunning, J. H. (1992) *Multinational enterprises and the Global Economy*, Wokingham: Addison-Wesley.

Durlauf, S. D. (1993) 'Non ergodic economic growth', *Review of Economic Studies*, 60, 349–366.

Duysters, G. (1996) *The Dynamics of Technical Innovation. The Evolution and Development of Information Technology*, Aldershot: Edward Elgar.

Eaton, B. C. and Lipsey, R. G. (1978) 'Freedom of entry and the existence of pure profit', *Economic Journal*, 88, 455–469.

Edquist, C. (ed.) (1997) *Systems of Innovation*, London: Cassel.

Egidi, M. and Narduzzo, A. (1997) 'The emergence of path-dependent behaviors in cooperative contexts', *International Journal of Industrial Organization*, 15, 677–709.

Eliasson, G. (1989) 'The dynamics of supply and economic growth. How industrial knowledge accumulation drives a path-dependent economic process', in Carlsson, B. (ed.) *Industrial Dynamics. Technological Organizational and Structural Changes in Industries and Firms*, Boston: Kluwer Academic Publishers.

Ergas, H. (1987) 'Does technology policy matter?', in Guile, B. R. and Brooks, H.

(eds) *Technology and Global Industry: Companies and Nations in the World Economy*, Washington, DC: National Academy Press.

Eswaran, M. and Gallini, N. (1996) 'Patent policy and the direction of technological change', *Rand Journal of Economics*, 27, 722–746.

Farell, J. (1995) 'Arguments for weaker intellectual property protection in network industries', in Kahin, B. and Abbate, J. (eds) *Standards Policy for Information Infrastructure*, Cambridge, MA: MIT Press.

Farell, J. and Saloner, G. (1985) 'Standardization compatibility and innovation', *Rand Journal of Economics*, 16, 70–83.

Farrell, J. and Saloner, G. (1987) 'Competition compatibility and standards: the economics of horses penguins and lemmings', in Gabel, L. H. (ed.) *Product Standardization and Competitive Strategy*, Amsterdam: Elsevier.

Feldman, M. P. (1994) *The Geography of Innovation*, Boston: Kluwer Academic Publishers.

Fellner, W. J. (1949) *Competition among the Few*, New York: Knopf.

Fellner, W. J. (1961) 'Two propositions in the theory of induced innovation', *Economic Journal*, 71, 305–308.

Fisher, R.A. (1930), *The Genetical Theory of Natural Selection*, Oxford: Oxford University Press.

Flaherty, M. T. (1980) 'Industry structure and cost-reducing investments', *Econometrica*, 48, 1187–1209.

Follmer, H. (1974) 'Random economies with many interacting agents', *Journal of Mathematical Economics*, 1, 51–62.

Folster, S. (1995) 'Do subsidies to cooperative R&D actually stimulate R&D investment and cooperation?', *Research Policy*, 24, 403–417.

Foray, D. (1989) 'Les modèles de competition technologique. Une revue de la littérature', *Revue d'Economie Industrielle*, 48, 16–34.

Foray, D. (1994) 'Users standards and the economics of coalition and committees', *Information Economics and Policy*, 6, 269–295.

Foray, D. (1995) 'The economics of intellectual property rights', in Hagedoorn, J. (ed.) *Technical Change and the World Economy*, Aldershot: Edward Elgar.

Foray, D. (1997) 'The dynamic implications of increasing returns: technological change and path dependent inefficiency', *International Journal of Industrial Organization*, 15, 733–752.

Foray, D. and Mowery, D. C. (1990) 'L'intégration de la R&D industrielle: nouvelles prospectives d'analyse', *Revue Economique*, 41, 501–530.

Foray, D. and Freeman, C. (1992) *Technology and the Wealth of Nations*, London: Francis Pinter.

Foray, D. and Lundvall, B. (1996) 'The knowledge-based economy: from the economics of knowledge to the learning economy', in OECD *Employment and Growth in the Knowledge-based Economy*, Paris: OECD.

Foster, J. (1991) 'Econometric methodology in an environment of evolutionary change', in Saviotti, P. P. and Metcalfe, J. S. (eds) *Evolutionary Theories of Economic and Technological Change*, Chur: Harwood.

Foster, J. (1993) 'Economics and the self-organization approach: Alfred Marshall revisited', *Economic Journal*, 103, 975–991.

Freeman, C. (1991) 'Networks of innovators: a synthesis of research issues', *Research Policy*, 20, 499–514.

Freeman, C. (1997) 'The national system of innovation in historical perspective', in

Archibugi, D. and Michie, J. (eds) *Technology Globalisation and Economic Performance*, Cambridge: Cambridge University Press.

Freeman, C. (1998) 'The economics of technical change' in Archibugi, D. and Michie, J. (eds) *Trade Growth and Technical Change*, Cambridge: Cambridge University Press.

Freeman, C., Clark, J. and Soete, L. (1982) *Unemployment and Technical Innovation. A Study of Long Waves and Economic Development*, London: Pinter.

Freeman, C. and Soete, L. (eds) (1990) *New Explorations in the Economics of Technological Change*, London: Pinter.

Freeman, C. and Soete, L. (1994) *Work for All or Mass Unemployment?*, London: Pinter.

Freeman, C. and Soete, L. (1997) *The Economics of Industrial Innovation*, 3rd edn, London: Pinter.

Gabel, L. H. (ed.) (1987) *Product Standardization and Competitive Strategy*, Amsterdam: Elsevier.

Gallouj, Faiz (1994) *Economie de l'innovation dans les services*, Paris: Editions L'Harmattan.

Geroski, P. (1991) *Market Dynamics and Entry*, Oxford: Basil Blackwell.

Geroski, P. (1995), 'Markets for technology: knowledge innovation and appropriability', in Stoneman, P. (ed.) *Handbook of the Economics of Innovation and Technological Change*, Oxford: Basil Blackwell.

Gennes, G. de (1976) 'La percolation: un concept unificateur', *La Recherche*, 72.

Geuna, A. (1998) *Resource Allocation and Knowledge Production: Studies in the Economics of University*, PhD Thesis, Maastricht University.

Gibbons, M. *et al.* (1994) *The New Production of Knowledge*, London: Sage.

Gibrat, R. (1931) *Les Inégalites économiques*, Paris: Recueil Sirey.

Greenstein, S. (1990) 'Creating economic advantage by setting compatibility standards: can "physical tie-ins" extend monopoly power?', *Economics of Innovation and New Technology*, 1, 43–62.

Greenwald, B. and Stiglitz, J. E. (1989) 'Toward a theory of rigidities', *American Economic Review*, 79, 364–369.

Griliches, Z. (1957) 'Hybrid corn: an exploration in the economics of technical change', *Econometrica*, 25, 501–522.

Griliches, Z. (1979) 'Issues in assessing the contribution of research and development to productivity growth', *Bell Journal of Economics*, 10, 92–116.

Griliches, Z. (ed.) (1984) *R&D Patents and Productivity*, Chicago: NBER.

Griliches, Z. (1986) 'Productivity R&D and the basic research at the firm level in the 1970s', *American Economic Review*, 76, 141–151.

Griliches, Z. (1992) 'The search for R&D spillovers', *Scandinavian Journal of Economics*, 94, 29–47.

Griliches, Z. (1995) 'Comments on measurement issues in relating IT expenditures to productivity growth', *Economics of Innovation and New Technology*, 3, 317–321.

Griliches, Z. (1997) 'The discovery of the residual', *Journal of Economic Literature*, 34, 1324–1330.

Grossman, G. M. and Shapiro, C. (1986), Research joint ventures: an antitrust analysis', *Journal of Law Economics and Organization*, 2, 315–337.

Habbakuk, J. C. (1962) *American and British Technology in the Nineteenth Century*, Cambridge: Cambridge University Press.

Hagerdoorn, J. (1995) 'Strategic technological partnership during the 1980s:

trends networks and corporate patterns in non-core technologies', *Research Policy*, 24, 207–231.

Hammersley, J. M. and Welsh, D. J. (1980) 'Percolation theory and its ramifications', *Contemporary Physics*, 21, 593–605.

Hart, P. (1962) 'The size and growth of firms', *Economica*, 29, 29–39.

Hawkins, R. W. (1993) 'Changing expectations: voluntary standards and the regulation of European telecommunications', *Communications & Strategies*, 11, 53–85.

Hayek, F. A. (1945) 'The use of knowledge in society', *American Economic Review*, 35, 519–530.

Hayek, F. A. (1976) *The Mirage of Social Justice*, Chicago: University of Chicago Press.

Hicks, D. (1995) 'Published papers tacit competencies and corporate management of the public/private character of knowledge', *Industrial and Corporate Change*, 4, 401–424.

Hirschman, A. O. (1958) *The Strategy of Economic Development*, New Haven: Yale University Press.

Hirschleifer, J. (1971) 'The private and social value of information and the reward to inventive activity', *American Economic Review*, 61, 561–574.

Hirschleifer, J. and Riley, J. C. (1992) *The Economics of Uncertainty and Information*, Cambridge: Cambridge University Press.

Hotelling, H. H. (1929) 'Stability in competition', *Economic Journal*, 39, 41–57.

Hulten, C. R. (1978) 'Growth accounting with intermediate inputs', *Review of Economic Studies*, 45, 511–518.

Hymer, S. and Pashigian, P. (1962) 'Firm size and rate of growth', *Journal of Political Economy*, 70, 556–69.

IMF (1992) *International Financial Statistics Yearbook*, Washington, DC: International Monetary Fund.

ISTAT (1987) *Tavola Intersettoriale dell'Economia Italiana*, Rome, 1987 and subsequent years.

ISTAT (1988) *Fatturato Prodotto Lordo Investimenti delle Imprese Industriali, del Commercio, dei Trasporti e Comunicazioni e di Alcuni Tipi di Servizi*, Rome, 1988 and subsequent years.

ISTAT (1988a) *Tavola Economica Intersettoriale 1985 a Prezzi di Mercato*, Rome.

Iwai, K. (1984a) 'Schumpeterian dynamics: an evolutionary model of innovation and imitation', *Journal of Economic Behavior and Organization*, 5, 159–190.

Iwai, K. (1984b) 'Schumpeterian dynamics part II: technological progress firm growth and economic selection, *Journal of Economic Behavior and Organization*, 5, 321–355.

Jacquemin, A. (1985) *Selection et pouvoir dans la nouvelle économie industrielle*, Paris: Cabay-Economica.

Jaffe, A. B. (1986) 'Technological opportunity and spillover of R&D: evidence from firms patents, profits and market value', *American Economic Review*, 76, 984–1001.

Jaffe, A. B. (1989) 'Real effects of academic research', *American Economic Review*, 79, 957–970.

Jaffe, A. B., Trajtenberg, M. and Henderson, R. (1993) 'Geographic localization of knowledge spillovers as evidenced by patent citations', *Quarterly Journal of Economics*, 108, 577–598.

Jorde, T. M. and Teece, D. J. (1990) 'Innovation and cooperation: implications for competition and antitrust', *Journal of Economic Perspectives*, 4, 75–96.

Kaldor, N. (1957) 'A model of economic growth', *Economic Journal*, 67: 591–624.

Kaldor, N. and Mirrlees, J. (1962) 'A new model of economic growth', *Review of Economic Studies*, 29, 174–192.

Kamien, M. I., Muller, E. and Zang, I. (1992) 'Research joint ventures and R&D cartels', *American Economic Review*, 82, 1293–1306.

Kamien, M. I. and Schwartz, N. L. (1982) *Market Structure and Innovation*, Cambridge: Cambridge University Press.

Katz, M. L. and Ordover, J. A. (1990) 'R&D cooperation and competition', *Brookings Papers on Economic Activity: Microeconomics*, 137–203.

Katz, M. L. and Shapiro, C. (1985) 'Network externalities competition and compatibility', *American Economic Review*, 75, 424–440.

Katz, M. L. and Shapiro, C. (1986) 'Technology adoption in the presence of network externalities', *Journal of Political Economy*, 94, 822–841.

Katz, M. L. (1986) 'An analysis of cooperative research and development', *Rand Journal of Economics*, 17, 527–534.

Kennedy, C. (1964) 'Induced bias in innovation and the theory of distribution', *Economic Journal*, 74, 541–547.

Kesten, H. (1982) *Percolation Theory for Mathematicians*, Boston, Basel and Stuttgart: Birkhauser.

Kiefer, N. M. (1988) 'Economic duration data and hazard functions', *Journal of Economic Literature*, 26, 646–679.

Kindleberger, C. P. (1983) 'Standards as public collective and private goods', *Kyklos*, 36, 377–396.

Kirman, A. P. (1992) 'Variety: the coexistence of techniques', *Revue d'Economie Industrielle*, 59, 62–74.

Kirman, A. P., Oddou, C. and Weber, S. (1986) 'Stochastic communication and coalition formation', *Econometrica*, 54, 129–138.

Kitch, E. (1977) 'The nature and function of the patent system', *Journal of Law and Economics*, 20, 265–290.

Klein, B. H. (1992) 'The role of positive sum games in economic growth', in Scherer, F. M. and Perlman, M. (eds) *Entrepreneurship Technological Innovation and Economic Growth*, Ann Arbor: University of Michigan Press.

Klemperer, P. (1987a) 'Markets with consumer switching costs', *Quarterly Journal of Economics*, 102, 375–394.

Klemperer, P. (1987b) 'The competitiveness of markets with switching costs', *Rand Journal of Economics*, 18, 138–150.

Klemperer, P. (1995) 'Competition when consumers have switching costs: an overview with application to industrial organization macroeconomics and international trade', *Review of Economic Studies*, 62, 515–539.

Klepper, S. and Graddy, E. (1990) 'The evolution of new industries and the determinants of market structure', *Rand Journal of Economics*, 21, 27–44.

Kogut, B., Walker, G. and Kim, D. (1995) 'Cooperation and entry as an extension of technological rivalry', *Research Policy*, 24, 77–95.

Kremer, M. (1993) 'The O-ring theory of economic development', *Quarterly Journal of Economics*, 108, 551–575.

Krugman, P. (1991) *Geography and Trade*, Cambridge, MA: MIT Press.

Krugman, P. (1996) *The Self-organizing Economy*, Oxford: Basil Blackwell.

Kuznets, S. (1930) *Secular Movements in Production and Prices. Their Nature and Bearing upon Cyclical Fluctuations*, Boston: Houghton Mifflin Company.

Kwon, M. J. and Stoneman, P. (1995) 'The impact of technology adoption on firm productivity', *Economics of Innovation and New Technology*, 3, 219–234.

Lamberton, D. (ed.) (1971) *Economics of Information and Knowledge*, Harmondsworth: Penguin.

Langlois, R. N. (ed.) (1986) *Economics as a Process: Essays in the New Institutional Economics*, Cambridge: Cambridge University Press.

Langlois, R. N. and Robertson, P.L. (1995) *Firms Markets and Economic Change. A Dynamic Theory of Business Institutions*, London: Routledge.

Layard, R., Nickell, S. and Jackman, R. (1994) *The Unemployment Crisis*, Oxford: Oxford University Press.

Lazonick, W. (1990) *Competitive Advantage on the Shop Floor*, Cambridge, MA: Harvard University Press.

Leonard Barton, D. (1995) *Wellsprings of Knowledge*, Boston: Harvard Business School Press.

Lilien, D. M. (1982) 'Sectoral shifts and cyclical unemployment', *Journal of Political Economy*, 90, 777–793.

Link, A. N. and Bauer, L. L. (1989) *Cooperative Research in the U.S. Manufacturing Industry*, Lexington: Lexington Books.

Link, A. N. and Tassey, G. (1987) 'The impact of standards on technology-based industries: the case of numerically controlled machine tools in automated batch manufacturing', in Gabel, L. H. (ed.) *Product Standardization and Competitive Strategy*, Amsterdam: Elsevier.

Loasby, B. J. (1991) *Equilibrium and Evolution. An Exploration of Connecting Principles in Economics*, Manchester: Manchester University Press.

Loasby, B. J. (1994) 'Understanding markets', Working Paper, Dept. of Economics, University of Stirling.

Loasby, B. J. (1995), 'The organization of capabilities', Working Paper, Dept. of Economics, University of Stirling.

Loveman, G. W. (1994) 'An assessment of the productivity impact of information technology', in Allen, T. J. and Scott Morton, M. S. (eds) *Information Technology and the Corporation of the 90s*, Oxford: Oxford University Press.

Lundvall, B. A. (1985) *Product Innovation and User-producer Interaction*, Aalborg: Aalborg University Press.

Lundvall, B. A. (ed.) (1992) *National Systems of Innovation. Towards a Theory of Innovation and Interactive Learning*, London: Pinter.

Lundvall, B. A. and Johnson, B. (1994) 'The learning economy', *Journal of Industry Studies*, 2, 23–42.

Machlup, F. (1962) *The Production and Distribution of Knowledge in the United States*, Princeton: Princeton University Press.

Machlup, F. (1984) *The Economics of Information and Human Capital*, Princeton: Princeton University Press.

Machlup, F. and Penrose, E. (1950) 'The patent controversy in the nineteenth century', *Journal of Economic History*, 10, 1–29.

Malerba, F. (1992) 'Learning by firms and incremental technical change, *Economic Journal*, 102, 845–859.

Malerba, F., Orsenigo, L. and Peretto, P. (1997) 'Persistence of innovative activities sectoral patterns of innovation and international technological specialization', *International Journal of Industrial Organization*, 15, 801–826.

Mankiw, N. G. (1985) 'Small menu costs and large business cycles: a macro-economic model of monopoly', *Quarterly Journal of Economics*, 100, 529–537.

Mansell, R. (1994) *The New Telecommunications*, New York: Sage.

Mansell, R. and Wehn, U. (eds) (1998) *Knowledge Societies: Information Technology for Sustainable Development*. Oxford: Oxford University Press.

Mansfield, E. (1961) 'Technical change and the rate of imitation', *Econometrica*, 29, 741–766.

Mansfield, E. (1962) 'Entry Gibrat's law innovation and the growth of firms', *American Economic Review*, 52, 1023–1051.

Mansfield, E. (1985) 'How rapidly does new industrial technology leak out', *Journal of Industrial Economics*, 34, 217–223.

Mansfield, E. (1991) 'Academic research and industrial innovation', *Research Policy*, 20, 1–12.

Mansfield, E. (1992) 'Academic research and industrial innovation: a further note', *Research Policy*, 21, 295–296.

Mansfield, E. (1995) 'Academic research underlying industrial innovations: sources characteristics and financing', *Review of Economics and Statistics*, 77, 55–65.

Mansfield, E., Schwartz, M. and Wagner, S. (1981) 'Imitation costs and patents: an empirical study', *Economic Journal*, 91, 907–918.

March, J. C. and Simon, H. A. (1958) *Organizations*, New York: John Wiley & Sons.

Marchionatti, R. (1992) 'Marshall on increasing returns and competition', *Quaderni di Storia dell'Economia Politica*, 10, 553–584.

Markham, J. W. and Papaneck, G. F. (eds) (1970) *Industrial Organization and Economic Development. In Honor of E. S. Mason*, Boston: Houghton Mifflin Company.

Marris, R. (1964) *The Economic Theory of 'Managerial' Capitalism*, London: Macmillan.

Marshall, A. (1919) *Industry and Trade*, London: Macmillan.

Marshall, A. (1920) *Principles of Economics*, London: Macmillan (I: 1890; VIII: 1920).

Martin, S. (1993) *Advanced Industrial Economics*, Oxford: Blackwell.

Matsuyama, K. (1995) 'Complementarities and cumulative processes in models of monopolistic competition', *Journal of Economic Literature*, 33, 701–729.

Matutes, C. and Regibeau, P. (1987) 'Standardization in multi-component industries', in Gabel, L. H. (ed.) *Product Standardization and Competitive Strategy*, Amsterdam: Elsevier.

Melvin, J. R. (1969) 'Intermediate goods and technological change', *Review of Economic Studies*, 36, 400–408.

Metcalfe, J. S. (1981) 'Impulse and diffusion in the study of technical change', *Futures*, 13, 347–359.

Metcalfe, J. S. (1989) 'Evolution and economic change', in Silberston A. (ed.) *Technology and Economic Progress*, London: Macmillan.

Metcalfe, J. S. (1992) 'Variety structure and change: an evolutionary perspective on the competitive process', *Revue d'Economie Industrielle*, 59, 46–61.

Metcalfe, J. S. (1994) 'Competition Fisher's principle and increasing returns to selection', *Journal of Evolutionary Economics*, 4, 327–346.

Metcalfe, J. S. (1995a) 'The economic foundation of technology policy: equilibrium and evolutionary perspectives', in P. Stoneman (ed.) *Handbook of the Economics of Innovation and Technological Change*, Oxford: Basil Blackwell.

Metcalfe, J. S. (1995b) 'Technology systems and technology policy in historical perspective', *Cambridge Journal of Economics*, 19, 25–47.

Metcalfe, J. S. (1997) *Evolutionary Economics and Creative Destruction*, London: Routledge.

Metcalfe, J. S. and Gibbons, M. (1988) 'Technology variety and organization. A systematic perspective on the competitive process', in Rosenbloom, R. S. and Burgelman, R. A. (eds) *Research on Technological Innovation Management and Policy*, Greenwich: JAI Press.

Metcalfe, J. S. and Miles, I. (1994) 'Standards selection and variety: an evolutionary approach', *Information Economics and Policy*, 6, 243–268.

Miles, I. *et al.* (1995) 'Knowledge-intensive business services', Bruxelles: EIMS.

Milgrom, P. and Roberts, J. (1990) 'The economics of modern manufacturing', *American Economic Review*, 80, 511–528.

Mody, A. (1993) 'Learning through alliances', *Journal of Economic Behavior and Organization*, 20, 151–170.

Mokyr, J. (1990) *The Levels of Riches*, Oxford: Oxford University Press.

Momigliano, F. (1975) *Economia Industriale e Teoria dell'Impresa*, Bologna: Il Mulino.

Mowery, D. C. (1983), 'The relationship between contractual and interfirm forms of industrial research in American manufacturing, 1900–1940', *Explorations in Economic History*, 20, 351–374.

Mowery, D. C. (1989) 'Collaborative ventures between U.S. and foreign manufacturing firms', *Research Policy*, 18, 19–32.

Mowery, D. C. (1995) 'The boundaries of the U.S. firms in R&D', in Lamoreaux, N. R. and Raff, D. M. G. (eds) *Coordination and Information*, Chicago: The University of Chicago Press for the National Bureau of Economic Research.

Mueller, D. C. (1972) 'A life cycle theory of the firm', *Journal of Industrial Economics*, 20, 199–219.

Mueller, D. C. (1986) *Profits in the Long Run*, Cambridge: Cambridge University Press.

Mueller, D. C. (1987) *The Corporation: Growth Diversification and Mergers*, Chur: Harwood.

Mueller, D. C. (1997) 'First mover advantage and path dependence', *International Journal of Industrial Organization*, 15, 827–850.

Mueller, D. C. and Tilton, J. (1969) 'Research and development costs as barriers to entry', *Canadian Journal of Economics*, 4, 570–579.

Nelson, R. R. (1959) 'The simple economics of basic scientific research', *Journal of Political Economy*, 67, 297–306.

Nelson, R. R. (1982) 'The role of knowledge in R&D efficiency', *Quarterly Journal of Economics*, 97, 453–470.

Nelson, R. R. (1987) *Understanding Technological Change as an Evolutionary Process*, Amsterdam: North Holland.

Nelson, R. R. (1990) 'Capitalism as an engine of progress', *Research Policy*, 19, 193–214.

Nelson, R. R. (1995) 'Recent evolutionary theorizing about economic change', *Journal of Economic Literature*, 33, 48–90.

Nelson, R. R. (ed.) (1993) *National Systems of Innovation*, Oxford: Oxford University Press.

Nelson, R. R., Winter, S. G. and Schuette, H.L. (1976) 'Technical change in an evolutionary model', *Quarterly Journal of Economics*, 90, 90–118.

Nelson, R. R. and Winter, S. G. (1982) *An Evolutionary Theory of Economic Change*, Cambridge, MA: Harvard University Press.

Nelson, R. R. and Wright, G. (1992) 'The rise and fall of American technological leadership: the postwar era in historical perspective', *Journal of Economic Literature*, 30, 1931–1964.

Newman, P. and Wolf, J. N. (1961) 'A model for the long-run theory of value', *Review of Economic Studies*, 29, 51–61.

Noble, D. (1977) *America by Design*, New York: Knopf.

Nonaka, I. and Takeuchi, H. (1995) *The Knowledge-creating Company*, Oxford: Oxford University Press.

North, D. C. (1991) *Institutions Institutional Change and Economic Performance*, Cambridge: Cambridge University Press.

OECD (1991) *Technology and the Economy*, Paris: OECD.

OECD (1992a) *Perspectives Economiques de l'OCDE*, Paris: OECD.

OECD (1992b) *Employment Outlook*, Paris: OECD.

OECD (1993) *Labour Force Statistics (1971–1991)*, Paris: OECD.

OECD (1994) *Main Science and Technology Indicators*, Paris: OECD.

Orlean, A. (1990) 'Le rôle des influences interpersonnelles dans le fonctionnement des marchés financiers', *Revue Economique*, 41, 839–868.

Orlean, A. (1992) 'Contagion des opinions et fonctionnement des marchés financiers', *Revue Economique*, 43, 685–698.

Ordover, J. A. (1991) 'A patent system for both diffusion and exclusion', *Journal of Economic Perspectives*, 5, 43–60.

Ordover, J. A. and Baumol, W. J. (1988) 'Antitrust policy and high technology industries', *Oxford Review of Economic Policy*, 4, 13–34.

Ordover, J. A. and Willig, R. D. (1985) 'Antitrust for high-tehnology industries: assessing research joint ventures and mergers', *Journal of Law and Eonomics*, 28, 311.

Parrinello, S. (1993) 'Non-pure private goods in the economics of production processes', *Metroeconomica*, 44, 195–214.

Pasinetti, L. L. (1981) *Structural Change and Economic Growth*, Cambridge: Cambridge University Press.

Pasinetti, L. L. (1988) 'Growing subsystems vertically integrated sectors and the labor theory', *Cambridge Journal of Economics*, 12, 125–134.

Pavitt, K. (1984) 'Sectoral patterns of technical change: towards a taxonomy', *Research Policy*, 13, 343–373.

Pavitt, K. (1987) 'What we know about the strategic management of technology', *California Management Review*, 32, 17–26.

Pavitt, K. (1991) 'What makes basic research economically useful?', *Research Policy*, 20, 109–119.

Pavitt, K. and Soete, L. (1982) 'International differences in economic growth and the international location of innovation', in Giersch, H. (ed.) *Emerging Technologies: Consequences for Economic Growth Sructural Change and Employment*, Tübingen: J.C.B. Mohr (Paul Siebeck).

Penrose, E. (1959) *The Theory of the Growth of the Firm*, Oxford: Basil Blackwell.

Perrin, J. (1991) Analyse des systèmes techniques', in Boyer, R., Chavance, B. and Godard, O. (eds) *Les Figures de l'irreversibilité en économie*, Paris: Editions de l'Ecole de Hautes Etudes en Sciences Sociales.

Perroux, F. (1935) 'La pensée économique de Joseph Schumpeter', introduction to the French translation of Schumpeter, J. (1912) *Theorie der Wirtschaftlichen Entwicklung*, Paris: Dalloz.

Perroux, F. (1964) *L'Economie du XXème siecle*, Paris: Presses Universitaires de France.

Petit, P. (1988) *La Croissance Tertiaire*, Paris: Economica.

Phillips, A. (1962) *Market Structure Organization and Performance*, Cambridge, MA: Harvard University Press.

Phillips, A. (1970) 'Structure conduct performance and performance conduct structure', in Markham, J. W. and Papanek, G. F. (eds) *Industrial Organization and Economic Development. In Honour of E. S. Mason*, Boston: Houghton Mifflin Company.

Phillips, A. (1971) *Technology and Market Structure*, Lexington: Lexington Books.

Polanyi, M. (1958) *Personal Knowledge. Towards a Post-Critical Philosophy*, London: Routledge & Kegan Paul.

Porter, M. (1990) *The Competitive Advantage of Nations*, New York: Macmillan.

Preissl, B. (1995) 'Strategic use of communication technology: diffusion processes in networks and environments', *Information Economics and Policy*, 7, 75–100.

Quéré, M. (1994) 'Basic reasearch inside the firm: lessons from an in-depth case study', *Research Policy*, 23, 413–424.

Quintas, P. and Guy, K. (1995) 'Collaborative pre-competitive R&D and the firm', *Research Policy*, 24, 325–348.

Reich, L. S. (1985) *The Making of American Industrial Research*, Cambridge: Cambridge University Press.

Richardson, G. B. (1962) *Information and Investment*, Oxford: Oxford University Press.

Richardson, G. B. (1972) 'The organization of industry', *Economic Journal*, 82, 883–896.

Rohlfs, J. (1974) 'A theory of interdependent demand for a communications service', *Bell Journal of Economics and Management*, 5, 16–37.

Romer, P. M. (1986) 'Increasing returns and long run growth', *Journal of Political Economy*, 98, 1002–1037.

Romer, P. M. (1990) 'Endogenous technological change', *Journal of Political Economy*, 98, S71–S102.

Rosenberg, N. (1976) *Perspectives on Technology*, Cambridge: Cambridge University Press.

Rosenberg, N. (1982) *Inside the Black Box: Technology and Economics*, Cambridge: Cambridge University Press.

Rosenberg, N. (1990) 'Why do firms do research (with their own money)?', *Research Policy*, 19, 165–174.

Rosenberg, N. (1994) *Exploring the Black Box*, Cambridge: Cambridge University Press.

Rosenberg, N. and Nelson, R. (1992) 'American universities and technical advance in industry', *Research Policy*, 23, 323–348.

Rosenberg, N. and Frischtak, G. (1994) 'Technological innovation and long waves', in Rosenberg, N. (ed.) *Exploring the Black Box*, Cambridge: Cambridge University Press.

Rosenstein Rodan, P. N. (1934) 'The role of time in economic theory', *Economica*, 2, 77–97.

Sah, R. and Stiglitz, J. E. (1986) 'The architecture of economic systems: hierarchies and polyarchies', *American Economic Review*, 76, 716–727.

Sahal, Devendra (1981) *Patterns of Technological Innovation*, Reading, MA: Addison-Wesley Publishing.

Saloner, G. (1990) 'Economic issues in computer interface standardization', *Economics of Innovation and New Technology*, 1, 135–156.

Salter, W. E. G. (1966) *Productivity and Technical Change*, Cambridge: Cambridge University Press.

Samuelson, P. (1954) 'The pure theory of public expenditure', *Review of Economics and Statistics*, 36, 387–389.

Saviotti, P. P. and Metcalfe, J. S. (eds.) (1992) *Evolutionary Theories of Economic and Technological Change*, Chur: Harwood.

Saxenian, A. (1991) 'The origins and dynamics of production networks in silicon valley', *Research Policy*, 20, 423–437.

Scheinkman, J. A. and Woodford, M. (1994) 'Self-organized criticality and economic fluctuations', *American Economic Review*, 84, 417–421.

Scherer, F. M. (1984) *Innovation and Growth: Schumpeterian Perspectives*, Cambridge, MA: MIT Press.

Scherer, F. M. and Ross, D. (1990) *Industrial Market Structure and Economic Performance*, 3rd edn, Boston: Houghton-Mifflin Company.

Schmalensee, R. (1986) Advertising and market structure', in Stiglitz, J. E. and Mathewson, G. F. (eds) New Developments in the Analysis of Market Structure, Cambridge, MA: MIT Press.

Schmookler, J. (1966) *Invention and Economic Growth*, Cambridge, MA: Harvard University Press.

Schmookler, J. (1957) 'Inventors past and present', *Review of Economics and Statistics*, 39, 321–333.

Schumpeter, J. A. (1934) *The Theory of Economic Development* (I: 1912), Cambridge, MA: Harvard University Press.

Schumpeter, J. A. (1939) *Business Cycles: A Theoretical Hstorical and Statistical Analysis*, New York: McGraw-Hill.

Schumpeter, J. A. (1954) *History of Economic Analysis*, New York: Oxford University Press.

Scitowsky, T. (1954) 'Two concepts of external economies', *Journal of Political Economy*, 62, 143–151.

Scotchmer, S. (1991) 'Standing on the shoulders of giants: cumulative research and the patent law', *Journal of Economic Perspectives*, 5, 29–41.

Scott Morton, M. S. (ed.) (1991) *The Corporation of the 1990s*, Oxford: Oxford University Press.

Senker, J. (1995) 'Tacit knowledge and models of innovation', *Industrial and Corporate Change*, 4, 425–448.

Shapiro, C. and Stiglitz, J. E. (1984) 'Equilibrium unemployment as a worker discipline device', *American Economic Review*, 74, 433–444.

Simon, H. A. (1951) 'Effects of technological change in a Leontieff model', in Koopmans, T.C. (ed.) *Activity Analysis of Production and Allocation*, New York: Wiley, 260–281.

Simon, H. A. (1982) *Models of Bounded Rationality*, Cambridge, MA: MIT Press.

Simon, H. A. (1983) 'Rationality in psychology and economics', *Journal of Business*,

59, S209–S224. Special issue edited by Hogarth, R. M. and Reder, M. W., *The Behavioral Foundations of Economic Theory*.

Simon, H. A. and Bonini, C. P. (1958) 'The size distribution of business firms', *American Economic Review*, 48, 607–617.

Soete, L. (1987) 'The newly emerging information technology sector', in Freeman, C. and Soete, L. (eds) *Technological Change and Full Employment*, Oxford: Basil Blackwell.

Spence, M. (1980) 'Notes on advertising economies of scale and entry barriers, *Quarterly Journal of Economics*, 94, 493–507.

Steedman, I. (1987) 'Free goods', in J. Eatwell, M. Milgate and P. Newman (eds) *The New Palgrave: A Dictionary of Economics*, London: Macmillan.

Steedman, I. (1992) 'Substitution and the representation of alternative methods of production', *Economics of Innovation and New Technology*, 2, 165–170.

Steindl, J. (1947) *Small and Big Business*, Oxford: Basil Blackwell.

Steindl, J. (1952) *Maturity and Stagnation in American Capitalism*, Oxford: Basil Blackwell.

Stephan, P. E. (1996) 'The economics of science', *Journal of Economic Literature*, 34, 1199–1235.

Stigler, G. J. (1951) 'The division of labor is limited by the extent of the market', *Journal of Political Economy*, 59, 185–193.

Stiglitz, J. E. (1987) 'Learning to learn localized learning and technological progress', in Dasgupta, P. and Stoneman, P. (eds) *Economic Policy and Technological Performance*, Cambridge: Cambridge University Press.

Stiglitz, J. E. (1988) 'Technological change sunk costs and competition', in Baily, M. N. and Winston, C. (eds) *Microeconomics. Brookings Papers on Economic Activity*, Washington, DC: The Brookings Institution, 883–947.

Stoneman, P. (1983) *The Economic Analysis of Technological Change*, Oxford: Oxford University Press.

Stoneman, P. (1987) *The Economic Analysis of Technology Policy*, Oxford: Clarendon Press.

Stoneman, P. (ed.) (1995) *Handbook of the Economics of Innovation and Technological Change*, Oxford: Blackwell.

Sutton, J. (1991) *Sunk Costs and Market Structure*, Cambridge, MA: MIT Press.

Sutton, J. (1997) 'Gibrat's legacy', *Journal of Economic Literature*, 35, 40–59.

Swann, P. (ed.) (1994) *New Technologies and the Firm: Innovation and Competition*, London: Routledge.

Swann, P. and Prevezer, M. (1996) 'A comparison of the dynamics of industrial clustering in computing and biotechnology', *Research Policy*, 25, 1139–1157.

Swann, P. and Shurmer, M. (1994) 'The emergence of standards in PC software: who would benefit from institutional intervention?', *Information Economics and Policy*, 6, 295–318.

Swann, P., Prevezer, M. and Stout, D. (eds) (1998) *The Dynamics of Industrial Clustering*, Oxford: Oxford University Press.

Sylos Labini, P. (1962) *Oligopoly and Technical Progress*, Cambridge, MA: Harvard University Press.

Sylos Labini, P. (1984) *The Forces of Economic Growth and Decline*, Cambridge, MA: MIT Press.

Teece, D. J. (1977) 'Technology transfer by multinational firms: the resource costs of transferring technological know-how', *Economic Journal*, 87, 242–261.

Teece, D. J. (1986) 'Profiting from technological innovation', *Research Policy*, 15, 285–305.

Teece, D. J. (ed.) (1987) *The Competitive Challenge*, Cambridge: Ballinger.

Teece, D. J. (1993) 'The dynamics of industrial capitalism: perspectives on Alfred Chandler's "Scale and scope"', *Journal of Economic Literature*, 31, 199–225.

Teubal, M. *et al.* (eds) (1996) *Technological Infrastructure Policy. An International Perspective*, Boston: Kluwer Academic Publishers.

Tylecote, A. (1991) *The Long Wave in the World Economy*, London: Routledge.

Utterback, J. M. (1994) *Mastering the Dynamics of Innovation*, Boston: Harvard Business School Press.

Utterback, J. M. and Afuah, A. N. (1998) 'The dynamic "dyamond": a technological perspective', *Economics of Innovation and New Technology*, 6(1–2).

Vernon, R. (1966) 'International investment and international trade in the product cycle', *Quarterly Journal of Economics*, 81, 190–208.

Veugelers, R. (1997) 'Internal R&D expenditures and external technical sourcing', *Research Policy*, 26, 303–315.

Von Hippel, E. (1988) *The Sources of Innovation*, Oxford: Oxford University Press.

Von Hippel, E. (1994) 'Sticky information and the locus of problem solving: implications for innovation', *Management Science*, 40, 429–439.

Von Tunzelmann, N. G. (1978) *Steam Power and British Industrialization to 1860*, Oxford: Oxford University Press.

Von Tunzelmann, N. G. (1981) 'Technical progress during the industrial revolution', in Floud, R. and McCloskey, D. N. (eds) *The Economic History of Great Britain Since 1700*, Vol. 1. Cambridge: Cambridge University Press.

Von Tunzelmann, N. G. (1995) *Technology and Industrial Progress. The Foundations of Economic Growth*, Aldershot: Edward Elgar.

Von Tunzelmann, N. G. (1998) 'Localized technological search and multi-technology companies', *Economics of Innovation and New Technology*, 6 (1–2).

von Weizsäcker, C. C. (1984) 'The costs of substitution', *Econometrica*, 52, 1085–1116.

Wasserman, S. and Faust, C. (1994) *Social Network Analysis: Methods and Applications*, Cambridge: Cambridge University Press.

Watkins, T. A. (1991) 'A technological communications costs model of R&D consortia as public policy', *Research Policy*, 20, 87–107.

Weiss, M. B. H. and Sirbu, M. (1990) 'Technological choice in voluntary standards committes: an empirical analysis', *Economics of Innovation and New Technology*, 1, 111–134.

Williamson, O. E. (1975) *Markets and Hierarchies: Analysis and Antitrust Implications*, New York: The Free Press.

Williamson, O. E. (1985) *The Economic Institutions of Capitalism*, New York: The Free Press.

Williamson, O. E. (1993) 'The logic of economic organization', in Williamson, O. E. and Winter, S. G. (eds) *The Nature of the Firm*, Oxford: Oxford University Press.

Wilson, D. D. (1995) 'IT investment and its productivity effects: an organizational sociologist's perspective on directions for future research', *Economics of Innovation and New Technology*, 3, 235–252.

Winter, S. G. (1981) 'Attention allocation and input proportions', *Journal of Economic Behavior and Organization*, 2, 31–46.

Winter, S. G. (1984) 'Schumpeterian competition in alternative technological regimes', *Journal of Economic Behavior and Organization*, 5, 287–320.

Winter, S. G. (1987) 'Knowledge and competence as strategic assets', in Teece, D. J. (ed.) *The Competitive Challenge*, Cambridge: Ballinger.

Winter, S. G. (1993) 'On Coase competence and the corporation', in Williamson, O. E. and Winter, S. G. (eds) *The Nature of the Firm*, Oxford: Oxford University Press.

Witt, U. (1997) 'Lock-in vs. critical mass. Two views on industrial change under network externalities', *International Journal of Industrial Organization*, 15, 753–775.

Wright, B. D. (1983) 'The economics of invention incentives: patent prizes and research contracts', *American Economic Review*, 73, 691–707.

Wright, G. (1990) 'The origins of American industrial success, 1879–1940', *American Economic Review*, 80, 651–668.

Zaratiegui, J. M. (1997) 'Twin brothers in Marshallian thought: knowledge and organization', *Review of Political Economy*, 9, 295–312.

Zucker, L., Darby, M. and Amstrong, J. (1994) 'Intellectual capital and the firm: the technology of geographically localized knowledge spillovers', NBER Working Paper No. 4946.

Zuscovitch, E. and Arrous, J. (1984) 'La diffusion intersectorielle des matériaux synthétiques. Evolution et bilan économique', in BETA, *La Chimie en Europe*, Strasbourg, 1984.

Young, A. (1928) 'Increasing returns and economic progress', *Economic Journal*, 38, 527–542.

Index